AF872316

Praise for *Precision Manufacturing, Precision Business* and Paul Van Metre

"Paul brings a rare perspective to this book: the experience of a former shop owner, the insight of a manufacturing expert, and the heart of someone who genuinely wants manufacturers and their people to succeed. *The Machinery's Handbook* has long been one of the most important references in manufacturing. I believe Paul's book has the potential to become equally important—not simply as a technical reference, but as essential reading for anyone who wants to understand how successful manufacturing companies are built, led, and sustained. This is practical manufacturing wisdom from someone who has lived it."

— *Scott Shortess, Advanced Plastics and Machining*

"I've spent years pulling data from the Top Shops survey, and the pattern in this book matches what that data shows: margin traces back to job costing accuracy more than machine count or headcount. Van Metre backs the argument with real numbers instead of the usual advice to work smarter. That specificity is exactly what makes this book worth an owner's time."

— *Brent Donaldson, Modern Machine Shop Magazine*

"Buying and running a machine shop is one of the hardest things I've done, and there's no manual for it — until now. Paul has done the work of talking to hundreds of us so the rest of us don't have to learn everything the hard way. This book is the guide I wish I'd had five years ago."

— *Matt Fortner, Progress Machining Inc.*

"If you want to own or operate a machine shop, follow 'Paul's path' for your best chance of success. What makes *Precision Manufacturing, Precision Business* invaluable is not that it teaches you how to machine better—it assumes you already know that part. What it teaches you is how to think like a business designer instead of a technician always putting out fires. That shift is everything. The book is comprehensive enough to serve as a reference, practical enough to act on immediately, and grounded in the reality of this industry in ways most business books never achieve. If you're serious about building a machine shop that's profitable, scalable, and valuable—not just one that keeps the lights on—this book deserves to be on your desk and in your operating decisions."

—John Newman, Athena Manufacturing

"*Precision Manufacturing, Precision Business* puts words to lessons that many machine shop owners, myself included, have learned the hard way. It captures the struggles, hard-earned wisdom, and genuine satisfaction that come with building a successful manufacturing business. This book is a powerful tool for accelerating the maturity of any machine shop that wants to move beyond dependence on heroics and compete at the highest level."

— Dwain Dyer, Concise Manufacturing

"This is the book I wish existed when I started my machine shop. I could always find books on business, and I could always find books on machining. What I couldn't find was a book that explained how to build a machine shop into a great business. Running a machine shop is different. The problems are different. The systems are different. The way you make money is different. Reading this book, I could see every stage of my own journey—from running a passion project to building a real business. If you're serious about growing your shop, this book will save you years of figuring it out the hard way."

—James Marzilli, Marzilli Machine Co.

"Paul has been an inspiration to this industry through his podcasts, and his passion for it can't be replicated. What impresses me most about this book is how he takes hard subjects and makes them simple — using real people, real experiences, real advice. That's a rare skill, because it's far easier to make something complicated than it is to make it simple. Well done."

— Scott Harms, MetalQuest

"Paul Van Metre understands that producing precision parts is only half the challenge—the business surrounding those parts must be operated with the same discipline. Precision Manufacturing, Precision Business is an insightful and practical guide for machine shop leaders who want to replace firefighting with systems, build a stronger team, improve profitability, and create a company built to last."

—Jason Davis, D&D Enterprises

"I first met Paul as the owner and co-founder of ProShop, the ERP system our shop runs on. But it didn't take long to realize he wasn't just a vendor—he'd clearly cut his teeth in the trade himself, and he quickly became more of a partner to our business than a supplier. *Precision Manufacturing, Precision Business* is an inside look at the good, the bad, and the reality of running what might be the hardest business in the world. It's a genuinely interesting read—the kind that sparks curiosity for more rather than satisfying it and moving on. The best comparison I can make is to Warren Miller and what he did for backcountry skiing in the '80s and '90s—taking an experience only a select few had ever lived and turning it into something the masses could see, understand, and get excited about. That's what this book does for precision manufacturing. It's educational, yes, but it's more than that. It comes from a perspective that maybe only one person on earth actually has: someone who's owned a shop, been a vendor and partner to hundreds more, and interviewed countless successful shop owners of the modern era.

— Mitch Olson, Olson Custom Designs

"Reading *Precision Manufacturing, Precision Business* has me looking at all aspects of how I run my own shop. It brings a lot of lessons and experiences from people who have already been through it into one place. Instead of trying to figure everything out on my own as I go, this book has me thinking about how I can apply the lessons and ideas from the many people who contributed to it. I'd highly recommend it to anyone who owns or is thinking about owning a manufacturing business. I will be reading it again and taking notes!"

— Jereme Rogers, Axis CNC

Precision Manufacturing, Precision Business

How the Best Machine Shops Turn Discipline into Profit

Paul Van Metre

ThankAMachinist Publishing

First edition.

Paperback: 979-8-9947458-0-9
eBook: 979-8-9947458-1-6
Hardback: 979-8-9947458-2-3
Audio book: 979-8-9947458-3-0

I dedicate this book to the countless owners, leaders and workers in the precision manufacturing industry, past, current, and future. Without your incredible efforts, sacrifices, grit, ingenuity, perseverance, blood, sweat and tears, we would have no nation, no economy, no other industries. You make up the bedrock of the economy. Although 90% of people don't understand that you exist or the value of your work, those that do, like I, are grateful. Thank you.

I also want to thank my family, friends and coworkers who have supported me in my journey. What we've achieved is a team result. I love you all.

Table of Contents

FOREWORD XVII

PREFACE XXII

INTRODUCTION 1

Precision Is the Business 3

How to Read This Book 4

Who This Is For (and Who It Isn't) 5

The Map Ahead 6

PART I: WHY THIS BUSINESS MATTERS

CHAPTER 1: Made Here, Built Right 11

The Multiplier Effect 14

What Offshoring Cost Us 17

Why Now Matters 20

The Responsibility This Carries 22

A Different Kind of Service 24

Why It's So Hard, and So Often Missed 25

CHAPTER 2: The Hardest Business in the World **27**

Restaurants, Construction, and Where Machining Actually Lives 29

Why Great Machinists Make Hard Owners 32

Three Forces That Compound 35

Busy but Behind 38

The Myth of Heroics 40

When Hard Work Stops Working 42

PART II: FROM MACHINIST TO BUSINESS OWNER

CHAPTER 3: The E-Myth of Machining **47**

Technician vs. Owner 50

Which Expert Are You? 53

The E-Myth, Applied to Steel 56

Lessons from *The Goal* **58**

Designing for Someone Else to Run 60

Systems First, Always 63

The Letting-Go Problem 66

What Has to Change First 67

CHAPTER 4: We Did It the Hard Way **71**

Six Kids, a Second Mortgage, and a Lot of Naivety 73

First Mistakes, First Breakthroughs 76

When Growth Broke What We'd Built 78

Where Discipline Finally Stuck 79

Seeing the Whole Thing as a System 82

How ProShop Came Out of the Pain 83

When Other Shops Started Doing It Too 85

What the Mistakes Were For 87

CHAPTER 5: Getting In Without Getting Killed 89

Why People Walk Into This 90

Build It or Buy It 93

The Paperwork Wall 96

What You'll Underestimate 98

Failure Patterns to Know Before You Sign 101

The Game You're Actually Choosing 104

PART III: SALES, MONEY, AND SURVIVAL

CHAPTER 6: The Riches Are in the Niches 109

Generalists and Specialists 111

Side by Side 113

Saying No When the Books Are Thin 114

Customer Parts You Love 116

Why Focus Has to Come Before Scale 118

CHAPTER 7: Sales Is a System **121**

Not a Personality, a System 124

Demand You Can Choose From 126

Inbound and Outbound, Used Together 128

Selling Trust, Not Parts 130

The Numbers That Tell You What's Coming 133

CHAPTER 8: Estimating and Pricing **137**

The Four Cost Buckets 139

Estimating ≠ Pricing 140

Engineering Brain vs. Market Reality 141

Where the Dollar Goes 143

Who Should Own Estimating 144

Closing the Loop 145

The First Run Right 147

CHAPTER 9: Numbers Don't Lie **151**

Numbers Over Opinions 153

The Chart of Accounts That Matter 156

What Job Costing Needs to Be Real 158

Variance Is a Conversation 159

Kill Your Losers Early 161

PART IV: PEOPLE, CULTURE, AND STANDARDS

CHAPTER 10: The Shop Is the People **167**

Culture Beats Talent 168

Hire for Attitude, Train for Skill 171

Apprenticeships and Your Pipeline 172

Onboarding That Works 174

Why People Stay 176

When It Falls Apart 179

CHAPTER 11: Growing Pains **181**

The First Real Layer 183

Breaking $2M, Breaking $10M 188

Stages of the Owner 192

Designing What Comes Next 196

CHAPTER 12: Certifications and Compliance **199**

The Truth Behind Standards 201

ISO, AS9100, CMMC, and What They Open 202

Someone Has to Own It 205

Burden or Structure 208

The Always-Audit-Ready Shop 210

Turning Burden into Leverage 212

CHAPTER 13: Stop Winging It **215**

The Franchise Prototype, Again 217

Systems Beat Fixes 219

Discipline Beats Software 222

Effort vs. Design 224

CHAPTER 14: Quote to Cash **227**

Before You Say Yes: Contract Review 229

Planning Before the Spindle Turns 232

Schedules and Kits 235

Quality, Built In 238

Visibility Is Profit 240

Where the Money Moves 243

CHAPTER 15: Where Precision Lives **245**

Kitting as Philosophy 247

Inspection That Catches Things 249

Where the Hours Go 253

The Weight of Unfinished Work 256

What "Good" Looks Like 258

Built to Excellence 261

CHAPTER 16: Never Finished **263**

Lean, Without the Lecture 264

Kaizen That Sticks 269

When the Floor Brings the Ideas 272

What Automation Reveals 275

When Things Get Busy 276

Stability and Momentum 279

PART V: THE CALL

CHAPTER 17: Myths and Realities of a Top Shop 283

What "Top Shop" Really Means 284

Reading the Benchmark 286

Finding the Soft Spots Before They Crack 290

The Four Numbers That Matter 292

From Data to Action 294

CHAPTER 18: Something Someone Would Buy 297

What Buyers Pay For 298

Working Yourself Out of a Job 302

EBITDA, Not Revenue 305

Systems Are the Multiplier 308

Concentrated But Stable 310

Building for Options 312

CHAPTER 19: Leaving Well 315

The Document Most Owners Skip 316

When Family Inherits 318

The Four Buyers (and What Each Wants) 321
The Years Before the Deal 323
Deal Killers 325
Stewardship After You're Out 328

CHAPTER 20: Something Worth Keeping **331**
What You Owe the People 332
What Actually Lasts 335
Pride and Mastery 337
The Final Charge 339

INDEX **342**

ACKNOWLEDGMENTS **366**

A NOTE TO READERS **368**

CONTINUE BUILDING **370**

ABOUT THE AUTHOR **372**

FOREWORD

Mitch Free, Founder and CEO of ZYCI

Those who know me know that I am not a big reader. In fact, I have probably read fewer than ten books cover to cover in my life. Yet I couldn't put this one down.

Paul Van Metre has filled the pages you are about to read with practical insights about building, leading, and improving a manufacturing business. Again and again, I found myself thinking about lessons I had learned the hard way—and about ideas I wish someone had shared with me much earlier in my career.

My own journey has taken me from working as a machinist to founding four consequential companies. Along the way, I've experienced extraordinary opportunities, difficult setbacks, rapid growth, and constant change. Yet, after all these years, I believe we are entering the most exciting period of my career.

Space exploration is accelerating. A new generation of defense companies is developing capabilities once thought impossible. Fusion energy is moving closer to commercial reality. Humanoid robots are leaving research laboratories and entering the real world. Artificial intelligence is transforming how companies design products, operate factories, make decisions, and compete.

Every one of these breakthroughs depends on manufacturing.

None of these industries can fulfill its promise, however, without companies capable of turning ambitious ideas into reliable, repeatable, physical products. That creates an extraordinary opportunity for the machine shops and manufacturing leaders willing to raise their level of performance.

I have spent most of my career believing something that, for a long time, was not especially popular to say: America wins when America makes things. And it's not because manufacturing is nostalgic or because we want to recreate the past. Every nation that leads the world has a strong industrial base, and America, as a superpower, is the least exempt to this rule.

Innovation begins with people who know how to design, build, test, and improve products. Without the ability to make things, even the best ideas remain ideas. Over the last several years, we have all been reminded of that reality.

Rebuilding that capability is not someone else's responsibility. It's *ours*. Every machine-shop owner, programmer, setup machinist, quality engineer, production leader, and apprentice learning to operate a CNC machine has a role to play in restoring America's industrial strength.

However, without the right business knowledge and tools, there is only so much we can do.

I have been fortunate to spend my career working alongside these people, and they are among the smartest, most resourceful, and most determined entrepreneurs I have ever known. Every day, machine shop professionals solve extraordinarily difficult problems, often with limited resources and unforgiving deadlines. They do it with ingenuity, persistence, and a commitment to quality that few outside our industry fully understand.

Still, **being a great machinist does not automatically make someone a great business owner.** The skills required to produce exceptional parts are not always the same skills required to build an exceptional company.

A shop can have talented people, advanced equipment, and a strong reputation for quality while still struggling with inconsistent processes, unclear responsibilities, poor communication, unpredictable delivery, and an unhealthy dependence on a few key employees. Technical excellence may win the work, but it takes leadership, systems, accountability, and sound business practices to build a company capable of performing consistently and growing sustainably.

That is why this book matters.

Precision Manufacturing, Precision Business addresses the challenges that determine whether a machine shop merely survives or becomes a truly exceptional company. It shows manufacturers how to build reliable systems, establish accountability, measure what matters, document what they learn, develop capable employees, and create a culture in which continuous improvement becomes part of the daily work rather than an occasional initiative.

As I read the book, I repeatedly recognized principles I have seen throughout my own career. The best companies do not depend on heroes to rescue them every day.

Paul understands these realities because he has spent decades inside the manufacturing industry. Through Machine Shop Mastery, ProShop ERP, and countless conversations with manufacturers across North America, he has studied what works, what fails, and why some shops continue to improve while others remain trapped by the same recurring problems.

I have known Paul for years, and he has always impressed me with both his knowledge of machining and his relentless pursuit of understanding what separates good shops from truly great ones. This book captures what he has learned. It is not a collection of motivational stories or recycled management clichés. It is a practical guide grounded in real shops, real challenges, and real solutions.

That guidance has never been more important. Manufacturing is changing faster today than at any other point in my career. The companies that adapt will be better positioned to grow. But technology alone will not make a business great. New equipment, better software, and artificial intelligence cannot compensate for weak leadership, poor processes, or a lack of accountability.

Paul shows that excellence is intentional, built one decision, one process, and one improvement at a time.

At ZYCI, we've built our company around a similar belief: when we help manufacturers become more capable, secure, reliable, and competitive, we strengthen more than individual businesses. We strengthen the entire industrial ecosystem. Together, we help secure America's future.

Whether you are opening your first machine shop, leading a family business that has operated for generations, or managing a manufacturing company with hundreds of employees, you will find practical ideas in these pages that can make your organization stronger.

Some chapters will confirm lessons you have already learned through experience. Others may challenge assumptions you have held for years. Both are valuable. The best manufacturers never stop improving. Neither should we. But before you begin reading, I would leave you with this thought: The future of American manufacturing will not be built by our largest companies alone. It will be built by thousands of small and mid-sized manufacturers that choose to become world-class.

It will be built by leaders who invest in people, embrace useful technology, pursue quality without compromise, and create businesses capable of outlasting their founders. That is the opportunity in front of us. I believe this book will help you seize it.

PREFACE

Making a Country, Making Parts

I wrote this book to help machine shop owners build more profitable businesses, but it isn't only about money.

There are times in a nation's life when the work of ordinary people becomes extraordinary—times when the work itself hasn't changed, but the stakes around it have. America is in one of those moments. Manufacturing has returned to the center of the economic and national conversation, and what happens in machine shops today will shape communities, supply chains, and sovereignty for decades.

For decades we were told that making things was for the low skilled, that manufacturing efficiency meant outsourcing and that strength is measured in corporate financial statements. The consequences are now obvious. Supply chains have become fragile, towns have emptied, and we have learned that a country that cannot manufacture cannot control its destiny.

Manufacturing is, at its core, a requirement for social and economic resilience. It takes manufacturing know-how to develop the processes and create the parts that build and support our economy and our nation.

Machine shop owners sit at the center of this reality whether they ask for it or not. They train skilled workers, anchor local economies, and create durable, middle-class jobs that strengthen and sustain entire communities. One well-run shop supports not only the team members on its payroll and the families that rely on them at home but also the other local businesses that form manufacturing hubs across our great nation. Few industries shoulder this level of critical economic underpinning and yet fly almost completely under the radar of our day to day lives.

Voices from inside the industry run throughout this book. Many of the quotes come from interviews I conducted on the Machine Shop Mastery Podcast (part of the MakingChips network) and from the Manufacturing Transformed Podcast, the substance and spirit of each conversation bring home the message of what is facing actual shops, the people and teams that are quietly maintaining and growing our manufacturing capabilities as a nation through all the constraints and consequences, intended and unintended, of holding down this industry that is critical to our nation.

Nate Ankrom of Genuine Machine Products puts the stakes plainly: “Every great nation produces goods. And if you stop producing goods, you become a weaker nation.” On the global supply chain shift: “There’s a huge onshoring effort going right now. We are not ready for that.” On the obligation that creates: “We have all got to answer the challenge—our patriotic duty—to keep the work in country.” The machine shop is a piece of national tapestry distributed across thousands of unassuming addresses.

This book is about more than growth, efficiency, or valuation, though it will address all three. It is about responsibility: systems over chaos, foresight over firefighting, long-term excellence over short-term survival. When shop owners get that right, they don't only improve their own lives; they strengthen their communities and their country.

Today's moment demands more from manufacturing and offers more in return. Demand is rising, expectations are higher, the opportunity is real—but it won't be seized through heroics alone. It will be seized by shops that are intentionally designed, carefully run, and disciplined in execution. The work matters. The money follows. What you build now will matter far longer than the next job on the schedule.

In these times, machine shops don't only make parts—they make a country.

INTRODUCTION

Built to Tolerance

Precision machining respects a simple truth: outcomes come from systems doing what they were designed to do. Tolerance is a discipline. You don't "sort of" hit ±0.001. You design for it, measure it, control the variables that threaten it. When something drifts, you correct the process. Yet many shops that hit surgical precision on the floor tolerate chaos everywhere else.

Parts move through the process—quoting, scheduling, purchasing, machining, inspection, shipping—with microscopic care. The business around them runs on instinct, memory, and heroics. Owners chase fires. Schedulers reshuffle the board. Estimators guess. Leaders compensate with longer hours and personal sacrifice. The irony is hard to miss: shops capable of manufacturing aerospace-grade components run their businesses with looser tolerances than they'd ever accept in a spindle.

This book starts from a simple premise: if precision matters on the shop floor, it has to matter in the business, too. But first, I want to share a little bit about myself and why I wrote this book.

Like most people, I grew up knowing nothing about machining. I didn't even know the industry existed. I learned about it in college, fell in love with it, and entered at 24 as a recent college grad, co-founding a machine shop called Pro CNC near Seattle. We owned that company for 17 years until we sold it in 2014. For most of that time, we were also building software to run the place—software that would eventually become ProShop.

The years that followed were the ones that shaped this book. Meeting hundreds of shop owners, I was struck by the people and their stories, the good ones and the hard ones. This was also the period when I developed my "hardest business in the world" theory. I started a podcast as a vehicle to share those stories of success and hardship, triumph and loss, because I kept seeing people make the same mistakes over and over—mistakes others had made decades before. If I could help tell those stories, I figured, it could save current and future shop owners some hardship.

Years into running Machine Shop Mastery, I had the opportunity to move my podcast under the umbrella of the iconic MakingChips Podcast brand and become a co-owner with Mike Payne of Hill Manufacturing and Nick Goellner of Hennig. We've since grown the MakingChips network to over a dozen shows, with the mission to Equip and Inspire the Metalworking Nation. It's meaningful work to me.

However, not everyone listens to podcasts, and not everyone learns best through audio. This book is a natural progression: what I've learned from hosting hundreds of conversations, in a format that might be more useful for some.

Precision *Is* the Business

A machine shop is a system—a living, interconnected one—where decisions in sales affect quality, scheduling shapes morale, training drives margin, and a lack of visibility bleeds profit. Ignore those connections and the shop survives on brute force. Design them deliberately and the shop begins to compound: financially, operationally, culturally.

Most shop owners never set out to become business theorists. They came up through the trade, learned by doing, and solved problems with their hands, their heads, and their work ethic. That background isn't a weakness; it's the foundation of everything good in this industry. But technical excellence alone can't carry the weight of a modern machine shop. Complexity has increased. Margins are thinner. Customers are more demanding. Compliance is non-negotiable. The old model of "work harder and it'll work out" no longer scales.

Mitch Free of ZYCI describes the trap most owners fall into without naming it. "In his mind, it hasn't occurred to him that he's no longer a machinist. He's now an entrepreneur, he's a business owner, right? If you're out of the shop making parts, who's taking care of the business side of the business?" Free's conclusion is the line every owner has to internalize: "The goal should be to work on the business, not in the business."[1] That shift—from technician to designer of a company—is the single largest reframe most owners ever make, and the one this book is built around.

1 Machine Shop Mastery, Episode 16.

This is a design problem, not a talent problem. Step back and look at the best shops—the ones that grow, endure, and become valuable assets—and you see the same pattern. Clear workflows. Clear ownership. Clear feedback loops. Clear standards. They're designed the way good parts are designed: intentionally, systematically, and with respect for reality.

How to Read This Book

The book is organized the same way successful machine shops are built. Part I establishes the stakes—why this business matters now, not just economically but socially and nationally. If the work feels heavy at times, that's intentional. Responsibility precedes freedom.

Part II marks the first real transition—from machinist to owner. Many shops stall here, not because the owners lack skill but because they underestimate how different the job is. These chapters surface the traps, the myths, and the early decisions that determine whether a shop compounds or caps out.

Parts III and IV move into survival and scale. Sales, pricing, job costing, people, leadership, compliance—this is where most shops quietly bleed. Visibility precedes improvement.

Part V is the spine. Systems aren't bolted on later; they're the architecture that makes everything else work. Quote-to-cash, shop floor execution, and continuous improvement stop being slogans and become design choices.

Jamie Marzilli of Marzilli Machine articulates the right test for any system you build. "One, the rule can't say Jamie in it. A lot of people like to write rules. They say, well, first you do X, then you do Y, then you ask Jamie what to do next. That's an awful rule," he explains. He then highlights the necessity of future-proofing the workflow: "And then the second one is, will this scale? So, if you're taking the time to invent a system, will this system scale?"[2] That's the standard. Read this section slowly.

The final parts look forward. Excellence, value, exits, and legacy come from discipline, not size. Whether you intend to sell, pass it on, or run it for decades, businesses designed well give their owners options. Businesses held together by heroics don't.

You can read this book straight through, or you can live with it. Mark it up, argue with it, return to it as your shop evolves. Clarity allows precision; precision allows something worth keeping.

Who This Is For (and Who It Isn't)

This book is for machine shop owners and leaders, and anyone who takes the work seriously. It's for people who feel the weight that comes with signing paychecks, quoting jobs, meeting compliance standards, deciding what kind of company they're building when no one is watching. If you want your shop to run better, earn more, and last longer—and you're willing to examine how it's designed—this book is for you.

---

2 Machine Shop Mastery, Episode 8.

This book is for owners who came up through the trade and now realize technical excellence isn't enough. For leaders tired of fighting the same fires every week. For those who suspect their business could be calmer, clearer, and more profitable through better structure. And for first-time buyers and would-be founders who want to enter this industry with eyes open.

This book isn't for people looking for hacks, tricks, or silver bullets. It promises neither overnight growth, nor effortless scaling, nor freedom without discipline. If you believe working harder will always fix a broken system, you'll find parts of this book frustrating. If you're unwilling to measure reality, confront uncomfortable numbers, or change how decisions get made, you'll find it demanding.

This book also isn't for spectators. Reading alone won't transform a shop. The ideas here require implementation, repetition, and patience. They ask you to think like a designer, not a firefighter—to trade heroics for clarity, ego for structure. That kind of work compounds. It turns a difficult business into a durable one.

The Map Ahead

Everything that follows builds on one idea: a machine shop that runs well is designed, not just worked hard at. The chapters move deliberately—from why this business matters, to why it's so difficult, to how the best shops endure.

Mike Fritz of American Precision Partners urges owners to think about the end game. "Everybody should run their business like they're going to sell it," he advises. "You should run your business so that a person like me would want to come in and buy it. And the only reason I say that is because it will force you to put in SOPs, KPIs, your key performance indicators, if you're not familiar with those acronyms."[3]

Whether a sale is ever in the cards or not, the discipline that prepares a business for one is the same discipline that makes it worth running. What follows is meant to sharpen how you see your business—to give language to problems you've felt but may not have named. Some chapters will confirm what you already know. Others may challenge assumptions you've relied on for years. That tension is part of the work.

Read this book in order. Let the ideas accumulate. What comes next is grounded in reality, built for this industry, and written for a moment when getting this right matters more than ever.

3 Machine Shop Mastery, Episode 57.

PART I

Why This Business Matters

CHAPTER 1

Made Here, Built Right

The Business That Builds Everything Else

In the early 1940s, the United States did something that still feels almost impossible to comprehend. In the middle of the Great Depression's aftermath, with an economy that had been battered for more than a decade, the country retooled itself into the most formidable manufacturing engine the world had ever seen. Factories that once made consumer goods were converted almost overnight to build tanks, ships, engines, and aircraft. At the peak of World War II, American plants were producing a B-17 bomber roughly every hour—sixteen planes a day, around the clock.

The Allies didn't win the war by strategy alone. They won it by capacity—the ability to take raw material and turn it into reliable, repeatable output at a scale no adversary could match. Machine shops sat at the foundation of that effort. They made the tooling, the fixtures, and the components that made everything else possible. When the war ended, that capacity flowed straight into the postwar boom, fueling decades of growth, industrial leadership, and a broad, stable middle class.

This history surfaces a first principle most people have forgotten: manufacturing is the sector that makes the others possible. You take something low in value—ore, resin, billet, forgings—and through skill, process, and discipline turn it into something exponentially more valuable.

That act of transformation is where economic leverage lives.

Bob Mosey of Mosey's Production Machinist puts it plainly. "Without manufacturing, we have nothing," he states flatly.[4] I echoed Bob during our interview, pointing at the immediate reality of our own conversation: "We couldn't be sitting here recording without machine parts or machines at the core of everything that we're touching or working with." It sounds obvious once you hear it, and yet the country has spent forty years letting this fact slip out of its economic vocabulary—an erasure that has shaped policy, education, and culture in ways most people never connect back to the shop floor.

Machine shops occupy the foundation. The equipment used in construction, forestry, energy, agriculture, transportation, and defense begins in machining. Even industries that appear far removed from heavy manufacturing—technology, entertainment, medicine—

---

4 Machine Shop Mastery, Episode 14.

depend on precision-made components. When machining is strong, the industrial stack above it grows more resilient. When it weakens, everything downstream feels the strain.

This is why manufacturing carries political and geopolitical weight. A country that can make things at scale has options: it can respond to crises, it can defend itself, and it can innovate faster because production and design live close together.

The numbers reinforce what history already shows. For every manufacturing job, roughly 4.8 additional jobs are created elsewhere in the economy—the highest multiplier of any sector.[5] And manufacturing isn't the province of mega-corporations. Three-quarters of manufacturing firms employ fewer than twenty people; more than ninety percent employ fewer than one hundred.[6]

That distribution isn't unusual for American business—most industries skew small. What's unusual is the weight those small firms carry. A twenty-person marketing agency going under is a local event. A twenty-person shop holding a sole-source position on a landing gear component is a schedule slip for an aircraft program. The industrial base isn't a handful of large institutions with the resources to plan for a decade. It's tens of thousands of owner-operators making decisions at the kitchen table, and the country's capacity is the sum of those decisions.

---

5 "The Multiplier Effect: How American Manufacturing Supports Other Industries," AmericanMade-Products.com.

6 U.S. Bureau of Labor Statistics / U.S. Census Bureau. https://nam.org/mfgdata/facts-about-manufacturing-expanded/

What follows in this chapter:

- The multiplier effect of machining, and how one well-run shop can carry a whole town.
- The hidden cost of offshoring, and the skills, schools, and pipelines we lost before we noticed.
- Why this moment matters now—reshoring, supply chain shock, and a narrow window for capable shops to respond.
- The responsibility this moment carries, and the discipline it demands of every owner.
- Why machining is a type of a national service—and a durable opportunity.
- Why this work is so hard and so often misunderstood, even when the work is there.

The Multiplier Effect

When a machine shop grows, the impact reaches far beyond its walls. New jobs appear in trucking, logistics, maintenance, material supply, food service, retail, and housing. Small towns and rural areas, where much of manufacturing still lives, gain resilience. A single successful shop becomes a quiet engine of stability.

Consider Northside Machine Company in Dugger, Indiana. The shop sits in a prominent downtown location and employs roughly seventy people in a town of about eight hundred. Apply the standard manufacturing multiplier to those seventy direct jobs and the ripple stretches to roughly 350 local jobs supported, directly or indirectly, by what happens inside one machine shop. In a town that size, that isn't a contribution to the local economy. It is the local economy. Remove the shop and you don't lose a business; you lose a community.

Matt Wardle of JD Machine has lived this. "The economic impact of small family-owned businesses," he explains, "I don't think you can put a value on it."[7] The two hundred families on JD Machine's payroll in Ogden aren't line items. They're mortgages paid, kids in school, weekend coaches funded, churches and food banks staffed, restaurants and hardware stores kept in business.

Manufacturing is durable in a way few sectors are. Tourism can vanish overnight. Finance and tech can concentrate wealth without building local capacity. Machining turns a dollar of raw input into ten dollars of lasting value, most of which stays close to where it was created.

It's difficult to name an industry that doesn't depend on machining once you start pulling on the thread. Aerospace is the obvious example: every airframe, engine, actuator, landing system, and control surface traces back through tiers of suppliers to shops that hold tolerances, document quality, and deliver consistently. The same pattern repeats across the economy.

Pull on almost any thread of the economy, and machining is what holds it together:

7 Machine Shop Mastery, Episode 49.

Industry	What machining produces
Aerospace & defense	Airframes, engines, actuators, landing systems, control surfaces, seats, galleys, lavatories
Automotive	Powertrains, suspensions, braking, steering, EV battery housings, body panels
Energy & infrastructure	Turbines, pumps, valves, transmission components
Medical/Dental	Surgical instruments, implants, imaging hardware, hand tools
Semiconductors & AI hardware	Chip-handling equipment, precision fixtures, cooling systems
Film, TV, broadcast	Cameras, lenses, mounts, rigs, lighting, audio gear
Agriculture & construction	Heavy equipment, hydraulics, attachments, drivetrain parts

When machining capacity erodes, entire industries stall. Shipbuilding is a sobering example. The United States once produced a dominant share of the world's ships; today, a single Chinese state-owned shipbuilder reportedly builds more commercial vessel tonnage in one year than the entire U.S. shipbuilding industry has produced since World War II. Ships, like aircraft, are systems of systems, and those systems depend on a deep, capable machining base. Without it, defense readiness, logistics and supply chain resilience grow fragile.

The same competition now plays out in advanced technologies. Countries that control the ability to machine critical components control more than factories—they control timelines, security, and leverage. Governments are reassessing supply chains once assumed to be permanently stable.

When manufacturing weakens, the first things to go are the hardest to rebuild: trade schools, apprenticeship programs, and the accumulated knowledge of experienced workers. Supply chains stretch and fracture. Middle-income jobs disappear—the ones that support families, fund schools, and stabilize communities. Innovation slows; manufacturing produces more than half of all patents, and when production moves away, research follows. Trade deficits grow, national security erodes, social cohesion frays.

What looks like an economic shift becomes a political and cultural one.

What Offshoring Cost Us

This brings us to offshoring, the economic driver behind the weakening of American manufacturing. From the 1970s through the early 2000s, offshoring was framed as progress. Companies reduced costs, consumers paid less, and balance sheets improved. In the short term, the logic appeared sound. The long-term costs, though, were both underestimated and unevenly distributed. What disappeared wasn't just production capacity, but the ecosystems that supported it: shop classes, vocational training, apprenticeship pipelines, and multi-generational skill transfer.

Aneesa Muthana of Pioneer Service lived the bottom edge of that decision-making firsthand. "In 2012, we lost 90% of our business. It went to China and Mexico. And that was extremely painful and challenging."[8] Numbers like that don't show up in trade statistics with a face attached, but every percentage point represents a shop somewhere making payroll decisions, a community absorbing a shock, and a base of skill quietly walking out the door.

Innovation suffered, too, because manufacturing produces the most private-sector research and development and accounts for the majority of patents. When production moved offshore, design and innovation increasingly followed. The separation of engineering from manufacturing slowed feedback loops and weakened the country's ability to improve processes quickly. Some capabilities, once lost, proved extraordinarily difficult to rebuild—particularly education infrastructure and tightly coupled domestic supply chains.

What changed inside these communities went far beyond employment statistics. When machine shops disappeared, so did the sense of continuity and purpose that had anchored generations. Work that once carried dignity and clear progression was replaced with uncertainty. Young people no longer saw a future in making things. Schools deprioritized shop classes. Guidance counselors steered students away from trades that had quietly sustained entire towns for decades.

Manufacturing didn't just lose workers; it lost legitimacy.

---

8 Machine Shop Mastery, Episode 15.

The damage compounded over time. As middle-income jobs vanished, inequality widened. Local governments struggled to fund schools, infrastructure, and public services. Health outcomes worsened, and substance abuse rose in regions that had lost their economic center of gravity. These weren't isolated failures of policy or culture; they were predictable consequences of removing the economic engine that had supported stable family formation, community investment, and long-term planning. Once that engine stalled, everything connected to it felt the shock.

Perhaps the most underestimated loss was capability. Skills decay faster than buildings. Teachers retire, master machinists leave the workforce, and tooling suppliers close. What had once been a dense, self-reinforcing ecosystem thinned out until rebuilding it required far more than capital alone. Education pipelines had to be re-created. Supply chains had to be reassembled. Trust between customers and domestic suppliers had to be re-earned. None of these are switches that can be flipped on demand.

Meanwhile, the country grew more exposed. Trade deficits widened, and dependence on foreign production deepened. National security risks multiplied as critical components, materials, and technologies were sourced from regions beyond domestic control. What once felt like an abstract economic tradeoff revealed itself as a strategic vulnerability. Offshoring cost the country optionality, not just jobs and lower wages.

Understanding this history isn't an argument for nostalgia or retreat. It's a call for realism. The lesson shouldn't be that manufacturing should return to what it was, but that it has to evolve into something stronger, more disciplined, and more resilient than before. Rebuilding capacity requires more than opening doors and buying machines. It requires intention, systems, leadership—in other words, a willingness to treat manufacturing not as a commodity, but as a strategic asset.

Why Now Matters

Something has shifted. For the first time in decades, manufacturing isn't an afterthought in national conversations about economic strength, security, and resilience. Supply chain failures, geopolitical instability, and the hard lessons of COVID exposed how fragile the system had become and how costly that fragility really is. What once looked like efficiency now looks like risk. What once seemed inevitable now looks reversible.

There's also a growing recognition that the old assumptions were wrong. The idea that advanced economies could abandon production and thrive on services and knowledge work alone has proven short-sighted. Manufacturing was never just another sector; it was the foundation that made the rest of the economy durable. Without it, innovation slows, middle-class opportunity shrinks, and national leverage erodes. Worse still, those who once worked in manufacturing lose a sense of dignity and purpose.

That reality is getting harder to ignore.

At the same time, demand has returned faster than capacity. Aerospace backlogs stretch for years with a backlog of more than 16,000 aircraft globally, and defense production struggles to scale. (One Tomahawk missile, for instance, takes 24 months to make.[9]) Infrastructure, energy, and advanced technology programs are competing for the same constrained supply base. In many sectors, the work is there, but the shops, people, and systems required to execute it aren't keeping pace. This gap is visible and growing.

Kristin Carlson of Peerless Precision sees this happening in her own quote queue, in real time. "Especially since the pandemic, we might have all slowed down a little bit for a period. But with the supply chain crunches that we're dealing with, more and more customers are bringing parts back from overseas," she notes. The influx is creating a new kind of bottleneck for her business. "It's getting to the point where it's hard to keep up with quoting," she explains. While discussing how this surge relates to other industry changes, she emphasizes that reshoring is the real driver. "Not everything is going overseas to Asia anymore. It's coming back."[10]

That last sentence is the one to sit with. After thirty years of an unbroken outbound trend, the work is moving in the other direction—and the shops capable of catching it are the ones that will define the next chapter of American manufacturing.

This creates a narrow window. Customers are actively looking for reliable domestic suppliers, governments

9 Is the US Defense Industrial Base Building Enough Tomahawk Missiles? https://nationalinterest.org/blog/buzz/is-us-defense-industrial-base-building-enough-tomahawk-missiles-hk-031526

10 Machine Shop Mastery, Episode 09.

are investing in reshoring and resilience, and capital is paying attention again. But windows like this don't stay open forever. If domestic manufacturing can't respond with speed, discipline, and consistency, demand will find another outlet, as it always does.

The Responsibility This Carries

So, what does all of this mean for the individual shop owner?

It means this moment carries responsibility: not in an abstract or political sense, but in a very practical one. Running a machine shop has always been about making money. It has to be. Profit keeps the doors open, pays employees, funds reinvestment, and rewards risk. But it's never been only about money. Shops create livelihoods, they anchor communities, and they quietly support industries and capabilities the country depends on. Whether they intend to or not, shop owners sit closer to the foundation than most people realize.

Because the model has a ceiling, that responsibility requires discipline. Discipline to stop relying on brute force and personal sacrifice as the primary operating model. Discipline to replace tribal knowledge with documented processes. Discipline to look honestly at numbers, bottlenecks, and behaviors, even when they're uncomfortable. Otherwise, it does not scale and cannot reach its full potential. The shops that endure aren't the ones with the most talented owners or the newest machines. They're the ones willing to run the business with the same rigor they apply to making parts.

Doing this work well doesn't mean turning into a corporate bureaucracy or losing the soul of the shop. It means becoming a student of the business itself. It means understanding that technical excellence and business excellence are different skills, and that both matter. Being great at machining doesn't automatically make someone great at pricing, scheduling, hiring, or leadership. Those are learned disciplines, and they deserve the same respect as the craft.

When shops commit to this level of professionalism, the upside compounds quickly. The business becomes more profitable, yes, but also more stable. Employees gain clarity instead of chaos. Customers gain consistency instead of excuses. Owners gain leverage instead of exhaustion. The shop becomes something rare—a place that people want to work for, want to buy from, and want to build on.

There's no real downside to embracing this mindset. The fears are understandable—fear of not knowing enough, fear of change, fear of losing control—but they're temporary. The benefits aren't. Shops that level up don't just survive tougher cycles; they become assets. They gain optionality. They earn the right to grow, to hand the business off, or to exit on their own terms.

Most shop owners already take pride in their work—pride in their people, their customers, and their contribution to the economy. This is simply the next step in honoring that pride. Excellence isn't a buzzword here; it's a responsibility. And, in this moment, stepping up isn't just good business. It's how this industry earns its future.

A Different Kind of Service

It's worth saying plainly what this responsibility looks like from the inside, because the framing so far has been national and the reality is personal.

We rightly honor the men and women who serve this country in uniform. There is another kind of service the country needs, and it asks something different. It asks people to build companies that make real things, to train skilled workers, to create jobs that support families for decades, to strengthen the industrial base a nation depends on when it matters most. It isn't the same sacrifice. But it is a genuine contribution, and it is one almost nobody thinks to name.

The owner reading this is doing several jobs at once: building stability for a family, creating opportunity for the families on the payroll, preserving skilled work that would otherwise disappear when the last person who knows how to do it retires, adding a small amount of capacity to a country that is short of it.

And here is the part that gets lost when the emphasis stays on difficulty: this work is not only necessary, it's attractive. The world will keep needing precision parts. It will keep needing trusted suppliers and technical capability and shops that can execute when the work actually matters. That demand doesn't evaporate with the next technology cycle. It is about as durable a foundation as any business can stand on.

Which is exactly why the difficulty is worth facing squarely. Yes, this may be the hardest business in the world—the next chapter makes that case in detail. But the difficulty is not a reason to look away from the opportunity; it *is* the opportunity. Hard businesses have fewer competitors. Hard businesses reward discipline in ways easy ones never do. For the owner willing to run this one with rigor and systems, a machine shop becomes more than a demanding job. It becomes a durable company, a family asset, a wealth-building engine, and a platform the next generation can stand on.

That's the honest version. Brutal, essential, and—done right—deeply rewarding.

Why It's So Hard, and So Often Missed

If manufacturing is foundational, and this moment demands more from shops than ever before, the next question is unavoidable: why does running a machine shop feel so relentlessly difficult, even when the work is there?

Most owners don't struggle because they're careless or incompetent. They struggle because machining combines a rare mix of complexity, capital intensity, and razor-thin margins that few other businesses face at the same time. Every job is different. Every mistake is expensive. Cash gets tied up long before it comes back. Small inefficiencies compound quietly until they become existential threats.

What makes this especially punishing is that the skills required to succeed as an owner aren't the same ones that make someone successful on the floor. Precision, problem-solving, and work ethic matter, but they aren't enough on their own. As shops grow, the business itself becomes the hardest system to run. Throughput gets harder to see. Bottlenecks multiply. Decisions made upstream ripple everywhere else. Owners often find themselves working harder than ever while feeling further behind.

That tension leads many shops to rely on brute force and heroics—long hours, constant firefighting, personal sacrifice—to keep things moving. It works for a while. Then it doesn't. Understanding why that happens is the first step toward fixing it. To move forward, we have to name the problem clearly. That starts by being honest about what kind of business this really is, and why skill alone has never been enough.

CHAPTER 2

The Hardest Business in the World

Why Machine Shops Play on Expert Mode

Most people outside manufacturing don't understand just how punishing this business can be. They see finished parts, busy shops, and skilled people making complex things, and they assume that if you're good at the craft, the business should take care of itself. They think you just load a piece of material into a machine, press a button, and a part comes out. Shop owners know better. They feel the weight every month—sometimes every day—of a business that demands constant attention and offers very little margin for error.

Machine shops don't just have to execute well; they have to execute consistently, across hundreds or thousands of details, while juggling customers, people, machines, cash, and time. One missed assumption can erase weeks of profit. One bad quote can turn a good month into a financial setback.

And unlike many other businesses, there's often no easy way to fix mistakes after the fact.

What makes this especially hard is that the work looks familiar to the people running it. Most owners came up through the trade. They know machining—they understand tolerances, setups, tooling, and quality. But running a machine shop isn't machining at scale; it's an entirely different discipline layered on top of it. That distinction is where many shops quietly struggle.

To understand why skill alone isn't enough, it helps to compare machining to other businesses commonly described as "hard." The contrast is revealing.

What this chapter covers:

- Machine shops compared with other "hard" businesses, side by side with restaurants and construction.
- Why skilled machinists so often struggle as owners.
- Complexity, capital intensity, and margins, and how each one amplifies the others.
- Throughput and visibility, and why busy shops still feel perpetually behind.
- The myth of brute force, and why heroics conceal the real problem instead of solving it.
- The point where effort alone stops working, and what has to replace it.

Restaurants, Construction, and Where Machining Actually Lives

Restaurants are often held up as the gold standard of difficult businesses. They're competitive, margins are thin, and failure rates are high. Running one requires long hours, tight coordination, and constant problem-solving. While restaurants are operationally complex, though, the work itself isn't technically complex. It doesn't take decades to learn how to cook well. Equipment costs are relatively modest. And mistakes, while painful, are usually survivable.

General construction is another example people point to. It can be demanding, physical, and schedule-driven. It's also far more forgiving than machining. A plumbing contractor can show up with a truck and a few bags of tools and bill a few hundred dollars an hour. Barriers to entry are lower. Competition is mostly local. Tolerances are loose enough that mistakes can often be corrected on-site without scrapping days of work.

Machining is different. A modern machine shop requires hundreds of thousands, often millions, of dollars in capital before the first part ever ships. A single CNC machine might cost $100,000 to $250,000 before tooling, fixtures, metrology, software, and supporting infrastructure are even considered. It takes years of experience to reliably produce complex work.

Competition, meanwhile, is global, not local.

The unforgiving nature of the work is what truly sets machining apart. Carpenters work within fractions of an inch. Machinists work in thousandths, or smaller. A missed tolerance of 0.0001" doesn't mean rework; it often means scrap. That scrap doesn't just cost material, it also wipes out labor, machine time, overhead, and opportunity. In a business with thin margins, that kind of precision cuts both ways.

Stack the three side by side, and the gap stops being rhetorical:

Dimension	Restaurant	General construction	Machine shop
Capital to start	Tens of thousands	Truck and tools	Hundreds of thousands to millions
Years to competence	Months to a few years	A few years	A decade or more
Tolerance for error	Survivable	Often correctable on-site	Often fatal to the job
Competition	Mostly local	Mostly local	Global
Pricing model	Menu, adjustable	Often time-and-materials	Firm fixed-price
Mistake recovery	Comp the meal, learn	Change order, rework	Scrap, absorb the loss

Allison Giddens of Win-Tech captures the asymmetry with the kind of dark humor that only an owner can earn, joking that "someone either has to be crazy or stupid to buy a machine shop." She explains the daily reality of the floor: "I always say, in a shop like this, you get a thousand chances to get a job wrong and one chance to get it right." To actually turn a profit, she notes, "The stars truly have to align to make the margin you quoted on it."[11] That ratio—a thousand ways to fail, one way to succeed—isn't a metaphor; it's a fairly literal description of how a part moves through a shop. Estimating, programming, material, setup, tooling, fixturing, in-process inspection, final inspection, paperwork, packaging, shipping. Any one of those steps can break the job, and most of them can break it silently.

Precision doesn't exist in isolation, either. It cascades through everything else the shop does. A small error upstream—an assumption in estimating, a missed detail in process planning, a rushed setup—shows up downstream as scrap, rework, expediting, or missed delivery dates. There's rarely a chance to renegotiate once the mistake is visible. The part either meets spec, or it doesn't. The customer either accepts it or they don't.

What makes this even more punishing is that most machine shop work is quoted as firm fixed-price. If costs run over, the shop absorbs them. There's no change order, no time-and-materials safety net. A job quoted with the hope of a 10% margin can turn into a total loss with one bad decision, or one bad day. That asymmetry is brutal: upside is capped, while downside is often unlimited.

11 Machine Shop Mastery, Episode 47.

Machining also stacks complexity in ways that are easy to underestimate. Material behavior, tool wear, machine condition, programming strategy, inspection methods, and operator skill all interact. Change one variable and the outcome can shift. Success isn't just about knowing how to make a part; it's about managing the conditions under which parts get made, repeatedly, by different people, across different machines, under real-world constraints.

This is where many comparisons fall apart. Other "hard" businesses can often compensate for mistakes with time, communication, or pricing adjustments. Machine shops don't have that luxury. Precision is binary. Either the system holds, or it doesn't. And when it doesn't, the cost shows up immediately on the shop's balance sheet. That unforgiving reality is what makes machining such a demanding business to run—and why relying on skill alone, no matter how deep, is rarely enough.

Why Great Machinists Make Hard Owners

The most common mistake skilled machinists make when they become owners is an understandable one: they assume that being good at machining will translate naturally into being good at running a machine shop. After all, the business exists to make parts. If you know how to do that well, how hard can the rest really be?

At first, the assumption even seems to hold. The owner can program, set up, troubleshoot, and keep machines running. Customers come through personal networks. Quality is strong. Early momentum feels earned. Before long, though, the demands start to compound—quoting takes more time, scheduling gets tighter, cash feels perpetually short, hiring gets harder. The work that once felt empowering starts to feel overwhelming.

Many new owners also underestimate how much of the job has nothing to do with machining at all. They assume the business is mostly about buying material, making parts, and sending invoices. In reality, those steps sit on top of a much larger structure: pricing strategy, capacity planning, workflow design, hiring and training, quality systems, customer communication, compliance, and cash management. Each one is its own discipline, and none of them improve automatically just because the parts are good.

Nick Preece of Preece Machining describes the trap with unusual honesty. "I am literally the best technician ever and I don't want to mess with any admin things. All I want to do is run a machine. It creates a whirlwind of chasing our tail."[12] That admission is more useful than any abstract diagnosis because it surfaces the actual emotional pull behind the problem. The work at the machine is satisfying. The admin work isn't. So the owner gravitates toward the spindle and away from the desk, and the business runs harder and harder on accumulated improvisation until the wheels finally start to come off.

Cash flow is often where this gap becomes impossible to ignore. Machine shops consume cash long before they generate it. The material is purchased upfront and labor

12 Machine Shop Mastery, Episode 29.

is paid weekly. Meanwhile, machines get financed and customers pay later, sometimes much later. Owners who didn't plan for this reality find themselves constantly short of oxygen, even when the shop is busy. It's common to hear, "We've got plenty of work, but there's never any money." That isn't bad luck. It's a system doing exactly what it was designed to do.

For some owners, this realization comes quickly, within the first few months. For others, it takes years. They assume things will smooth out once the shop "gets established." Instead of getting easier, though, the problems persist. They're working longer hours, carrying more stress, and still wondering why the numbers don't reflect the effort. At that point, it becomes clear that skill isn't the constraint.

None of this is a failure of character or work ethic. Machinists are problem solvers by nature. They're used to fixing what's broken by applying intelligence and effort directly. The problems in a growing shop, though, aren't always visible at the machine level. They live in the gaps between functions. They show up as missed handoffs, unclear priorities, bad assumptions, and unmeasured decisions. And those problems don't yield to effort alone.

The turning point for most owners comes when they recognize a hard truth: running a machine shop is a different job than machining. It requires a different way of thinking, a different set of tools, and a willingness to step back from the work to implement the system that produces it. Until that shift happens, even the most skilled machinists will find themselves fighting the business instead of building it.

Three Forces That Compound

What makes machine shops especially difficult to run is that complexity, capital intensity, and margins don't just coexist; they reinforce each other. Each one amplifies the consequences of the others. Complexity increases the chances of error. Capital intensity magnifies the cost of those errors. Thin margins leave very little room to absorb them.

Picture a real example of how the three forces braid together. A shop quotes a precision aluminum housing with a 12% target margin. The estimator assumes a four-hour cycle time based on a similar part run two years ago. Material arrives, but the heat treatment is slightly off-spec, so the first roughing pass results in the cutter getting gummed up and breaking, and a $300 end mill lasts 2 minutes. The second setup takes ninety minutes longer than planned and scraps two parts because the fixture, designed for a different revision, doesn't locate cleanly. Extra material is overnighted, run on overtime.

By the time the part reaches inspection, two features are at the edge of tolerance. One out of fifteen is scrapped, and you had to buy 18 blanks. The job ships on time, the customer is satisfied, and the shop loses 8% on what was supposed to be a profitable run. None of those small failures would matter on their own. Stacked together, on a job with a 12% target margin, they're the difference between a good day and a bad one. Multiply that across a year, and you get a shop that's busy, well-respected, and somehow never has any cash.

I have long said that this industry, with its capital-intensive nature, competitive, and technical nature, is the hardest business in the world. As Nate Bourgeois, founder of Ouroboros Space and Defense, says, "If you get into machining for the money, not only will you be sorely surprised, but you probably won't actually survive."[13] That isn't cynicism. Shops that survive long-term are run by people who care about the craft and the company in roughly equal measure. Run a shop purely as a financial bet, and the math will eventually find you out.

Start with fixed costs. Even in a slow month, a shop can't escape rent or a mortgage, utilities, insurance, software, and debt service on machines. Labor used to be considered variable, but in today's environment it rarely is. Skilled machinists are too hard to find and too valuable to let go. Lay them off during a downturn, and there's no guarantee you'll ever replace them. In practice, almost every employee becomes overhead, whether the machines are cutting chips or sitting idle.

Capital requirements shape every decision a shop makes. Moving into new materials, tighter tolerances, or different industries often requires dramatically more expensive equipment. A shop can't "test" its way into five-axis work or exotic alloys without real money on the line. Unlike many other businesses, there's no low-cost version of high-end machining. Capability is binary—either you can do the work, or you can't—and the price of entry is high.

---

13 Machine Shop Mastery, Episode 48.

Margins make this even more unforgiving. To earn a modest profit on a typical job, thousands of small things have to go right. The quote has to be accurate. Material has to arrive on time. Setups have to be efficient. Tools have to perform. Programs have to be clean. Inspections have to pass. The schedule has to hold. Miss any one of those details, and a job that looked like a 10% win can quickly turn into a total loss.

Unlike construction or consulting, machine shops usually can't pass overruns back to the customer. Most work is quoted as firm, fixed price. If the shop runs long, that cost belongs to the shop. If a tolerance is missed, the part is scrap. If a delivery is late, penalties—or worse—follow. There's no buffer. The system either produces margin, or it destroys it. This is why shops can feel financially fragile even when they're busy. Revenue masks risk. Machines are running, people are working overtime, and invoices are going out—but underneath, the business may be bleeding quietly. Cash gets tied up in work-in-process. Small inefficiencies compound. One bad month wipes out the gains of three good ones.

In a business like this, discipline isn't optional. You can't outwork structural problems forever. The combination of complexity, capital, and margins means the shop has to operate with intention—or it will default into chaos. And that's where many owners begin to feel like they're always behind, no matter how hard they push.

Busy but Behind

One of the most common frustrations shop owners voice is this: we're busy all the time, but it never feels like we're getting ahead. Machines are running. People are working overtime. Quotes are going out. And yet, cash is tight, schedules slip, and the pressure never really lets up. That disconnect isn't a mystery; it's a throughput and visibility problem.

Throughput is simply the rate at which the shop turns effort into finished, shippable work. When throughput isn't understood or managed deliberately, the shop stays busy without being effective. Work piles up. Jobs wait between steps. Priorities shift daily. Energy goes into expediting instead of executing. From the outside, it looks like productivity. Inside, it feels like chaos.

Lack of visibility makes this worse. When owners and managers can't clearly see where work stands—what's quoted, what's released, what's in process but taking longer than planned, what's late, and what's blocking progress—they lose the ability to plan. Without a plan, everything becomes reactive. Schedules turn into guesses. Commitments get overextended. The shop slides into constant firefighting mode.

Day to day, these problems don't announce themselves as crises. They show up gradually, in ways that feel manageable at first. Overtime stops being an exception and quietly becomes part of the baseline. Expediting becomes normal. Material arrives late, or it arrives wrong, and the shop absorbs the hit. Jobs get touched twice because something upstream wasn't fully thought through. As the quote often attributed to Jack Bergman states, "There's never enough time to do it right, but there's always enough time to do it over." People spend more time coordinating, clarifying, and moving work around than actually making parts. None of this feels catastrophic in isolation, but taken together, it steadily erodes margin without anyone being able to point to a single cause.

Poor throughput planning makes this erosion inevitable. When the shop doesn't have a clear, realistic view of its capacity, decisions get made on instinct instead of fact. Too much work gets accepted, or the right work gets run in the wrong order. Jobs are forced through out of sequence, setups stretch longer than expected, and machines wait on parts while other areas pile up. The cost doesn't appear as one dramatic failure; it accumulates quietly, through inefficiency layered on top of inefficiency. If I could summarize the most common realization from hundreds of ProShop implementations, it's this one. A little more time invested in planning up front pays back massive dividends on the back end.

The human toll is just as real. Most people in a machine shop take pride in their work. They want to do things right. They want to deliver quality parts and keep customers happy. When the environment feels constantly rushed and disorganized, that pride starts to wear down. Even when a team pulls off a save through sheer effort, the relief is fleeting, because everyone knows the next fire is already forming.

That's why so many shops feel perpetually behind. Not because the people aren't working hard enough, but because effort isn't being converted into results efficiently. Without visibility, throughput can't be managed. Without managed throughput, planning breaks down. And when planning breaks down, the business begins to dictate the owner's time and energy instead of the other way around.

The Myth of Heroics

When a shop falls behind, the response is almost instinctive. Effort increases, hours get longer, and the pace accelerates. Everyone leans in and does whatever it takes to hit the delivery. In the moment, it feels responsible, sometimes even noble. That impulse comes from a good place; machining is built on pride in the work, respect for the craft, and a deep sense of accountability. But what works at the machine doesn't always work at the level of the business.

The habits that solve individual problems don't scale when the problems are systemic. Over time, constant intervention replaces structure, and effort stands in for clarity. The shop keeps moving, but it does so by burning energy instead of building capability. That's the trap of heroics: they feel like leadership in the moment, but they quietly prevent the business from ever learning how to run without them.

Dave Capkowicz of CK Tool describes the personal cost in terms most owners will recognize, even if they'd rather not admit it. Reflecting on his early days, he admits, "my biggest fault in owning my own business when I first started is when way before the sun came up, I was at the shop, and I was at the shop way after the sun went down." He details the physical toll this schedule demanded: "I was averaging probably four or five hours of sleep. I just worked, and some days I slept in my office." He masked the lack of systems with sheer force of will, recalling his mindset at the time: "I was just like, okay, I got this. I have two people to help and we're going to get it done." He concludes simply: "But all the, all the negative stuff is, is man, I had no work life balance."[14]

That story isn't cautionary because Capkowicz failed; it's cautionary because that pattern of behavior is treated, in many shops, as the definition of a committed owner. The reality is closer to the opposite. An owner working off four hours of sleep a night is a leading indicator that the system has been substituted for, not built. Heroics are appealing because they produce short-term wins. What rarely happens afterward is a real examination of why the crisis happened in the first place. Instead of fixing the system that allowed the failure, the shop absorbs the cost and moves on. Over time, those costs stack up.

There's a simple exercise from lean manufacturing called the Five Whys. When something goes wrong, you ask why it happened. Then you ask why that happened. And you keep going, five times, until you reach the root cause in the system. Most shops never get past the first why. They stop at "We were busy," or "Someone made a mistake," and then throw more effort at the problem.

---

14 Machine Shop Mastery, Episode 35.

Brute force masks deeper issues; bad scheduling, poor planning, unclear processes. Owners stepping in to save the day conceals gaps in structure and accountability, keeping the shop going without allowing it to get better. In fact, the shop becomes more fragile because it now depends on constant intervention to function.

Eventually, something gives. Sometimes it's cash, with the business bleeding slowly until one bad quarter wipes out years of progress. Sometimes it's people, with burnout setting in and taking good employees away. The owner often becomes the bottleneck for every decision. Even when the shop survives financially, the cost shows up in exhaustion, stress, and a business that feels impossible to step away from.

The hardest truth is this: companies that require constant heroics are telling you something. They're telling you the system isn't working. Great shops don't eliminate problems, but they solve them in a way that makes the next day easier, not harder. They don't rely on brute force. They rely on design. And that's where the conversation has to turn next.

When Hard Work Stops Working

Up to this point, we've been naming the problem: why machine shops are uniquely difficult to run, why effort alone breaks down, and why so many capable, hardworking owners feel trapped inside businesses that won't stabilize. Diagnosis only matters, though, if it leads somewhere useful.

The next step isn't more motivation or harder work. It's a shift in how owners understand their role. The skills that make someone a great machinist are real, valuable, and hard-earned—but they aren't the same skills required to design and run a durable business. Confusing the two is one of the most common ways owners unintentionally sabotage themselves.

That confusion is exactly what Part II is about: setting expectations early and clearly, especially for owners who are talented, driven, and proud of their craft. It's about understanding why owning a machine shop is a fundamentally different job than working in one, and why treating it as such isn't selling out or going corporate, but taking responsibility seriously.

We'll start by unpacking a core idea that's shaped countless successful businesses across industries: the difference between being a technician and being an owner. From there, we'll look at what it actually means to design a shop as a system—one that can grow, adapt, and eventually operate without constant heroics. We'll share hard-earned lessons from building Pro CNC and ProShop, not as a success story, but as a record of mistakes, constraints, and breakthroughs that forced discipline into the business. Finally, we'll address the point where many people enter this industry: starting or buying a shop. We'll look honestly at why people do it, what they expect, and what they consistently underestimate, before the stakes get too high and the options get too narrow.

This is where the work shifts from reacting to problems to designing solutions. From pushing harder to building smarter. From surviving the business to actually owning it.

PART II

From Machinist to Business Owner

CHAPTER 3

The E-Myth of Machining

Machining and Business Are Two Different Jobs

Two books come up again and again in conversations about struggling machine shops: *The E-Myth Revisited* by Michael Gerber and *The Goal* by Eli Goldratt. They're often recommended, frequently quoted, and just as often misunderstood. You don't need to have read either of them to understand this chapter, but you do need to understand the problems they're trying to solve, because both books subtly shape the way the rest of this book is organized.

Although the two books take different angles, they challenge the same assumption: that working harder, being more skilled, or optimizing individual tasks will naturally produce a successful business. In practice, that assumption breaks down, especially in machining. The E-Myth focuses on a pattern that shows up in almost every trade. Someone becomes highly skilled at the technical work. They're reliable. They care. Eventually, they start a business, and what they don't realize is that owning a business that does technical work is a fundamentally different job than doing the work itself.

In machining, the most familiar version of that story is the machinist who buys a Haas and hangs a sign. But the pattern isn't about machinists. It's about excellence in one function being mistaken for readiness to run the whole. The estimator who knows exactly what work is worth. The quality engineer who can hold a system together under audit. The salesperson with a book of business. The finance-minded buyer who can read a deal better than anyone in the room. Each arrives with a genuine strength and a matching blind spot, and the blind spot is the part nobody warns them about. The skills don't transfer cleanly, and the habits that made them great technicians often work against them as owners.

While *The E-Myth* focuses on the technician's mindset, *The Goal* comes at the problem from a systems perspective. It argues that a business isn't a collection of independent activities; it's a system with a purpose. Optimizing individual steps doesn't matter if the system as a whole isn't improving. What matters is flow, constraints, and throughput. The goal isn't to be busy. The goal is to make money now and in the future.

Machining sits at the intersection of these two ideas in a particularly unforgiving way. The work is deeply technical. The tolerances are tight. The capital requirements are high. Mistakes are expensive. Because of that, shop owners are constantly pulled back into the details—programming parts, fixing problems, saving jobs, answering questions. It feels necessary. It feels responsible. And it's often exactly what keeps the business stuck.

This chapter is about drawing a clear line between two roles that are often blurred: the technician and the owner. It's about understanding why skill alone is never enough, why systems matter earlier than most people think, and why many shops stall not because of a lack of effort, but because of how that effort is applied.

Nick Preece of Preece Machining & Assembly described reading The E-Myth as a kind of uncomfortable mirror. "I read that book, The E-Myth, and I just was almost crushed," he said. "I remember just being like, that is me. I am the perfect technician. The bigger the mountain of stuff to do, the happier I am. How have I not thought at all about the business?"[15]

If you've ever felt indispensable to your shop, constantly busy, and still uneasy about the future, this chapter is for you—not because you're doing something wrong, but because you may be doing the right things for the wrong job. We'll start by breaking down the most common trap: confusing excellence at machining with competence at running a machining business.

What this chapter covers:

- The difference between being a technician and being an owner, and why the shift catches so many machinists off guard.

15 Machine Shop Master, Episode 29.

- What different owners see clearly and the most common blindspots.
- How the E-Myth applies to machining, and why machining amplifies the trap rather than escaping it.
- Lessons from The Goal: flow, constraints, and why local efficiency isn't enough.
- Designing the franchise prototype, even if you'll never actually franchise.
- Why systems have to come first, not later.
- The psychological shift the owner has to make, and the price of skipping it.

Technician vs. Owner

The day-to-day work of a great machinist is deeply satisfying in a way few jobs are. It's hands-on, precise, and honest. You're given a drawing, material, and a set of constraints, and your job is to figure out how to turn that into a real, physical part that meets spec. There's creativity in the process, but the outcome is binary. The part is either right, or it isn't. Tolerances don't care how hard you worked or how late you stayed. They only care about results.

Most machinists spend their days working largely on their own. Even in a busy shop, the work itself is solitary—programming, setting up, cutting, measuring, adjusting. You're solving problems directly, with your hands and your head at the same time. When something goes wrong, you can usually see it, touch it, and fix it. Progress is tangible. You can point to what you made at the end of the day and know whether it was good.

Owning a machine shop is nothing like that.

The work of an owner is abstract, indirect, and often uncomfortable, especially for someone who came up through the trade. Instead of working on parts, you're working on people. Instead of solving technical problems, you're dealing with coordination, priorities, tradeoffs, and uncertainty. The output of your work isn't a finished component; it's alignment. Are the right jobs being quoted? Are they priced correctly? Is work flowing through the shop the way you think it is? Will there still be work here three months from now?

That shift catches a lot of machinists off guard. Although the skills that made them successful on the floor don't disappear, those skills stop being the limiting factor. What starts to matter more is communication, planning, system design, and leadership. None of those show up on a print. None of them have tolerances you can measure with calipers. And none of them provide the same immediate feedback loop that machining does. The contrast looks something like this:

Dimension	Technician	Owner
Primary output	Finished parts	Aligned decisions
Time horizon	Hours and days	Months and years

Dimension	Technician	Owner
Feedback loop	Immediate, tactile	Delayed, indirect
Problem type	Technical, bounded	Systemic, ambiguous
Tools of the job	Calipers, programs, tooling	Numbers, conversations, structure
Measure of success	Did the part meet spec?	Is the system improving?
Source of pride	What you built today	What the company can do without you

This is why so many owners stay trapped in technical work long after the business is asking something different from them. The machine is familiar. The problems are solvable. The feedback is clear. Compared to that, sales, hiring, forecasting, and process design feel vague and risky. If you're the best machinist in the shop—and many owners are—it's even harder to step away. Every time you jump in to program a job, fix a setup, or save a delivery, you're rewarded with proof that you're still indispensable.

The problem is that indispensability doesn't scale.

When the owner remains the best machinist, programmer, or firefighter, the business quietly organizes itself around that fact. Questions bottleneck at one person. Decisions wait. Problems escalate upward instead of being solved where they happen. The owner becomes the center of gravity for everything technical, and often everything important. It feels like control. In reality, it's constraint.

At first, this can work. In a small shop, the owner's involvement can mask weak systems and missing structure. As volume increases, though, the cracks start to show. The owner is buried in today's problems while tomorrow's problems go unattended. Sales and marketing become reactive. The backlog shrinks without warning. The shop slips into feast-and-famine cycles—not because the owner isn't working hard enough, but because they're working on the wrong time horizon.

There's a moment, different for every shop, when technical competence stops being an asset and starts becoming a bottleneck. It's the moment when the business needs attention upstream but the owner is still downstream, making parts. Even though stepping away from the machine feels like losing control, staying there is what's actually putting the business at risk. This tension isn't a personal failure. It's structural. And it's exactly the trap that *The E-Myth* was written to describe.

Which Expert Are You?

The technician-to-owner story is usually told as a machinist's story, and that's fair enough; it's the most common path into this industry. But the trap isn't specific to machinists. It's specific to experts. Whatever function you came up through taught you to see the business through that function's lens. That lens is an asset. It's also the reason certain problems will be invisible to you for years.

Came up through	Sees clearly	Tends to underestimate
The floor	Capability, process, what the work actually takes	Sales cycles, pricing discipline, financial structure
Engineering or programming	Technical risk, design intent, what's achievable	Customer relationships, cash timing, people problems
Quality	Process discipline, documentation, systems thinking	Market risk, growth tradeoffs, commercial urgency
Estimating	What work is worth, where margin hides	Execution reality, throughput, team dynamics
Sales	Demand, relationships, market position	Technical complexity, operational constraints, capacity
Finance or acquisition	Deal structure, capital allocation, the numbers	Craft, culture, tribal knowledge, how long trust takes
The family business	History, customers, the accumulated why	Inherited assumptions nobody has questioned in thirty years

None of these columns describes a deficiency. They describe a starting position. The problem isn't having a blind spot—everyone has one. The problem is that the owner's blind spot doesn't stay personal. It becomes structural.

Here's how that works. The owner naturally spends time where they're competent, because competence is comfortable and feedback is fast. The areas they avoid get less attention, worse hiring, later systems, and thinner scrutiny. Over a few years, the company develops a shape that matches the owner's instincts—strong where they're strong, soft where they're soft. Employees learn what gets attention and what doesn't. Customers learn it, too.

Ask any experienced person to walk through an unfamiliar shop and they can usually tell you what the owner came up through within an hour. The tell isn't what's good. It's what's been neglected. That's why self-awareness isn't a soft skill in this context. It's a design input. If you don't know what you'll avoid, you can't staff around it, build systems for it, or hold yourself accountable to it.

There are structured ways to get at this. Kolbe, Working Genius, DISC, Myers-Briggs, and a dozen similar assessments all try to name how a person naturally approaches problems, and any of them can be useful for putting language to something you half-know already. The specific instrument matters far less than the honesty. You can arrive at the same insight with a legal pad and a willingness to write down the three parts of the business you've been quietly hoping someone else will handle.

What you do with the answer matters more than how you got it. The instinct most owners have is to lean into their strengths and hope the rest sorts itself out. The stronger move is to lean into the weaknesses—deliberately, by bringing in people who see what you don't, decide differently than you would, and act on different instincts. That's uncomfortable by design. People who think like you are easy to work with and confirm what you already believe. People who don't are the ones who catch what you miss.

Ownership isn't about becoming great at everything. That's not available. It's about building a business that isn't limited by what the owner personally does best. Which reframes the whole transition. It isn't machinist to owner. It's a functional expert to business designer—and the design has to account for the designer.

The E-Myth, Applied to Steel

At its core, *The E-Myth* (short for "entrepreneurial myth") challenges a common assumption: that being good at a craft qualifies someone to run a business built around that craft. Gerber argues that most small businesses are started by technicians—people who are excellent at doing the work—who are then surprised when the business itself demands a completely different set of skills. The myth is believing that technical expertise automatically translates into managerial or entrepreneurial competence. Machining fits this pattern almost perfectly, and in many ways, it amplifies it.

Machining is extraordinarily technical. It requires deep knowledge, years of experience, and constant problem-solving under tight tolerances and high stakes. It's also capital-intensive in a way many other trades aren't. While a carpenter or plumber can often scale their work incrementally, adding tools and helpers over time, a machine shop requires large, irreversible investments early—machines, tooling, inspection equipment, software—often before the owner fully understands what the business will demand of them.

That combination makes the E-Myth trap harder to escape. Because the work is so difficult, the technician-owner is often the most capable person in the building. And because skilled machinists are so hard to find, many shops quietly decide that they have to depend on the owner's expertise to survive. Over time, the business becomes structured around that dependence.

This is where machining adds extra complexity to Gerber's original idea. *The E-Myth* encourages owners to design their businesses like "franchise prototypes"—systems so clear and repeatable that the business could be replicated many times over. Franchises work not because the work is simple, but because the systems are robust. Every process is defined. Every handoff is intentional. Every role is clear.

In machining, that level of systemization can feel intimidating, even unrealistic. The work itself is variable. Materials move. Tolerances stack. No two jobs are exactly alike. Owners often assume that this variability makes strong systems impossible—or worse, that systems will dilute craftsmanship.

In reality, the opposite is true. The more complex the work, the more the business depends on systems. When tolerances are tight and margins are thin, tribal knowledge and heroics become liabilities. Without clear processes, information gets trapped in people's heads. Decisions get made inconsistently. Mistakes repeat themselves. And the owner gets pulled back into the details—not because they want to, but because the business has no other way to function.

This is why machining is especially vulnerable to the technician-turned-owner trap. The technical demands of the work make it easy to justify staying in the weeds. The difficulty of hiring reinforces that decision. The lack of visible structure makes it feel like there's no alternative. There is, though, and seeing it requires a different way of thinking about the shop—not as a collection of machines and problems, but as a system. That's where *The Goal* comes in.

Lessons from *The Goal*

While *The E-Myth* explains why so many machinists struggle as owners, *The Goal* explains what they're missing when they try to fix it.

Goldratt's book is a business novel built around a deceptively simple idea: the purpose of a business is to make money—now and in the future—and everything else is a means to that end. His insight wasn't just philosophical. It was operational. He showed that most organizations fail not because people aren't working hard, but because they're optimizing the wrong things.

The book introduces the Theory of Constraints: every system has at least one constraint that governs its overall performance. Improving anything other than that constraint doesn't meaningfully improve the system, and often makes it worse. Local efficiency does not equal global success.

This is where machine shops get into trouble. Most shop owners are excellent at improving local efficiency. They know how to shave seconds off a cycle time. They know how to tweak a setup, change a toolpath, or adjust feeds and speeds to get better performance out of a machine. Those improvements feel tangible. You can see them. You can measure them. You can take pride in them. Local wins, though, don't automatically translate into business results.

A machine that runs faster doesn't help if parts sit waiting for inspection. A perfect setup doesn't matter if the job was quoted wrong. A department running at full utilization can actually choke the rest of the shop by creating bigger queues, more WIP, and longer lead times. Without realizing it, owners optimize individual islands while the system as a whole slows down.

This is why so many shops feel busy but stuck. People are working hard. Machines are running. Problems are getting solved—and yet margins stay thin, deliveries slip, and stress never seems to ease. From the owner's perspective, it feels like fighting fires nonstop. From the system's perspective, it's predictable.

Even though the daily experience inside the shop feels chaotic, *The Goal* forces a shift in thinking that makes that chaos legible. Instead of asking, "How do I make this machine faster?" it asks, "What is actually limiting my ability to ship good parts, on time, profitably?" Instead of managing departments independently, it demands that you see how work flows—or fails to flow—across the entire business.

For machine shop owners, this is often the first time the business itself becomes visible as a system. Scheduling, quoting, purchasing, production, quality, and cash flow stop being separate concerns and start looking like interconnected parts of a single process. Decisions get evaluated not by how efficient they feel, but by whether they improve throughput at the constraint.

Taken together, *The E-Myth* and *The Goal* deliver a hard but liberating message: the problem isn't effort, intelligence, or commitment. The problem is design. The rest of this chapter builds on that foundation, showing why owning a shop is a fundamentally different job than machining, why systems have to come before growth, and why letting go of the work you love is often the price of building something that lasts.

Designing for Someone Else to Run

Once you start seeing the shop as a system, a new question naturally follows: What would this business look like if it had to run without me? Not for a day. Not for a vacation weekend. But for thirty days, or longer, without things quietly falling apart. That question sits at the heart of *The E-Myth*'s most challenging idea: the franchise prototype. The concept isn't that you should actually franchise your machine shop. It's that you should design it as if you could. Every role, every process, every handoff should be clear enough, repeatable enough, and visible enough that another competent person could step in and execute it.

John Shegda of KMM Group describes the same idea in practical terms: "It's all about the systemization of your business. You may never franchise your business, but if you were, what systems would you need in order to be able to do that?"[16] That is the real point of the franchise prototype. It is not about cloning the shop. It is about making the work clear enough that the business does not depend on memory, personality, or constant owner intervention.

For many shop owners, this idea feels foreign, even threatening. Their business didn't start as a clean-sheet design. It grew organically. Maybe it started in a garage. Machines were added wherever they fit. Processes evolved in response to problems, not as part of a master plan. Knowledge lives in people's heads. Decisions get made because "that's how we've always done it." That works... until it doesn't.

The moment the owner imagines being gone for an extended period, the cracks become obvious. Phones would ring. Questions would pile up. People would make the best decisions they could with the information they had, but not necessarily the right ones. Jobs would slip. Materials wouldn't get ordered on time. Customers wouldn't get called back. Not because people don't care, but because the system depends too heavily on one person's judgment.

Designing a franchise prototype forces you to confront that dependency. It means thinking about the business the same way you think about a part: as something that has to function reliably under real-world conditions. The questions that fall out of that frame are the ones most owners have never asked out loud:

---

16 Machine Shop Mastery, Episode 22.

- **Flow.** How does work actually move through the shop, from quote to cash, and where does it stall?
- **Information.** Where does each piece of information originate, and where does it most often get lost?
- **Decision points.** Which decisions are made repeatedly, by whom, and why aren't they standardized yet?
- **Handoffs.** What happens at each transition between roles, and what falls through when someone is out?
- **Ownership.** Who owns quoting, scheduling, and quality planning—and would they give the same answer the owner would?
- **Definition of "good."** What does excellent execution look like in each role, and how does someone know if they're hitting it?
- **Continuity.** What happens when a key person leaves or a new one starts? How long until full productivity?

This kind of design isn't abstract. It gets very concrete, very fast. Floor layouts matter. Data flow matters just as much as material flow. Although owners often worry that designing for replaceability will dilute craftsmanship, in reality it does the opposite. When information is democratized and expectations are clear, skill can actually compound. People don't have to guess. They don't have to rely on tribal knowledge or interrupt the owner for every decision. They can focus on doing excellent work inside a structure that supports them.

This is also where many shops hit a ceiling, often around a few million dollars in revenue. Growth increases complexity, but without systems and delegation, the owner becomes the bottleneck. Everything routes back through one person. Progress slows. Stress rises. The business stalls or even shrinks. Designing the franchise prototype is how you break through that ceiling. It's how you decouple the owner from daily execution without losing control. It's how you turn a shop that survives on effort into one that runs on intent. And it leads directly to a hard but necessary conclusion: systems can't come later. They have to come first.

Systems First, Always

There's a common belief that structure is something you add after the business has grown—once you're big enough, profitable enough, or stable enough to slow down and formalize how things work. Early on, the thinking goes, systems would only get in the way. They'd feel like overhead. Bureaucracy. A drag on momentum. And while that belief is understandable, it is also costly.

What actually happens is that complexity arrives whether you're ready or not. One customer becomes five. One machine becomes six. One person doing everything becomes a small team with different skill levels, habits, and assumptions. Every additional job, material order, and delivery date increases the number of details that have to be remembered and coordinated. Without systems, those details live in people's heads, inboxes, notebooks, and hallway conversations.

The two paths—with systems and without—feel similar in the early days, but they diverge sharply over time:

Inside the shop	Without systems	With systems
Where knowledge lives	Owner's head, inboxes, hallway	Documents, dashboards, defined roles
When something goes wrong	Owner gets pulled in to solve it	Process catches it; team owns the fix
New hire ramp-up	Months of asking and guessing	Weeks against a clear standard
Growth response	Each new customer adds chaos	Each new customer compounds capability
What scales	Owner exhaustion	Output and quality
Default mode under pressure	Firefighting	Execution

When complexity outpaces structure, the business starts dropping balls. A quote doesn't get followed up. Material gets ordered late, or not at all. A job sits because someone assumed someone else had it covered. A paper traveler goes missing. None of these failures feel dramatic in isolation, but together they create friction, rework, and missed commitments that quietly erode trust and margin.

This is how bad habits turn into structural debt. The longer a shop operates without clear systems, the more those habits get reinforced. Workarounds become normal. Firefighting becomes expected. People learn how to survive the chaos instead of improving it. By the time the owner finally decides it's time to get organized, they're not starting from zero—they're undoing years of embedded behavior.

Ironically, systems are easiest to design when the business is small. While there are fewer people, fewer jobs, and fewer exceptions, it's much easier to define how work should flow. The decisions are simpler. The feedback is faster. The cost of change is lower. We've seen even one-person shops adopt disciplined systems and outperform much larger competitors simply because their execution is clean. Adding people without systems doesn't relieve pressure—it multiplies it.

Without clear expectations and workflows, new hires are forced to invent their own ways of working. They make judgment calls without context. They rely on the owner for constant clarification. The result is a shop held together by daily acts of heroism: late nights, last-minute saves, and constant interruptions to keep things from going off the rails. That kind of effort feels productive, but it's fragile. It doesn't scale. And it burns people out.

Systems don't slow good shops down. They make progress repeatable. They turn effort into output. They allow learning to compound instead of resetting every time someone new joins the team. Most importantly, they give the owner room to step back and lead instead of constantly reacting. Which brings us to the hardest part of all—not the mechanics of systems, but the psychology of letting go.

The Letting-Go Problem

For many machinists-turned-owners, the hardest part of building systems isn't technical; it's personal. Stepping into the role of a true owner often feels like a loss long before it feels like progress. The work that once brought pride, clarity, and immediate feedback—solving problems at the machine, holding tight tolerances, rescuing difficult jobs—starts to slip out of reach. In its place are meetings, decisions, tradeoffs, and long-term bets whose results aren't always visible right away.

That transition cuts deep because machining isn't just a job; it's an identity. Many owners built their confidence and reputation by being the person who could figure it out when no one else could. They were the best programmer, the best troubleshooter, the one people trusted when things went sideways. Letting go of that role can feel like giving up control, relevance, or even self-worth. The dopamine hit of solving a technical problem is real, and leadership rarely provides the same immediate reward.

This is why some owners unconsciously resist the very systems they say they want. They design a process, then bypass it. They delegate responsibility, then step back in at the first sign of friction. Although ego plays a role, the deeper driver is habit and comfort. The business becomes dependent on their intervention, reinforcing the belief that they're still needed everywhere—which, in turn, makes it harder to step away.

The shift begins when success stops being measured by effort and starts being measured by outcomes. Working harder, staying later, and saving the day may feel virtuous, but they don't tell you whether the system is improving. Outcomes do. Delivery performance. Margin consistency. Throughput stability. Employee clarity. When those measures become the focus, the owner's role naturally changes from hero to designer, from firefighter to architect.

Respecting the business as a craft in its own right is what makes that shift possible. Just as a precision part requires every variable to come together correctly—material, process, tooling, inspection—a business requires its own form of precision. Sales, operations, finance, people, and systems all have to align. None of them can be left to intuition alone. Designing the business becomes an act of craftsmanship, demanding the same discipline and intentionality as machining itself.

When owners make that psychological shift, they don't abandon the craft—they protect it. They create an environment where good work is repeatable, where people can succeed without constant supervision, and where the business can grow without consuming the person who built it. That mindset is the real dividing line in this book, and it determines how much value the reader will get from everything that follows.

What Has to Change First

Before the rest of this book can be useful, one thing has to be accepted: being good at machining doesn't mean being good at owning a machine shop. That's not an insult. It's a recognition of reality. The skills that make someone exceptional on the floor aren't the same skills required to design, lead, and scale a business that produces consistent results. Until that distinction is clear, everything that follows risks being misapplied.

This is also why tools, tactics, and software don't work on their own. Without the mindset shift this chapter introduces, they become surface-level fixes. They might improve something here or there—maybe ten percent—but they won't change the trajectory of the business. Systems only work when the owner believes the business itself deserves to be designed with the same care as a precision part. This idea is where the title of this book came from. It is critical to apply the same precision to building the business as it is to machining a precision part.

The owners who get the most value from the chapters ahead aren't necessarily the most experienced or the most skilled. They're the ones willing to be honest about where they're guessing, where they're compensating with effort, and where they've been confusing control with involvement. They're open to the idea that their role has to change if the business is ever going to change.

Even if this chapter is skipped or ignored, the rest of the book will still offer useful ideas. Some processes will tighten up. Some mistakes will be avoided. The deeper transformation, though—the shift from being trapped inside the business to intentionally designing it—won't happen. That requires humility first, and systems second.

With that foundation in place, the next chapters turn from diagnosis to direction. They move from why this work matters to how owners actually step into it, starting with the real-world decisions around entering the business in the first place.

CHAPTER 4

We Did It the Hard Way

What Pro CNC Taught Us Before ProShop Existed

One misconception people sometimes have about ProShop ERP, the company I co-founded, is that it started as a software idea. It didn't. ProShop came out of necessity, not inspiration. Before there was software, there was a machine shop, Pro CNC, funded by a second mortgage, started in 1997 by a group of recent college grads who were ambitious, undercapitalized, and inexperienced. We didn't come from the industry. We learned by doing, and by getting a lot of things wrong.

If this story were told only as a software success, it would miss the point entirely. Everything we know about running a machine shop—what matters, what breaks, what scales, and what doesn't—came from building Pro CNC first. That business was the foundation. Without it, we wouldn't have known which problems were real, which ones were academic, and which ones were simply distractions.

The mistakes I'll describe in this chapter are the same ones most shop owners make, especially early on. That's why they're easier to hear. When lessons come from lived experience, they land differently. They're not instructions handed down from the outside; they're observations from someone who's been in the same position, making the same tradeoffs under the same pressure.

What this story is not is a blueprint to copy step by step. Most readers won't have six founders. They won't be starting in the late 1990s. The industry, the competitive landscape, and the capital environment are all different now. Some parts of our journey were uniquely hard; others were uniquely fortunate. The value here isn't in imitation; it's in understanding what the journey revealed.

What Pro CNC ultimately taught us had very little to do with luck, timing, or even machining skill. It taught us how unforgiving this business really is—and how essential systems, discipline, and design are if you want to build something that lasts.

What this chapter traces:

- The early days of Pro CNC, started by six undercapitalized 20-somethings with no industry background.
- Our first mistakes and breakthroughs, including the 9/11 cash crisis and the advisor who refused to sugarcoat any of it.

- The scaling pains that surfaced once growth returned, and why every weakness we hadn't designed for got amplified.
- The discipline and process adherence that forced their way into the business.
- How seeing the shop as a system changed everything we did next.
- How ProShop came out of that shop's pain, and what we learned when other shops started using it.

Six Kids, a Second Mortgage, and a Lot of Naivety

Before there was Pro CNC, there was a group of students at Western Washington University who were obsessed with building race cars. Kelsey, Tim, Mason, Mark, and myself were part of the Vehicle Research Institute team, competing in Formula SAE, spending long hours designing parts, machining what we could, solving problems under pressure, and learning how to work as a real unit. We fell in love with the craft—and, just as much, with the teamwork and the momentum that comes from trying to build something ambitious together.

The original dream wasn't "let's start a machine shop." The dream was to build cars, specifically, to start a small niche car company. The problem was obvious: we didn't have the money, the resources, or the credibility to do that out of the gate. So we came up with what we thought was a clever stepping stone. We told ourselves that if we started a machine shop—since it used many of the same tools, processes, and skills—we'd generate cash flow, build capability, and then use that platform to launch the car company later.

So Kelsey's brother, Darcy, joined as the sixth business partner, and took out a second mortgage on his house. We found a small warehouse space near Seattle, bought a Haas VF4 and some basic support equipment, opened the doors, and tried to figure out how to run a business—let alone a machine shop. And here's how naive we were: we honestly believed that within a couple of years we'd have plenty of free time, evenings and weekends, and enough money in the bank to start building a prototype car. In hindsight, that's almost funny. At the time, it felt completely reasonable.

We assumed a lot of things that didn't hold up. Looking back, the gap between what we believed and what was actually true is almost embarrassing to lay out—but it's also exactly the gap most first-time owners walk into:

What we assumed	**What turned out to be true**
Finding customers wouldn't be that hard.	Sales is the hardest, longest-cycle work in the business.
We'd make profit on most of the jobs we ran.	Many "good" jobs were quietly losing money once everything was counted.
If we stayed busy, the money would take care of itself.	Busy and profitable are very different things, and revenue masks both.

What we assumed	What turned out to be true
Effort would be the main variable.	Structure was the main variable; effort just hid the lack of it.
A few part numbers of experience was enough to start.	Becoming a competent machinist is a multi-year apprenticeship of its own.
We'd have evenings, weekends, and a prototype car within two years.	We had none of those things, on no foreseeable timeline.

Kelsey Heikoop and I had been on three different teams across three different years, and between all that experience we'd probably designed, programmed, and machined maybe fifty-part numbers. In the grand scheme of machining, that isn't much. We were minimally experienced machinists and completely inexperienced businesspeople, which made us a worst-case example of what *The E-Myth* describes. We weren't just technicians trying to become entrepreneurs; we were technicians still becoming technicians, while also trying to run a company.

And yet, we did have early wins. We found some good customers. We were able to grow quickly. Within four years, we had roughly a dozen to fifteen employees. It felt like proof. It felt like we were figuring it out. Looking back, though, it's clear we were riding a strong economic wave as much as we were riding skill. Although we thought we were good businesspeople, the truth is that we didn't yet understand what the business was actually demanding from us.

First Mistakes, First Breakthroughs

The first real cracks didn't show up when things were slow. They showed up when things were busy. We were working hard, adding people, shipping parts, and convincing ourselves that momentum meant progress. Underneath, though, the same problems kept resurfacing. Jobs were harder to track than they should've been. Schedules were fragile. Cash felt tighter than it ought to have. And every fix seemed to require more attention, more follow-up, and more heroics.

One of the earliest warning signs was how much of the business lived in our heads and in spreadsheets. To his credit, Kelsey was always a systems thinker. He built some incredibly sophisticated Excel tools using Visual Basic—macros that spawned worksheets, automated job tracking, and helped us organize work in ways that were well ahead of what most small shops were doing at the time. For a while, it worked. Then we ran headfirst into the limits of what spreadsheets could handle.

That's when we went looking for software. Like most shops back then, we had a set of green Thomas Register books sitting on a shelf in the office. We pulled down the one for software vendors and started inviting companies in for demos, genuinely excited to see what was out there. What we found was shocking. Every system did fine with the bookends of the business—quotes, purchase orders, invoices, inventory. The middle, though, the part that actually mattered, was untouched. Shop floor execution was still paper. Travelers. Clipboards. Manual updates. The most complex, variable part of the business was being managed with the least support.

We were dumbfounded. By that point, we already had computers at every machine and were using Excel directly on the floor. Going backward to paper wasn't an option. So instead of buying software, we hired someone to build our own. A programmer named Matt Carrico came in with the simple goal of turning our spreadsheets into something more robust. We thought it would take a few months. Maybe a year. What actually happened was that once we saw what was possible, our list of "one more thing" never stopped growing.

Around the same time, reality hit hard. We were overly reliant on the aerospace industry. After 9/11, the big OEMs paused all their new airplane orders and work dried up fast. Orders were canceled. New work stopped coming in. Within a couple of months, the owners stopped taking a paycheck. With a new wife and a one-year-old at home, I lost a lot of sleep through that period. Although we didn't want to lay anyone off—we were a tight group, and it felt unthinkable—we also weren't managing cash well, and we weren't actively driving enough new sales. Catastrophes have a way of humbling you like nothing else can. Within weeks, we were close to insolvency and were on the brink of losing everything. Busy had masked fragility, and now the margin for error was gone.

That low point forced the first real breakthrough. Through the local Small Business Development Center, we found an advisor named Tom who didn't sugarcoat anything. He told us we had to gain control of our budget, cut costs, and—most importantly—become sales- and marketing-driven. We had to create what we later came to call positive sales pressure: enough demand that we could be selective about the work we took on, instead of saying yes to everything out of fear.

It was painful. We laid people off. We owned our mistakes. And then, slowly, things started to change as we focused on systems, on visibility, and on building a business that could survive without constant intervention. We didn't realize it at the time, but this was the moment when effort stopped being enough—and design became unavoidable.

When Growth Broke What We'd Built

Once we stabilized, the business began to grow again, and this time, it was real growth. Orders came back, we rehired most of the people we'd laid off, and revenue increased. From the outside, Pro CNC looked like a success story. Inside, though, the pressure never really went away. In fact, it intensified. Growth didn't simplify anything; it amplified every weakness we hadn't fully addressed.

At a smaller scale, gaps in the system were survivable. While there were only a few machines and a handful of jobs running at once, we could keep things straight with memory, informal conversations, and extra effort. As volume increased, that stopped working. More jobs meant more handoffs. More people meant more assumptions. More customers meant more urgency. The same problems kept showing up, just faster and with higher stakes.

Some systems failed outright under the load. Scheduling became guesswork. Quoting accuracy lagged reality. Information didn't move cleanly from sales to the floor, or from the floor back to management. Decisions that once felt simple now had unintended consequences elsewhere in the shop. We'd fix one bottleneck only to create another. It became clear that optimizing pieces of the business in isolation wasn't enough.

Adding people sometimes made things worse instead of better. New hires needed context that didn't exist outside of someone's head. Without clear ownership and standard processes, responsibility blurred. Jobs stalled because no one knew who was supposed to act next. Small misunderstandings turned into delays, rework, and frustration. The more we grew, the more the business demanded coordination we hadn't explicitly designed for.

Day to day, this showed up as constant tension. We were busy and, on paper, successful—but always behind. Always expediting. Always juggling priorities. There was no sense of control, only motion. We were working harder than ever, yet the business felt fragile, as if one bad month could undo years of progress. That contradiction—growth without relief—was the clearest signal yet. The problem wasn't effort, talent, or even demand. It was structure. We hadn't designed the business to operate at this level, and growth was forcing that reality into the open. If Pro CNC was going to keep moving forward, we couldn't just scale what we were doing. We had to rethink how the shop actually worked.

Where Discipline Finally Stuck

As Pro CNC matured, we learned a hard lesson: designing systems is the easy part. Living inside them is much harder.

On paper, many of our processes were solid. We had defined workflows, checklists, and tools meant to keep work moving smoothly. In practice, though, those processes were often treated as guidelines instead of requirements. And every small deviation carried a cost.

At first, skipping steps didn't feel dangerous. Someone would jump ahead to "save time," bypass a review because they were confident, or make a judgment call instead of following standard work. In isolation, those decisions made sense. The problem was cumulative. Each shortcut created a small amount of variance, and that variance rippled downstream. By the time a job reached final inspection or assembly, the original deviation was invisible—but its impact was not.

Throughput suffered quietly. Jobs that should have flowed predictably started stalling. Setups took longer than expected. Machines waited on information, tools, or material that should have been ready. We didn't lose days at once—we lost minutes and hours everywhere. That inefficiency was hard to spot in the moment, but brutal in aggregate. The shop felt busy, yet progress was slower than it should have been.

Discipline became the uncomfortable word no one wanted to say out loud. Enforcing process felt rigid. People worried it would slow them down or remove flexibility. What we eventually realized was that the opposite was true. The lack of discipline was what created chaos. Flexibility without structure wasn't adaptability—it was unpredictability.

The turning point came when we stopped treating adherence as optional. Processes weren't there to constrain good people; they were there to protect throughput and quality. Standard work became the baseline, not the ideal. Deviations required explanation, not justification. Once that expectation was clear, something shifted. Problems surfaced earlier. Planning improved. Firefighting decreased.

Most importantly, effort started converting into results. The same people, using the same machines, produced more consistent outcomes with less stress. Discipline didn't make the shop slower; it made it calmer. And that calmness created the conditions for real improvement. That's when we began to see the shop differently. Not as a collection of machines and people, but as a system—one where every part affected the whole. And once you see that, you can't unsee it.

The calmness also showed up as observations from outsiders. They'd walk our shop floor, watching people quietly work, not walking around much, and they'd ask us "Are you guys staying busy?" To which we'd answer, "we're setting records each month." Keep in mind, we'd hardly ever visited another shop before so we didn't know what the comparison was. But these visitors who'd been in hundreds of shops, commented that they'd hardly ever seen a shop look so calm and un-busy.

In hindsight, that calmness was lack of chaos. Things weren't being expedited, machines weren't being torn down to throw on a hot job with late material, there weren't rework operations being setup on the manual mill.

It's like my racing instructors told me, the fastest drivers are incredibly calm to watch, not thrashing the wheel, but finessing each apex by inches and smooth controlled motions in the cockpit.

Seeing the Whole Thing as a System

For a long time, we treated problems as isolated events. A late job meant fixing that job. A quality issue meant correcting that part. A missed delivery meant pushing harder the next time. Each response was local, focused, and well-intentioned. Over time, though, a pattern emerged: we were solving symptoms, not causes.

The shift happened when we started looking at the shop as a single, interconnected system rather than a collection of independent activities. A delay in programming wasn't just a programming issue—it affected scheduling, setups, machine utilization, inspection, and shipping. A change made to help one area often created friction somewhere else. Once we saw that, quick fixes became less appealing, because we could finally see their downstream cost.

Some bottlenecks surprised us. Machines weren't always the constraint—information was. Jobs sat idle not because capacity was unavailable, but because priorities weren't clear, tooling wasn't staged, or decisions were being made too late. We had assumed the limiting factor was always spindle time. In reality, it was flow.

Throughput thinking changed how we made decisions. Instead of asking, "Is this machine busy?" we asked, "Is this job moving?" Instead of optimizing individual departments, we focused on keeping work progressing through the entire system. Scheduling became less about filling calendars and more about protecting flow. Fewer jobs in process meant fewer surprises, even if it felt counterintuitive at first.

This was where the lessons from *The Goal* stopped being theoretical. Constraints weren't just something you identified once—they shifted depending on volume, mix, and discipline. Improving one part of the system without understanding the whole often made things worse. Real improvement requires coordination, not optimization.

Seeing the shop as a system forced humility. It meant accepting that no single person—owner included—could hold everything in their head. The business needed a way to make work visible, priorities explicit, and decisions consistent. That realization didn't just change how we ran Pro CNC. It made something else obvious. If the system mattered this much, it couldn't live only in spreadsheets, whiteboards, or tribal knowledge. It had to be built into how the shop actually operated—every day, on the floor. That realization led directly to the next phase of our story.

How ProShop Came Out of the Pain

What pushed us toward software wasn't ambition; it was frustration. We weren't trying to start a tech company. We were trying to survive and improve a machine shop that had outgrown spreadsheets, whiteboards, and tribal knowledge. The problems we kept running into weren't exotic or edge cases; they were the same problems, over and over, just wearing different disguises. Missed details upstream that showed up as scrap downstream. Jobs that looked profitable on paper but somehow lost money in reality. Schedules that worked until one thing slipped—and then everything unraveled.

We tried to solve those problems the way most shops do at first: better spreadsheets, more discipline, more communication. In the early days, Kelsey built increasingly sophisticated Excel tools, complete with macros and automation, and for a while they helped. Every improvement, though, revealed another limitation. Spreadsheets could show information, but they couldn't enforce behavior. They depended on people remembering to update them, interpreting them correctly, and using them consistently. As the shop grew, that dependency became a liability.

What we eventually realized was that the problem wasn't effort or intelligence; it was the absence of a single, integrated system that reflected how the shop actually worked. Office software handled purchasing, invoicing, and inventory. The shop floor—the place where value was actually created—was left to paper travelers, tribal knowledge, and memory. The most important part of the business lived in the least-controlled environment.

Hiring Matt to turn our spreadsheets into software wasn't a strategic decision at first. It was a practical one. We wanted the same tools we'd built to stop breaking under scale. Once those tools moved onto the shop floor, though, something changed. Information stopped lagging. Decisions stopped relying on guesses. Problems became visible earlier, when they were cheaper and easier to fix. For the first time, the system—not the owner—was doing the heavy lifting.

At some point, it became clear that the software wasn't just supporting the business. It was the system. It embodied the rules, the discipline, and the feedback loops that we'd learned the hard way. And just as important, it didn't rely on heroics to work. It assumed people were busy, imperfect, and human—and it was designed to keep the business stable anyway.

That's why ProShop focused on enforcing discipline instead of adding flexibility. Although flexibility is seductive, in a complex environment it often turns into ambiguity. We'd lived that ambiguity. We'd paid for it in stress, cash flow scares, and near-misses that could've ended the business. The goal wasn't to make the shop more rigid—it was to make it more resilient. The system needed to make the right way the easy way, every day, without constant intervention.

We didn't build ProShop because we wanted to sell software. We built it because we couldn't find anything that solved the problems we were actually facing. Once we saw what happened when those problems were solved—first in our own shop—it was hard to ignore what that might mean for others.

When Other Shops Started Doing It Too

The real turning point came when other shops started using what we'd built and seeing the same results. At first, we assumed ProShop worked because it was tailored to our business, our people, and our quirks. When our largest machining customer and even competitors implemented it and began reporting similar changes—better visibility, calmer operations, improved margins—it became clear that the problems we'd been fighting weren't unique. They were structural.

Shop owners from different industries, sizes, and regions described the same patterns we'd lived through: busy days with little to show for them, schedules that looked good until reality intervened, and a constant feeling of being behind no matter how hard everyone worked. What surprised us wasn't that they had problems—it was how consistent those problems were. Different machines, different customers, different materials. Same breakdowns.

What translated most cleanly wasn't any specific workflow or metric. It was the idea that the shop had to be treated as a single system, not a collection of departments doing their best. When quoting, scheduling, purchasing, machining, inspection, and shipping were finally connected by shared data and clear ownership, behavior changed. Decisions improved. Accountability increased. And most importantly, owners started getting their time back.

Not everyone welcomed that change. Some shops resisted structure, seeing it as a loss of flexibility or autonomy. Others struggled with the discomfort of visibility—because once the numbers are clear, excuses disappear. The shops that leaned in, even reluctantly, tended to see the same thing we did: structure didn't limit them. It freed them. It reduced chaos, protected margins, and made growth less painful.

That's when we knew this wasn't just about Pro CNC or even ProShop. It was about a set of principles that applied anywhere machining happened. The software was simply one way—our way—of enforcing those principles. The real value was in the thinking behind it.

What the Mistakes Were For

This story isn't meant to be a blueprint to copy. It's not an argument that everyone should build software, scale aggressively, or sell their shop for a certain number. The details are specific to our path. The lessons aren't. What matters is what the experience revealed about how machine shops actually work—or fail to work. We didn't succeed because we were smarter, more disciplined, or more talented than other owners. In many ways, we started at a disadvantage: young, undercapitalized, and inexperienced. What changed the trajectory wasn't effort. It was learning, sometimes painfully, that systems matter more than intentions.

If there's one takeaway, it's this: good shops don't run on heroics. They run on clarity. They make work visible. They define ownership. They design workflows that hold up under pressure instead of collapsing when things get busy. Those principles apply whether you're running five machines or fifty, whether you use ProShop or spreadsheets, whether you plan to grow or stay small.

There are mistakes we'd want every first-time owner to avoid—assuming cash flow will take care of itself, underestimating how hard sales really is, believing culture can substitute for process. There are also habits worth adopting early: measuring what matters, documenting what works, and treating the business with the same seriousness as the parts it produces.

More than anything, this journey taught us humility. The shop doesn't care how hard you work. Reality doesn't bend to optimism. Systems either work or they don't—and when they don't, the cost is real. The flip side is just as true, though: when the system is designed well, the business becomes calmer, more profitable, and more resilient. Owners get their lives back. Employees do better work. Customers feel the difference.

That's the deeper point of this chapter: not that we figured it out, but that it can be figured out, if you're willing to stop relying on effort alone and start designing deliberately.

CHAPTER 5

Getting In Without Getting Killed

Starting vs. Buying a Shop and Surviving the First Five Years

Few industries attract people as deliberately as machining. This isn't a business people stumble into. Starting or buying a machine shop usually follows years of consideration—the capital is real, the learning curve steep, the margin for error thin.

Yet people keep entering. Some because they love the craft. Others because they see an opportunity. Increasingly, some because they believe manufacturing matters—economically, culturally, even morally. They see machine shops as anchors: places where value is created, skills passed on, communities stay resilient.

This chapter is about how people enter the industry—and why so many underestimate what they're stepping into. It's not a warning against starting or buying a shop. It's a reality check. There are good reasons to do this. There are also bad assumptions that quietly destroy otherwise capable owners.

What this chapter covers:

- Why people enter the machining business, the two paths in, and the motivations that drive them.
- Starting from scratch versus buying an existing shop, and the very different risk profile of each.
- Entity structures and funding, and how early paperwork shapes everything that comes after.
- What new owners consistently underestimate—cash flow, complexity, hiring, and the silent cost of personal time.
- Failure stories and the warning signs that get rationalized away before they bite.
- The game you're actually choosing, and what it asks of you over five years rather than one.

Why People Walk Into This

People arrive at machine shop ownership through three paths. The first comes from outside the industry—professionals with successful careers (engineering, finance, operations, even private equity) who choose manufacturing. They understand that machining sits at the foundation of the economy and want to build something tangible: create jobs, contribute locally, leave behind a business that produces real value.

Stories like this are becoming more common. Two young professionals in Vancouver, British Columbia, left private equity to buy a machine shop—not because it was easy, but because they believed it mattered. They wanted to invest their energy in something that employed people, supported the regional economy, produced work they could point to with pride. The language is consistent: contribution, legacy, stewardship.

The second path is more traditional. Machinists start their own shops—sometimes because they believe they can do better than their employer, sometimes for financial reasons, often for autonomy and pride in ownership. Many want a place where work is done right, people are treated fairly, quality matters. They understand the importance of the work and want to create jobs and pass on skills.

The third path starts inside the shop that already exists. A son or daughter takes over from a parent. A key employee buys out a retiring owner. A general manager who has run the floor for a decade finally puts a name on the door. These owners arrive with something the other two don't have: they already know the customers, the machines, the people, and the accumulated history of decisions that made the shop what it is. That familiarity is an advantage and a trap. Inherited assumptions are the hardest kind to see, and the shop that raised you is the last one you'll think to question.

What matters isn't which door you came through; it's knowing what that door taught you to see and what it left out. The machinist arrives fluent in capability and vague on cash. The finance-minded buyer arrives fluent in structure and vague on craft. The next-generation owner arrives fluent in history and blind to the assumptions inside it. Each of these is a real strength attached to a real gap, and the gap doesn't announce itself. It just quietly shapes the company until someone names it.

Where all three groups get into trouble isn't motivation; it's expectation. Most new owners expect the first few years to be hard. What they don't expect is how hard, or why it's hard in ways that have nothing to do with making parts. Cash flow becomes constant pressure. Customer management consumes more time than anticipated. Hiring, compliance, quoting, scheduling, insurance, equipment maintenance, and financing quickly dominate the calendar. The business demands attention in places that feel far removed from the craft that drew them in.

This is where expectations are almost always wrong.

Machinists often assume that being good at machining will translate into being good at running a machine shop. It doesn't. Technical excellence and ownership are different jobs. Meanwhile, outsiders tend to underestimate the depth of the craft itself. CNC machines may be computerized, but machining remains one of the most demanding technical trades in existence. Tight tolerances, material behavior, process planning, and quality requirements leave little room for casual learning.

Matt Fortner of Progress Machining describes the outsider arrival in terms any new buyer with a non-technical background will recognize. He bought his shop from an 81-year-old owner. "He didn't even turn the lights on. And

I know why now. I'm walking through this dark shop and he's pointing stuff out and I'm looking at CNC machines and I don't know a Haas from a Doosan from an Okuma," he recalls. The learning curve was steep: "I don't really even know the difference between a lathe and a mill."[17] Both groups discover the same truth the hard way: this business is less forgiving than it looks. Understanding why you're getting into the business isn't enough. You need a sober view of what ownership demands—before the money is spent and the responsibility becomes permanent.

Build It or Buy It

At some point, anyone serious about ownership runs into the same fork: start from scratch or buy an existing shop. People debate as if one path is inherently smarter. Both can work, and both can go very wrong, depending on what the owner values and how prepared they are for the tradeoffs.

Starting from scratch appeals to people who want a clean slate. They want to build the company exactly the way they envision it, without inherited problems, cultural baggage, or outdated systems. A greenfield shop feels pure. Every process, every hire, every customer relationship reflects the founder's intent.

Starting from zero can work if a few conditions are met. The founder typically has industry connections—customers willing to take a chance, suppliers extending fair terms—and enough financial runway to survive a long ramp-up. Early profitability is rare; the bigger threat is duration. Sales

17 Machine Shop Mastery, Episode 93.

cycles are longer than expected, mistakes are expensive, and the business stays fragile longer than most people anticipate.

Scott Harms of MetalQuest Unlimited captures the brutal reality of starting cold: "I did not have a customer on day one. So I bought a machine and literally said, I've got this. Can you please send me something to fill it?"[18] That's the unvarnished version. The buildings get built, the machines get bought, the doors open—then the work has to actually walk through them. There's a long stretch when nothing about the business is working except the founder's belief that it eventually will.

Buying an existing shop trades creative freedom for momentum. An acquisition comes with customers, employees, vendor relationships, and cash flow—things that take years to build organically. The business already functions. Work is being quoted, parts shipped, invoices paid. That baseline alone removes a massive amount of existential risk.

Many first-time buyers underestimate how valuable that momentum is. Winning customers takes years, and trust compounds slowly. An established shop may have decades of relationship equity baked into it. That equity can't be replicated quickly, no matter how skilled the new owner is.

No acquisition is clean. Existing businesses carry baggage. Financials may look acceptable on paper while hiding issues underneath—unsellable inventory counted as assets,

---

18 Machine Shop Mastery, Episode 62.

deferred maintenance, outdated equipment, informal practices that don't scale. Cultural issues are harder to uncover. Employees may say the right things during a transition; some never buy in.

Customer risk is another hidden variable. In many small shops, customer loyalty is tied as much to the previous owner as to the business itself. Without careful decoupling, revenue that looked stable can erode fast. Capital structure matters too. Buyers sometimes spend everything acquiring the business only to realize afterward that the shop needs immediate investment in equipment, facility upgrades, systems, or people.

None of this means buying a shop is riskier than starting. It means the risks are different. The contrast looks like this:

Dimension	Starting from scratch	Buying an existing shop
When risk concentrates	Early—before revenue exists	Later—as hidden issues surface
What you inherit	Nothing, good or bad	Customers, culture, systems, and baggage
Customer base	Built one relationship at a time	Already in place, but tied to the prior owner
Cash flow	Negative for a long stretch	Functional from day one
Speed of momentum	Slow; years to build trust	Immediate, but fragile during transition

Dimension	Starting from scratch	Buying an existing shop
Hidden costs	Underestimating ramp-up duration	Deferred maintenance, obsolete tooling, tribal knowledge
Best fit for	Founders with capital, contacts, and patience	Buyers ready to manage change without breaking what works

Starting from scratch concentrates risk early, when cash flow is thin and mistakes are unforgiving. Buying a shop concentrates risk later, when hidden issues surface and change becomes necessary. In both cases, the danger isn't the path—it's failing to understand what that path actually demands.

The Paperwork Wall

Most people treat entity structure and funding as paperwork. These early choices quietly shape everything that comes after: risk exposure, tax burden, flexibility, and how much pressure the business operates under when things get tight.

The goal is simple: limit personal liability, avoid unnecessary taxation, preserve flexibility. Different structures optimize for different outcomes. Many first-time owners default to a sole proprietorship because it's fast and simple. That simplicity is deceptive—it offers no liability protection. The owner is personally responsible for everything from debt to lawsuits. For a capital-intensive operation like a machine shop, this creates unnecessary exposure.

Most shops operate as some form of limited liability entity. LLCs are common because they offer flexibility in ownership while limiting personal liability. S Corporations are popular for smaller businesses because they allow profits to flow through without double taxation. C Corporations tend to make sense only when outside investors or future equity transactions are part of the plan.

The structure isn't the point—the intent behind it is. Owners need to ask hard questions early. Do I plan to bring in partners later? Will I seek outside investment? Is this business meant to stay small, or to grow and eventually be sold?

Funding decisions create more pressure than entity structure. Most owners underestimate how much capital it takes to survive the early years, especially when sales cycles are long and margins thin. Reality frequently underperforms even the worst case. Costs creep. Customers pay late. Capital that looked enough becomes dangerously insufficient. People who promised you work won't return a call once you need to keep spindles busy.

Starting underfunded forces bad decisions. Owners price work too low to keep machines running. They delay maintenance. They hire the wrong people because they're desperate. These aren't character flaws—they're structural consequences of financial pressure. Debt can be useful but it's unforgiving. Loans don't care if a customer paid late. They apply pressure every month. Without buffers, debt turns minor operational problems into existential ones.

A common funding mistake is spending everything to get started and leaving no margin for error. Equipment and build-outs feel tangible. Cash reserves don't. But the reserves are what determine whether the business can absorb mistakes long enough to learn from them.

Many experienced owners say the same thing: I would have started with more money. Not for luxury—for time. Time to learn, time to make mistakes, time to build systems before chaos set in. In some cases, the only reason the business survived was because personal expenses were low or a partner's income covered basics. I wouldn't have survived the first few years of Pro CNC without my partner's income, and cheap rent in my future in-law's basement. That's not a strategy. It's a vulnerability.

Capital is about stability, not just growth. Adequate funding gives owners the ability to say no to bad work, invest in systems early, and make decisions based on long-term health instead of short-term survival. Businesses don't fail randomly. They fail along the fault lines created by early decisions.

What You'll Underestimate

Across hundreds of conversations with shop owners, the same handful of surprises come up again and again. They're not exotic. They're the quiet underestimations that turn manageable problems into existential ones over the first few years:

- **Cash flow lags everything.** Winning work feels like making money. It isn't. It's committing cash now for a promise later.
- **Complexity compounds invisibly.** Quoting, scheduling, purchasing, programming, inspection, shipping, and accounting all happen in parallel—at first, all in one person's head.
- **Hiring multiplies, not divides, the chaos.** Without clear roles, new employees create more questions than they answer.
- **Sales is the longest-cycle work in the building.** Customer trust compounds slowly. It can't be willed into existence with effort or marketing spend alone.
- **The shop's structure ages faster than its equipment.** Bad habits formed in year one are still costing the business in year five.
- **Personal time becomes the silent cost.** Vacations feel risky. Evenings disappear. The business takes more than the financials show.

The first shock comes from cash flow. On paper, a job can look profitable while demanding cash long before it produces any. A $10,000 job might require thousands in material upfront, plus tooling and outside processing before a chip is cut. Meanwhile payroll continues every two weeks. Even if the job goes perfectly, the profit—often modest—doesn't arrive until months later, if it arrives on time at all.

That delay catches people off guard. Winning work doesn't mean having money. It means committing cash now for a promise later. When multiple jobs overlap, the business can be profitable on paper and starving for cash. That tension just becomes more visible as volume increases.

Many owners remember the first "big" job they won and how exciting it felt. Five thousand dollars. Ten thousand. Then reality sets in. Margins are thin. One late delivery, one scrapped part, one underestimated setup can wipe out most of what was supposed to be earned. When the money finally arrives months later, it rarely feels like a win. It feels like relief.

The second major underestimation is complexity. Making parts is hard; running a shop is harder. New owners think in linear terms: quote, buy material, make, ship, invoice. What they don't see is the web of coordination underneath—quoting accuracy, vendor lead times, inspection planning, scheduling tradeoffs, quality documentation, customer communication.

Early on, the owner absorbs all of this personally. They don't realize they're doing the jobs of ten or twelve different roles because it's all happening inside their head. Sales, estimating, purchasing, planning, programming, machining, inspection, shipping, accounting blend into one long day. It works—until it doesn't.

When roles aren't defined, everything depends on memory. When processes aren't written down, every task becomes improvisation. When systems aren't designed early, they get bolted on later under stress. Hiring amplifies this.

Even good people end up doing work differently, creating inconsistency. The owner becomes the translator, referee, and fixer.

None of this feels urgent at first. The shop is busy. Parts are shipping. Customers seem happy. The cost shows up quietly: missed details, late jobs, rework, strained relationships, constant mental load on the owner. What new owners underestimate isn't their ability to work hard. It's how quickly complexity compounds when structure lags reality. The business doesn't collapse all at once. It slowly becomes heavier to carry.

Failure Patterns to Know Before You Sign

Failure in machining rarely looks dramatic. It doesn't usually arrive as a single catastrophic event. More often, it shows up as slow erosion—of cash, energy, clarity, or confidence—until one bad quarter exposes how thin the margin for error really was.

Running out of money is the most common endpoint, but rarely the root cause. Cash problems are usually the symptom of poor pricing, weak costing, overreliance on a few customers, lack of sales pressure, or systems that don't surface problems early. By the time the bank account makes the problem obvious, the damage has been accumulating for months or years.

Another failure pattern is subtler: realizing too late that ownership didn't deliver the freedom promised. Many owners discover they didn't build a business—they bought themselves an exhausting, expensive job. Vacations feel risky. Most owners remember vividly the first time payroll felt uncertain. People's livelihoods depend on decisions you made months earlier. At Pro CNC, I felt proud when the local paper wrote about the 75 employees on our team. In private, it was a crushing burden when our backlog was thin and I knew 75 families were relying on me personally to bring in the work.

Before failure becomes unavoidable, there are usually warning signs that get rationalized away. One of the most dangerous is overconcentration in a single customer. Landing a big customer feels like validation—work is steady, the shop gets busy fast. That dependence quietly increases risk. If the customer slows, changes buyers, or disappears, the shop can be exposed overnight.

Matt Wardle of JD Machine watched a version of this play out in real time. "I had a customer that said, Hey, you know, you've done a great job as a prototype shop. We want you to be a production shop, go out and buy production-related Swiss machines and multi-turreted lathes and all that stuff to build these products," he recalls. Wardle moved the company onto that bet, investing in a new building and millions in capital equipment. "They called me as soon as I had a new building and it wasn't even finished. I was standing in the dirt and a semi rolled up with one of the first of our four-star screw machines. And they said, uh, we're going to start our own shop and we're not going to need suppliers." When Wardle pushed back about the signed contract: "And they say, yeah, but you know, there's fine print that says we'll only guarantee two weeks of finished goods and six weeks of raw materials."[19]

That's what concentration risk looks like when it goes wrong. The customer didn't just leave—they walked away from a commitment Wardle had built an entire production posture around. Almost every shop that's been around long enough has a version of this story.

Another warning sign is operating without clear, enforced processes. From the inside, things feel manageable. From the outside, cracks are obvious. Jobs rely on memory. Schedules shift. Firefighting becomes normal. As volume grows, the cost of improvisation rises. Missed details turn into late deliveries. Late deliveries turn into strained relationships. Strained relationships eventually turn into lost work.

The hardest lessons are often the ones learned last.

Culture is one of them. Every shop has a culture, whether the owner shapes it or not. If it isn't cultivated, it grows by default. That culture determines how problems surface, how accountability works, whether the shop improves or stagnates. The leaders at KMM Group put it in terms any shop owner can picture: your company culture is like dirt. Tend it, take care of it, fertilize it, and you can plant almost anything in it and watch it grow. Ignore it and what comes up is potluck. Changing it later is far harder than shaping it early.[20]

---

19 Machine Shop Mastery, Episode 49.

20 Machine Shop Mastery, Episode 22.

The shops that survive long-term aren't the ones that avoid mistakes. They're the ones that recognize patterns early, respond honestly, and adjust before pressure turns into collapse. The real question isn't whether you should start or buy a shop, but whether you're prepared to design one deliberately.

The Game You're Actually Choosing

Starting or buying a machine shop isn't a single decision—it's a series of commitments that compound. The first is financial; the more consequential ones are psychological and structural. You're choosing a pace, a pressure level, and a responsibility profile few businesses demand.

What trips people up isn't ignorance. It's underestimating the duration of the challenge. Many owners can endure a hard year. Fewer are prepared for five. The real test isn't whether you can survive the early chaos—it's whether you're willing to design your way out instead of normalizing it.

The owners who build durable businesses accept early that machining skill is only part of the equation. They invest in structure sooner than feels comfortable. They treat culture, cash flow, and systems as first-order concerns, not afterthoughts.

This chapter isn't meant to discourage ownership. It's meant to clarify it. Chosen with open eyes and a willingness to design deliberately, machining can be one of the most meaningful ways to build a company that matters—to customers, employees, and community. The difference between surviving and building something lasting is rarely effort. It's design.

PART III

Sales, Money, and Survival

CHAPTER 6

The Riches Are in the Niches

Why "Yes to Everything" Is the Fastest Way to Lose

There comes a moment in almost every machine shop when the owner realizes something uncomfortable: being able to make nearly anything is not the same as being good at running a business. In the early years, versatility feels like strength. You take whatever comes through the door—aluminum, stainless, plastics. One week tight-tolerance aerospace; the next, agricultural brackets. You quote everything, say yes often, learn fast. If you're scrappy enough, you survive.

Over time, survival starts to look like stagnation. Margins stay thin, firefighting becomes the default, and every job feels like a new puzzle rather than a refinement of something you've mastered. You compete on price because there's always another shop that can "also do that." As overhead climbs, the generalist strategy that kept the lights on can no longer carry the weight.

This chapter is about that inflection point: when breadth stops being an asset and starts becoming a tax. It's about recognizing when focus becomes leverage, and developing the discipline to walk away from work that doesn't belong to you. Choosing customers and parts intentionally—rather than accepting whatever fills machine time—is one of the most consequential decisions an owner makes.

The idea is simple. Generalists compete on availability; specialists compete on value. Value is where margin, stability, and freedom live. What follows looks at the operational, financial, and cultural consequences of choosing a niche—and why focus, contrary to how it feels in the moment, is liberating rather than restrictive.

What this chapter covers:

- The difference between generalists and specialists—and why one path compounds while the other compresses margin.
- Saying no when the books are thin, and why mismatched work costs more than empty capacity.
- How to recognize the customers and parts that actually fit the shop you're trying to build.
- Why focus has to come before scale, not after.

Generalists and Specialists

Most shops begin as generalists because it's the easiest way to keep machines running. When you're small, it makes financial sense to cast a wide net—you call anyone within driving distance who might need machined parts, you quote anything that hits your inbox, you try to make whatever metal part fits your equipment. In those early days, that's the only way to generate revenue, build relationships, and accumulate experience.

The problem isn't starting as a generalist—it's staying one too long. When you're not truly excellent at something, being able to make "anything" becomes a liability. You compete with everyone—other shops, better-equipped specialists, the guy in a garage willing to quote at half your rate. When nothing distinguishes you, price becomes the deciding factor, and price-based competition is a race almost no shop wins. Nate Bourgeois at Ouroboros Space and Defense puts it more bluntly than most: "A generalist in machining has very, very hard path to success. I don't want to know that you can machine every part because that doesn't help me at all. When I'm looking at a part, I need to know who can specialize in this [...] Because if someone says they can do everything, they probably can do nothing."[21] That's how the buyer sees it, and the buyer's perception is the market.

As the shop grows, the math turns against generalism in another way. More employees, more rent, more insurance, more compliance—higher fixed costs mean you need stronger margins. The low-dollar, highly variable work that once kept a two-person operation afloat cannot support a

21 Machine Shop Mastery, Episode 48.

real organization. You can't charge the same hourly rate at fifteen people that you did at two, but the market doesn't care what your overhead is.

Specialization changes the dynamic in almost every direction. Once a shop commits to a niche, sales sharpens because instead of chasing every RFQ, you pursue specific companies within a defined industry or application. The niche itself—medical implants, aerospace brackets, high-volume aluminum housings, tight-tolerance stainless—matters less than the commitment. Your offering becomes distinctive. You become known for something. That's the beginning of pricing power.

Internally, the operation begins to align around excellence in a category rather than breadth across many. You invest in the right machines, the right workholding, the right inspection equipment. Programmers see the same geometries repeatedly; machinists encounter familiar tolerances and materials. The "gotchas" that used to ambush you become predictable, eventually preventable. Instead of constantly solving brand-new problems, you refine known solutions. That's the real mechanism behind margin improvement. Generalists survive on adaptability; specialists compound knowledge.

Specialization, when taken to the extreme, changes everything. I've seen shops achieve EBITDA margins of 50% to 60% alongside double-digit growth. They get there in two ways: through highly specialized automation or by focusing on parts for extreme-demand industries that are larger, more complex, or simply much harder to make.

When you become the shop that can make parts no one else can—or when you refine a process to the point where your costs are a fraction of the competition's—you aren't just running a machine shop anymore. You're a specialized hardware manufacturer, and you're hitting margins five times the industry average. That puts profitability in the same neighborhood as high-growth software companies.

Once EBITDA climbs into the tens of millions, the dynamics of the business change entirely. You aren't just another competitor; you're a strategic asset. I know of one sub-20-person shop that sold for nearly $90 million in 2025. When a business hits that level of absolute EBITDA, you unlock a pool of buyers who are willing to pay aggressive multiples—often 9x or more. In chapter 17 we'll discuss the Top Shops program and the revenue per employee metric, but keep in mind that there are companies exceeding $1,000,000 per employee.

It's easy to shake your head and dismiss those numbers as outliers. But that shop started exactly where everyone else does: one machine, one customer, no differentiation. The difference wasn't the machines they bought or the location they were in. It was the strategy they chose and the discipline they used to execute it. Just knowing these examples exist, I hope is inspiring and shows what is possible when everything is in alignment.

Side by Side

The practical differences show up across almost every part of the business. The table below is a useful frame for thinking about where your shop sits now—and where you'd prefer it to sit a few years from now.

Dimension	Generalist Shop	Specialist Shop
Basis of competition	Availability and price	Capability and value
Sales posture	Reactive; quote whatever comes in	Proactive; pursue targeted accounts
Knowledge accumulation	Novel problems each week	Repetition compounds into expertise
Tooling and inspection	Broad but shallow	Optimized for recurring geometries
Margin profile	Thin, volatile	Stronger, more predictable
Owner's role at scale	Central problem-solver	Architect of systems others run

Saying No When the Books Are Thin

When capacity opens up and machines aren't fully scheduled, the instinct is almost always to fill the gap. A job lands on your desk that isn't quite in your niche but will "keep the spindle turning." Taking it feels responsible—revenue is revenue, and empty capacity feels like money burning. The discipline question is whether all revenue is actually equal. It almost never is.

Work outside your sweet spot generally costs more than the quote suggests. Your team hasn't seen the geometry. Tooling isn't optimized. Inspection isn't dialed in. What looked like a decent margin starts eroding through extra setup time, slower cycle times, rework, frustration. By the time parts ship, you may have made far less than expected. Meanwhile, the right job may walk through the door while you're tied up with the wrong one.

There's an opportunity-cost dimension that's easy to miss. Open capacity, properly used, isn't a problem to be solved by reflexive quoting—it's an asset that should be spent on sales and marketing within your niche, building pipeline and creating positive sales pressure. Fill every gap with mismatched work and you slip into a defensive posture, reacting instead of leading. That's the psychological shift that converts a shop with potential into a shop that's merely busy.

Allison Giddens at Win-Tech has seen this pattern repeatedly, and her advice cuts against the reflex to quote everything: "When you get all kinds of requests for quotes, it's tempting to just quote it all. I think that the best advice though is just to get really, really good at the stuff that you want to be really, really good at, and I think that's gonna ultimately make you invaluable to your customers and to the market."[22] The argument isn't that you leave the quote box empty. It's that the work you accept should serve the shop you're trying to build, not just the week you're trying to get through.

22 Machine Shop Mastery, Episode 47.

Disciplined shops resist the drift because they understand that bad work costs more than its direct expenses. It drains morale when machinists wrestle with parts the shop isn't set up to make well. It introduces variability into scheduling and quality, and forces unnecessary investments in tooling, inspection, or processes that don't support the long-term strategy. The ripple effects extend beyond a single job—they reshape habits, expectations, and the shop's internal sense of what kind of business it is.

The strongest organizations protect their focus even under pressure. They stay proactive in sales, build a war chest during good times so they aren't desperate during slow ones, and lean on standardized systems rather than scrambling for table scraps. A focused shop under pressure behaves like a well-engineered submarine—its systems and margins form a thick hull. Saying no isn't arrogance; it's alignment.

Customer Parts You Love

Choosing a niche isn't only about the type of work—it's also about who you do it for, which owners underweight most often. A perfect customer isn't simply one who sends volume or pays on time, though those matter. A perfect customer's values align with yours: open to communication, collaborative, willing to listen when you offer feedback about design, manufacturability, or pricing. They see the relationship as a relationship, not a transaction.

You can usually tell which kind of customer you have by how they respond when something doesn't go perfectly.

Say, "We made a mistake and next time we'll need to price it differently," and a strong customer leans in—they want to understand, they're thinking long term. A purely transactional customer may immediately threaten to re-bid. The best customers understand something many shops forget: a healthy vendor base requires healthy vendors, and supplier instability eventually becomes the customer's problem too.

A simple evaluation framework becomes powerful here. Disciplined shops score their customer base against a consistent set of criteria. Over time, the patterns are hard to argue with. Some customers energize the business; others quietly drain it. A practical starting point:

- **Profitability.** Do the jobs actually make money once setup, rework, and admin are counted?
- **Communication quality.** Are drawings, revisions, and expectations clear and timely?
- **Payment behavior.** Do they pay on terms, or treat your company as a short-term lender?
- **Growth potential.** Is there a realistic path for the account to expand within your niche?
- **Strategic alignment.** Do the parts they send fit the shop you're trying to build?
- **Cultural fit.** Do they treat your team with respect, or as interchangeable vendors?

The same logic applies to parts. A "wrong" part isn't necessarily one with a low price—it's one you can't produce cost-effectively, inspect reliably, or execute without trial and error. If every order feels like a science experiment, it's a poor fit regardless of revenue. A "right" part aligns with your strengths: familiar material, proven tolerances, geometry that matches your equipment. You can make it profitably through a repeatable system, not through late nights and heroics.

When shops ignore this fit, everything becomes a firefight. Variability increases. Cash flow becomes erratic. Stress rises, and good people leave—not because they dislike machining, but because they dislike chaos. Fit isn't a luxury. It's a filter—and the clearer the filter, the more stable the business behind it.

Why Focus Has to Come Before Scale

Growth doesn't fix a lack of focus—it exposes it. When a shop is small, lack of clarity can be masked by sheer effort. The owner keeps work in their head, problems are solved in real time. It feels scrappy but manageable. Add volume and the structure holding everything together begins to fracture.

Scale introduces problems that weren't problems before. You need real structure: team leads, clear reporting lines, defined responsibilities. Five people reporting to the owner is intense but survivable; fifteen is chaos. Mental tracking systems collapse. What once lived in memory now demands dashboards, scheduling discipline, real process control. Highly variable work makes it worse—complexity compounds faster than systems can absorb.

Physical constraints show up too. Racking for WIP runs out. Cutting-tool management becomes critical. Digital file organization turns from minor annoyance into real liability. Small inefficiencies become systemic bottlenecks.

A focused shop scales with far less friction because repetition is what makes systems work. Doing similar parts over and over, you can design around them. You know the flow, the pitfalls. Continuous improvement stops being a slogan and becomes practice.

Focus also changes the owner's role. In a variable shop, the owner stays the central problem-solver—the one who has "seen something like this." In a focused shop with standardized processes, knowledge embeds into the system itself. The team owns outcomes. Leaders emerge from within. You can scale without focus, but it hurts more than it has to. With focus, scale becomes a force multiplier.

Focus isn't isolation, though. It doesn't mean turning away every customer with a need outside your wheelhouse. It means knowing which work belongs to you and building relationships with trusted partners for the rest. A well-built network of specialists, each strong in their own lane, beats a group of generalists competing on price every time.

None of this makes focus easy to adopt. Narrowing your scope feels risky, especially when you've built a habit of saying yes to everything. In practice, the opposite is true.

By deciding what you'll be excellent at, you stop competing on desperation and start competing on capability. Every successful business you can name is known for something—defined by a category it dominates. Machine shops are no different. Focus doesn't limit you; it clarifies you.

Clarity creates stability, margin, and eventually freedom.

CHAPTER 7

Sales Is a System

Why Waiting for the Phone to Ring Is Not a Strategy

Word of mouth is where almost everyone starts. You know a few people in the industry. A larger shop sends you offload work. A former employer gives you a chance. A friend in aerospace or oil and gas shares your name. That first work comes through relationships, not campaigns.

In the beginning, that's fine. Word of mouth, however, isn't a strategy. Referrals feel stable until they aren't. If the larger shop slows, they pull that work back in-house. If your primary customer gets acquired or changes buyers, your order book can evaporate overnight. You didn't lose on quality. You lost because you built your business on someone else's demand.

Mike Fritz of American Precision Partners frames the underlying problem in a single observation: "They focus their entire career on getting the part made well, and none of their career or very low amounts of their career, figuring out how to get people to say, will you make this part? And that is the [...] crux of why you're seeing these shops where demand is increasing and shops are declining. It has nothing to do with their ability to make a part."[23]

Read that twice. Shops that are struggling aren't losing on capability. They're losing on the work that should have been done long before the part ever hit the spindle—the work of building, naming, and managing demand on purpose.

There's another subtle risk. Word of mouth often pulls you into a single industry by default. Aerospace people know aerospace people. Oil and gas buyers know oil and gas buyers. Over time, you may find yourself concentrated in one sector without ever choosing it deliberately.

Industry focus isn't automatically bad. It can be powerful. But there's a difference between being intentionally niched and accidentally concentrated. A healthy niche is often defined by geometry, materials, tolerances, and process expertise—not just the logo on the customer's building. At Pro CNC, we became known for small, intricate aluminum parts that required tiny tools and careful process control. Those parts showed up in aerospace, medical, and tech. The niche wasn't the industry. It was the capability.

When sales aren't intentional, risk hides in plain sight. There's customer concentration risk—shops where 70% or 80% of revenue comes from one customer. That may feel efficient, even comfortable, until the customer's forecast

23 Machine Shop Mastery, Episode 58.

swings or their buyer retires and someone new decides to "rebalance suppliers."

At that point, your business isn't really yours.

There are macro risks too—economic downturns, industry contractions, acquisitions, regulatory changes. These are outside your control but become existential when you're overly exposed. Then there's the micro risk: the lumpiness of orders. You win a wave of POs, spend so much energy executing that you stop selling, and the backlog shrinks quietly. A few months later revenue drops below overhead. You may be capable, but your sales process isn't consistent.

Word of mouth breaks down because it isn't repeatable, measurable, or controllable. Strong shops don't eliminate referrals—they build systems around them. They track leads, RFQs, win rates, order value, backlog, revenue. They know their numbers. They keep selling, even when they're busy.

Sales and marketing aren't personality traits. They're operational disciplines. What follows looks at what a real sales system looks like in a machine shop, why owner-led quoting becomes a bottleneck, how to create positive sales pressure, and which metrics actually matter.

Hoping for work isn't a strategy. What is a strategy is designing demand.

What this chapter covers:

- Why sales has to be a system, not a personality—and what stops working once it's just one person.
- Building enough demand that you can choose which work to take.
- Inbound and outbound channels, used together rather than as alternatives.
- Selling trust, not parts—how buyers actually decide.
- The pipeline numbers that tell you what's coming, before the slow month arrives.

Not a Personality, a System

In most small shops, sales is a person, not a department. Usually that person is the owner. When an RFQ comes in, it feels too important to hand it off. Quoting requires judgment—materials, outside processes, setup time, cycle time, tooling risk, inspection requirements, margin. Too low, you lose money. Too high, you lose the job.

So owners stay glued to their desks building quotes. Meanwhile the floor needs attention. A setup may be running long. A part may be scrapped. A customer may call with a change. The owner is pulled between operations and estimating, and whichever problem feels most urgent wins. If production is on fire, quoting slows. If quoting is backed up, production decisions get rushed.

This is why many shops stall: they never build a sales system that functions beyond one individual.

A real sales system has structure. At the top is marketing: brand awareness and lead generation. A strong website, SEO, Google Ads, LinkedIn outreach, trade shows, targeted campaigns. Marketing doesn't require deep machining expertise—it requires consistency. An intern, virtual assistant, employee, or agency can manage much of it.

Below marketing sits the quoting and estimating engine, where most bottlenecks occur. Estimating doesn't need to be a solo act. Strong shops build collaborative quoting: purchasing gathers material and outside process pricing; a programmer or lead machinist estimates setup and cycle times; an estimator compiles inputs and applies margin strategy. The owner reviews high-risk jobs but isn't responsible for every number.

Over time, the process becomes documented and data-driven. Historical jobs inform new pricing. Win rates are tracked. Margins are analyzed. The shop builds a repeatable method for pricing work profitably.

After the quote goes out, follow-up becomes its own discipline. Many shops send quotes and wait. Strong shops track open quotes, follow up consistently, adjust when necessary. Account management can also be delegated, freeing the owner for strategy.

When sales becomes repeatable, the business stabilizes. Revenue becomes more predictable. The shop stops scrambling to fill machines and becomes more selective. Pricing discipline improves because desperation decreases. Sales can't be something you do only when you're slow. It has to run continuously.

Demand You Can Choose From

Many shops only chase work when they feel the pain of being slow. The machines open up, backlog thins, sales becomes urgent. By the time that urgency hits, it's already late.

Sales has a lead time just like production does.

Even when relationships exist, work doesn't appear overnight. A buyer has to send an RFQ. You have to review the drawings. Materials must be priced. The quote built and submitted. If you win, you still need to order material, schedule, run, inspect, ship, and invoice. From first outreach to cash collected can easily span months. Chasing work only when you're slow guarantees lumpy revenue.

This creates a cycle. When the shop is busy, everyone focuses on parts. Sales activity drops. Backlog shrinks. Then the shop hits a dry patch and panics. Owners juggle fires on the floor while trying to fill the funnel. The most urgent problem wins, and long-term stability suffers.

My co-founder Kelsey Heikoop, who lived this with me at Pro CNC, has put it about as plainly as it can be put: "The first thing that I think everybody should hear like really clearly is that you have to be sales driven. You can't be driven by what you hope will happen in the future or [...] some kind of promise that should arrive. It's got to be based on what you can really sell right now."[24] The shops that survive long-term internalize this early. The ones that don't spend years confusing pipeline optimism with actual revenue—and pay for it every time the optimism turns out to be wrong.

There's also a catch-22 in smaller shops. You need more people to specialize and build systems, but you need consistent profit to afford those people. Owners and team members will inevitably wear multiple hats in the early stages. The key isn't eliminating that reality overnight—it's gradually building structure so quoting, marketing, and operations aren't constantly competing for the same attention.

Strong shops manage demand intentionally. They define clear stages in the sales funnel and know the numbers at each: leads, RFQ volume and value, close rate, value of new orders won, backlog, monthly revenue shipped. These signals tell leadership whether growth is sustainable or fragile.

If a shop needs $1,000,000 a year to operate profitably and wins roughly 25% of its quotes, it has to quote about $4,000,000 in work. If quoting volume drops, leadership knows months in advance that revenue will suffer. If win rates decline, pricing or positioning may need adjustment. The system provides visibility before a crisis hits.

24 Machine Shop Mastery, Episode 23.

Intentional demand management enables positive sales pressure: slightly more demand than capacity, not dramatically less. With a healthy backlog and active quoting, a shop can be selective. It prioritizes higher-margin work. It declines poor-fit jobs without fear. It plans hiring and capital based on real data rather than guesswork.

The difference between reactive and proactive shops isn't effort. It's discipline. Reactive shops treat sales as an emergency response. Proactive shops treat it as an engineered process. One lives with constant swings between overload and drought. The other smooths the curve.

Inbound and Outbound, Used Together

Inbound marketing works when a shop has built enough visibility and credibility that customers come to them consistently. The website ranks for relevant searches. The company shows up on Google. Ongoing activity reinforces expertise—case studies, certifications, thought leadership. Done well, inbound creates a steady stream of RFQs without the shop initiating every conversation.

For many shops, this starts with strong fundamentals: a professional website optimized for search, a well-managed Google Business profile, targeted Google Ads. LinkedIn can also be powerful in B2B. Sharing new equipment investments, technical capabilities, team expertise, or complex projects builds credibility over time. Inbound works best when it's consistent and speaks directly to a clearly defined niche.

Outbound is proactive: cold emails, cold calls, LinkedIn outreach, plant visits, trade show engagement. It's particularly effective when a shop wants to enter a new industry, pursue specific target accounts, or accelerate growth beyond what organic traffic can support. It lets leadership deliberately choose the kinds of companies they want to work with instead of waiting to be discovered.

The two approaches solve different problems and call on different muscles:

Dimension	Inbound	Outbound
What it does	Pulls customers toward you	Pushes you toward customers
Best for	Long-term credibility, steady RFQ flow	Targeted growth, new industries, specific accounts
Primary channels	SEO, Google Ads, LinkedIn content, case studies	Cold email, calls, plant visits, trade shows
Time to results	Slow build; compounds over time	Faster, but only with sustained effort
What it requires	Consistency, content, technical clarity	Discipline, list-building, follow-through
Risk if neglected	Funnel quietly empties between projects	Growth ceiling; dependence on luck

Not all channels perform equally. Google search, SEO, and LinkedIn work because buyers and engineers actively use them. General social platforms like Facebook or Instagram are typically less effective for acquiring customers, though they may help with recruiting or brand awareness.

The right balance depends on the shop's goals. A company aiming for 10% growth may rely on steady inbound. A company targeting 30–50% growth, or entering aerospace or medical, will need more aggressive outbound combined with targeted inbound.

One principle holds: sales and marketing have to continue even when the shop is busy. If all attention shifts to operations during peak periods, the funnel quietly empties. By the time the backlog shrinks, it's too late.

Someone has to own marketing. Sales—estimating, quoting, follow-up—has to be clearly assigned. Operations focuses on execution. Finance ensures the numbers support the strategy. Sales & Marketing, Operations, Finance—three pillars that all have to function. If one weakens, the stool tips.

Balanced correctly, inbound builds long-term credibility and trust while outbound creates intentional opportunity. Together, they form a system that replaces hope with predictability.

Selling Trust, Not Parts

When customers buy from a machine shop, they're not just buying a part. They're buying certainty—that their supply chain won't be disrupted, that their production schedule won't stall, that their reputation won't be damaged by late or defective components. For procurement, purchasing is fundamentally a risk mitigation function.

If a buyer issues a PO and parts arrive late, out of tolerance, or improperly documented, the downstream cost can far exceed the order. Production lines stop. Engineers scramble. In that context, price is one variable among many. Reliability matters more.

Jason Davis of D&D Enterprises captures what reliability actually looks like from the buyer's side, and it isn't what most shops assume. "If you're an extremely good vendor [...] your job is to make your buyer forget you. Because you want your buyer to place orders and now everything's on a portal, or [...] it's all electronic [...] You want them to order parts, and you want to deliver parts and there to be zero interaction. Your name never comes up on any meetings, on the quality reports, nowhere."[25] That's the inversion most owners never quite accept. The goal isn't to be the supplier the buyer raves about. It's to be the supplier the buyer doesn't have to think about. Memorability, in this business, almost always means something has gone wrong.

Claiming "high quality and on-time delivery" isn't enough. Every shop says that. What differentiates a strong shop is the method. Customers want to understand how you ensure quality. What systems are in place? How are jobs tracked? How is inspection handled? What happens when something goes wrong?

---

25 Machine Shop Mastery, Episode 63.

A senior supply chain manager once said that when he walked into a shop he could "smell the chaos" immediately. Disorganized tooling, unclear job travelers, inconsistent documentation—these are signals. They communicate risk long before a single part is inspected. Shops that rely on brute force may occasionally deliver good results, but they can't convincingly communicate reliability.

Strong shops communicate process discipline. They show how work flows through the company. They demonstrate how revisions are controlled, traceability maintained, corrective actions implemented. The "how" is what builds trust.

Certifications reinforce trust, especially in regulated industries. In aerospace, medical, and defense, certain certifications aren't optional—without them, a shop can't enter the conversation with OEMs or prime contractors.

In other sectors, certifications may not be strictly required but can strengthen credibility and open doors to higher-tier customers. If the goal is to serve major OEMs or Tier 1 suppliers, process discipline and formal certifications become part of the sales strategy.

Ultimately, customers are buying peace of mind. They want to know that when they send an order, it will be handled by a system that produces consistent outcomes. Shops that understand this, and communicate it clearly, stop selling parts and start selling confidence.

The Numbers That Tell You What's Coming

If sales is a system, it has to be measured. Shops that grow intentionally know their numbers at every stage of the funnel. They understand how opportunities turn into revenue, and where the system is weak.

The funnel can be broken into a small number of metrics that, taken together, tell the whole story:

Metric	What it measures	Why it matters
Lead count	Companies that could become customers	Without leads, nothing else in the funnel matters
RFQ count and value	Quoting volume and dollar size	Volume tells you about activity; value tells you about fit
Close rate	% of quoted dollars that become orders	A 25% close on $4M is a different shop than 10% on the same
Backlog	Won orders not yet shipped	The single best leading indicator of revenue stability
Monthly revenue shipped	Dollars actually invoiced	Where the funnel finally meets cash flow
Customer concentration	% of revenue from top accounts	Reveals fragility long before the numbers do

Backlog deserves special attention. If orders received exceed monthly shipments, backlog grows. If shipments outpace new orders, backlog shrinks. That trend tells you whether you're building momentum or consuming it. Monthly revenue—what's actually shipped and invoiced—translates the pipeline into cash flow. It's possible to win significant work and still feel cash pressure if deliveries are spaced out.

A healthy pipeline isn't one magic number—it's clarity. Owners should be able to recite their lead count, RFQ volume, close rate, backlog, and revenue targets without scrambling for a spreadsheet.

Diversification is the other side of pipeline health. Even a strong funnel becomes fragile if too much revenue comes from one customer or industry. Practical rules disciplined shops apply:

- **Single customer cap.** No customer should represent more than roughly 15–20% of total revenue.
- **Industry cap.** No industry should represent more than roughly 30–35% of total revenue.
- **The profit-percentage rule.** Limit any single customer's revenue share to no more than your net profit percentage. If your net profit is 15%, no single customer should be more than 15% of revenue.
- **The break-even test.** If your largest customer disappeared overnight, would you still break even? If the answer is no, you're overconcentrated regardless of what the percentages say.

The exact numbers vary by shop and industry, but the principle is consistent: no single relationship should have the power to destabilize the business. The profit-percentage rule is the one most worth internalizing. Its logic is simple: if a customer disappeared overnight, you'd feel it, but you wouldn't be instantly underwater.

Strong shops treat these metrics as early warning signals. If RFQs slow, they respond immediately. If close rates decline, they examine pricing. If backlog shrinks, they increase sales activity before machines sit idle. The pipeline isn't something to review quarterly. It's something to watch continuously.

When you understand your numbers, you stop reacting emotionally to slow weeks and busy weeks. You start making decisions from data. That discipline transforms sales from a source of anxiety into a source of control.

CHAPTER 8

Estimating and Pricing

Two Different Functions with One Shared Truth

Most shops conflate two things that should never be confused: what a job costs to make and what a customer is willing to pay for it. They're related, not the same. Estimating is the internal measure—what will it actually cost us? Pricing is the external measure—what will the market bear? The space between is where profit lives, or where it disappears.

That distinction sounds simple. In practice, it's the area where most shops quietly bleed margin. Owners build estimates with rough rules of thumb, add what feels like a fair markup, then either lose work because the price is too high or win work that loses money because the price was too low. They don't know which jobs are profitable. They don't know which customers subsidize the others. They look at the bank account at month-end and read tea leaves.

Dave Kapkowicz of EBITDA Growth Systems puts it more bluntly than most: "A lot of business owners, nine out of ten business owners that we interface with think they understand their costs, but at the end of the day, they don't fully understand their costs. They aren't asking a hundred percent of the right questions. When you dig into [...] the bills that you pay and the things that actually cost you, your labor, material, tooling, et cetera [...] do you focus, do you factor utilization into that? Because you're paying for it. If it's not running, you're still paying for it. It isn't just the hours that you work."[26] That gap—between thinking you understand your costs and actually understanding them—is what this chapter is about.

The shop owner who closes the gap gains something rare: the ability to walk into a quoting conversation knowing what costs really are, what margin needs to be, and where pricing has to land to win without giving the work away. The owner who doesn't close the gap operates on faith. In a business with margins this thin, faith is an expensive operating principle.

What this chapter covers:

- The four cost buckets every shop has, and the one most owners mishandle.
- Why estimating and pricing are different jobs—and what happens when they're conflated.
- The engineering brain that builds accurate costs, and the market reality that sets the price.

26 Machine Shop Mastery, Episode 35.

- Where every dollar of revenue actually goes once the work is done.
- Who should own estimating as the shop grows, and how to close the feedback loop that makes it sharper over time.
- Why the first run on a job matters as much as the hundredth.

The Four Cost Buckets

Every machine shop's costs fall into four buckets. Most owners know three of them well and mishandle the fourth. Getting this right is the difference between estimating that reflects reality and estimating that hides what the business is doing.

- **Out-of-pocket cost.** Money you spend with another company on behalf of the job—raw materials, hardware, outside processes like heat treat or anodize, special tooling for that customer.
- **Direct labor.** The cost of people whose hands directly touch the job—programmers, machinists, inspectors—for the time they actually spend on it.
- **Direct overhead.** The cost of the equipment used to make the part. Each machine has its own hourly cost based on what it costs to buy, what it costs to run, and how many billable hours it earns in a year. A five-axis with a pallet pool has a very different cost per hour than a 1995 Bridgeport.

- **Indirect overhead.** Everything else that keeps the company running: SG&A, sales and marketing, rent, insurance, software, office staff. These costs don't change much when a particular job runs. They're absorbed by every billable hour the shop produces.

The first three together make up cost of goods sold. The fourth—indirect overhead—is the one most shops handle poorly. It doesn't change month to month (rent is rent), but the number of billable hours your shop produces does change. If you typically run 15,000 billable hours a year, your indirect overhead per hour is one number. If a slow quarter drops you to 12,000, that overhead spreads over fewer hours, and your real cost per hour is higher than your estimating rate reflects.

The fix isn't to reprice work mid-quarter—you can't tell a customer, "We had a slow March, so we're raising your price." The fix is to set your indirect overhead rate based on a realistic average of billable hours, review it at least yearly (quarterly when something significant changes), and run sales hard enough that slow months don't break your math. Without enough billable hours, no estimating system saves you.

Estimating ≠ Pricing

Once the four buckets are clear, the next discipline is keeping estimating and pricing separate, even though they meet at the bottom of the quote. Estimating produces one number: what it will cost. Pricing produces another: what you're going to charge. The space between is your margin.

Most shops eventually learn this. The trap that persists longer is the way they adjust the two numbers when something feels off. The instinct, when a quote comes back too high to win, is to sharpen the pencil on time. "Maybe it'll only take 45 minutes instead of an hour." That's a terrible move—and the single most common pricing error in the industry.

Time and cost should be as accurate as humanly possible, regardless of what the customer is willing to pay. If you think a job will take an hour, your estimate should say one hour. If the customer's budget says the price needs to come down, that's a margin conversation, not a time conversation. Adjusting time to make the price work corrupts the only number that should be sacred: actual cost.

There are two clean ways to handle this. Estimate the time accurately, build the price the customer needs, and accept the lower margin. Or estimate the time accurately, build the price you want, and accept that you may not win this job. Both keep your data clean. Both let you compare quoted versus actual on the back end. What you can't do is keep playing with time inputs to make the math come out right.

Engineering Brain vs. Market Reality

Most owners come to estimating from the engineering side of the brain. They started as machinists; they know how parts get made. Looking at a print, they see operations, fixtures, tool paths, inspection steps. That's a strength on the cost side—but it's also a trap. Engineering accuracy is necessary, not sufficient. The other half—what the market will bear—lives somewhere most engineering brains aren't naturally tuned to.

Pricing isn't about adding a standard markup to a cost. There's no industry table that says "aerospace pays 22%, oil and gas pays 17%." What the market will bear varies by region, niche, customer relationship, available capacity, what competitors are charging. Shops that win consistently don't guess. They track win rates. They ask customers for feedback when they lose work. They occasionally ask other shops to quote things to calibrate where the market actually is.

Then there's a deeper issue most owners hit eventually: the trap of using a single flat shop rate for every machine. It's easy to quote with. But it creates a problem—the wrong machines get used. Your most expensive equipment (five-axis with pallet pool, high-end Swiss) ends up underpriced relative to what it actually costs. Customers, even unconsciously, route work toward whoever's cheapest for that geometry. Over time, your most capable equipment gets overloaded while your older machines sit idle.

Nate Bourgeois of Ouroboros Space and Defense lived this and walked himself out of it: "I had been using a flat shop rate because I considered my guys to be my biggest price-driving asset. That was pretty effective, but then we noticed that we were selling a lot of our bigger machines, our expensive hardware. And then some of our smaller equipment, those weren't getting sold when we were pricing them the same as these other machines." Once he switched to machine-specific costing, the picture changed: "I know what it's going to take to get that part done. Now we are able to keep all of the spindles turning pretty much all the time."[27] That second sentence is the operational payoff. Accurate machine-specific cost data changes which equipment runs, and which equipment earns its keep.

Where the Dollar Goes

It's worth taking a step back to the customer's side of the table. When a buyer sees a $1,000 invoice for a precision part, the natural reaction is to assume the shop is making a fortune. Even employees inside the shop sometimes assume this. The reality of most jobs is that the profit margin is much smaller than anyone outside the business would guess.

Of every dollar of revenue a machine shop brings in, the breakdown roughly looks like this:

Where the dollar goes	Average shop	Good shop	Great shop
Out-of-pocket cost (material, outside processes)	$0.30	$0.28	$0.27
Direct labor	$0.25	$0.22	$0.18
Direct overhead (machine cost)	$0.18	$0.18	$0.18
Indirect overhead (rent, admin, sales, software)	$0.20	$0.20	$0.15
Profit retained by the shop	$0.07	$0.12	$0.22

Illustrative breakdown. Actual figures vary by industry, niche, and shop maturity.

27 Machine Shop Mastery, Episode 48.

The numbers in that last row are the ones to internalize. Average shops keep six to nine cents of every dollar. Good shops—disciplined estimating, lean operations, healthy mix of repeat work—keep ten to fifteen cents. The truly high performers, typically specialized in regulated industries with high barriers to entry, can keep twenty to twenty-five cents. Those shops are rare, and their margins reflect specific structural advantages.

If your numbers fall well below the average column, the chapter has done its job by getting you to look. Single-digit profit almost always traces to one of three things: estimates that don't reflect actual costs, prices that don't reflect what the market would pay, or an indirect overhead burden spread across too few billable hours. The diagnosis usually isn't that the shop is bad at machining—it's that the financial data isn't accurate enough to support the decisions it's making.

Who Should Own Estimating

In most small shops, the owner owns estimating. It's often one of the very last things they let go of. Estimating sits at the intersection of technical judgment, customer relationships, and profitability, and the owner is the only person whose interests are aligned across all three. A salesperson optimizing for closing may quote too low. A manufacturing lead optimizing for not getting blamed may pad the numbers. Neither failure mode helps the company.

Whoever owns estimating has to be invested in the overall success of the company, not just one slice. That can be the

CEO. It can be a chief revenue officer or sales director—but only if their compensation is tied to profitability rather than booked revenue. The KPI shouldn't be "did we win the job?" It should be "did we win the job at a price that produces the margin we needed?" Until that's the metric, the function drifts toward whichever stakeholder shouts loudest.

As the shop grows, the owner has to give parts of estimating away, and the parts to give away are clearer than most owners realize. Out-of-pocket costs—material pricing, outside processes—can move to procurement. Setup and cycle time estimates can move to engineering or experienced machinists, who often have better intuition than the owner does anyway. The owner's role becomes review and final pricing on high-risk jobs, plus the strategic work of refining the rates and overhead burdens.

The barrier to delegating usually isn't trust—it's the absence of a system. While owners hold onto estimating, they're holding onto a body of unwritten knowledge: which rates apply to which machines, which jobs have hidden inspection burdens, which customers always slip in revisions. Until that knowledge is captured in a system, delegating estimating means betting the shop's margin on a coin flip. Build the system first; delegation gets easy after.

Closing the Loop

A good estimate has two things going for it: it gets the plan right, and it gets the numbers right. Plan accuracy means the estimator correctly anticipated which machines would be used, in what order, with what setups and inspection steps. Number accuracy means time, labor, material, and overhead came in close to what actually happened on the floor. The first is qualitative, but easier to assess than people think. Compare the estimating plan to what manufacturing actually did, and the gaps are usually obvious.

The second is what most shops measure when they bother to measure anything: estimated cost versus actual. The target, perhaps surprisingly, is 100%. Not 110%. Not "safely above 100%." Exactly 100%. If you're consistently estimating high—quoting two hours when the job takes ninety minutes—you don't actually understand your cost structure. You're padding, and that padding costs you the next time you're bidding repeat or production work. If you're estimating low, you're losing money on every job, and you don't know which ones.

Dwain Dyer of Concise Manufacturing describes the moment a shop crosses from guessing to knowing: "I can compare theory versus reality. And I understand that when I come to you with a price, I can sit confidently in that price and say, no, I can't do it any cheaper. Or, hey, if you place that order for 800 pieces instead of 200 pieces, I can get you the price you want."[28] That confidence is the consequence of a system that closes the loop between what the shop quoted and what the job actually cost. Without that loop, every customer conversation about price reduces to a guess.

Closing the loop requires two pieces of clean data: the estimate as issued, and the actual cost as incurred. The actual cost is where most shops fall down. People don't

28 Machine Shop Mastery, Episode 34.

track their time. Machine costs aren't calculated accurately. Out-of-pocket costs get absorbed without being tied back to the job. Without that data, comparing theory to reality is impossible. Tracking accurately is unglamorous work. It's also the difference between a shop that improves and a shop that runs the same mistakes for ten years. Making that tracking easier has been our mission for the two past decades.

The First Run Right

How much does the first run of a job matter? It depends on what kind of work you do.

If your shop is high-volume, low-mix—a small number of part numbers running in quantity, repeating month after month—the first run matters less. You'll have many chances to optimize. Setup times will come down. Programs will get refined. The cost-benefit of an extra hour spent perfecting that first setup pays back across thousands of subsequent parts. If you're high-mix, low-volume—a true job shop with constantly new part numbers—the first run is often the only run. Every minute lost on a poorly planned setup is a minute you'll never recover.

Most shops want a balance. Repeat work provides predictability, scheduling stability, and the leverage of running parts you've perfected. New part numbers keep skilled employees engaged and create the pipeline for tomorrow's repeat work. The trap to avoid is being good at one mode and unable to price the other. Many shops that win lots of new-part-number work struggle on production work later, because they don't know how to lower labor percent through automation or recalibrate pricing for higher volume.

There's a related concept worth naming: the cost burden shift. When a job is underpriced—bad estimate, aggressive discount, non-recurring costs not charged to the customer—the shortfall doesn't disappear. It gets absorbed into indirect overhead, spread across every other job the shop runs. The losing job, in effect, takes its losses out of the margins of the winning jobs:

Scenario	Job A (priced right)	Job B (priced low)	Effect on the shop
Quoted profit per job	+$1,500	+$500	+$2,000 expected
Actual outcome	+$1,500	−$1,200	+$300 actual
What just happened	Shop kept the margin	Shop lost real money	Job A's margin paid for Job B

Cost burden shift: an underpriced job draws margin out of the rest of the work.

It's the same dynamic as a retail store absorbing the cost of theft. The shop doesn't notice it on any single transaction. It just notices, at year-end, that profit is lower than it should be. Multiplied across enough underpriced jobs, the cost burden shift is the difference between a healthy margin and a single-digit one. The fix is upstream: estimate accurately, price for the margin you need, and quote non-recurring costs separately when the customer will pay them. When you don't, your other customers end up paying them for you.

Lori Robertson of Cutting Edge Metals describes what closing the loop looks like once it actually works inside a shop—and the answer is more human than most owners expect: "As we go through and run the jobs in the future [...] I'll actually run the quoted versus actual report on a job and I'll show it to them and say, hey, look, we made $1,500 on this job or whatever the case may be. And it's interesting to watch them get excited about, wow, we really did it. We really nailed it."[29] That's the part most owners miss. Accurate estimating is cultural, not just financial. When the team sees that the numbers reflect their work, the estimate becomes a target the whole company is rowing toward, not a number on a quote that nobody on the floor ever sees.

That's the deeper point of estimating and pricing as disciplines. Done badly, they make the business operate in the dark. Done well, they give every part of the company a shared, accurate picture of what the work is actually worth. From there, every other decision gets easier.

29 Machine Shop Mastery, Episode 33.

CHAPTER 9

Numbers Don't Lie

Why Numbers Either Save or Kill the Business

A Swiss machine shop implemented real job costing for the first time and uncovered something hiding in plain sight. They'd been losing money for years. Not on everything—the company was busy, orders were flowing, the bank account wasn't empty—so nothing looked broken. But once ProShop allowed them to capture labor accurately, allocated machine costs properly, and tied real expenses to specific jobs, the picture changed.

Certain part numbers, parts they'd been running for years, were consistent losers. No one knew. The jobs felt fine. They didn't blow up schedules or cause constant scrap. They simply consumed more labor, more machine time, and more overhead than anyone realized.

For years, those parts quietly dragged down profitability. When the data finally made the truth visible, leadership faced a choice: raise prices and risk losing the work, or keep bleeding slowly. They assumed the customer would walk. Instead, they showed all the numbers. They explained in detail what it actually cost to make the parts. They asked for a significant increase.

The customer accepted it, and said they'd never seen a vendor so clearly show their cost structure. From then on, same machines, same people, same parts. The only thing that changed was visibility, and that visibility produced a $21,000 annual improvement in profitability for that customer. From losing about $11,000 per year to making about $10,000 profit per year..

What this chapter covers:

- Why numbers over opinions is the only path to real improvement.
- The chart of accounts that actually matter—and what most shops mishandle.
- What job costing needs to be real, not a spreadsheet exercise.
- Variance as a conversation, not an accusation.
- How to kill your losers early, before they bleed the rest of the shop dry.

Numbers Over Opinions

Owners often assume they know their numbers at a useful level of detail. They don't. They'll glance at the bank account and see more cash than last month. They'll remember that a job "went smoothly." They'll conclude things are fine. A healthy bank balance can mask unhealthy jobs.

Without disciplined data collection, everything is an assumption. At the job level the self-deception gets subtler. A part didn't create chaos. It shipped on time. No one complained, so it must have made money. Unless labor was tracked accurately, machine time captured properly, and out-of-pocket costs tied directly to that job, there's no way to know.

John Newman of Athena Manufacturing names the failure mode: "You can walk off the cliff if you get a big order, and you estimate that it's going to cost you $400 a part, and it costs you $800, and you sell it for $600. Every time you ship one, you're putting $200 in it."[30] That's the whole problem. The shop isn't losing money because it can't make parts; it's losing because it didn't know what the parts actually cost.

There's also the Pareto principle. In most shops, a small percentage of jobs cause the majority of losses. 20% of parts might create 80% of the pain, or more. When you niche down and become expert at a geometry or process, those losses shrink because you're no longer reinventing the wheel. In a generalist environment, the losses concentrate in unknown places.

---

30 Machine Shop Mastery, Episode 56.

Eliminating just a handful of those losing jobs can transform the business. At Pro CNC, this became formalized in what we called the "kill the losers" process. At shipping—or at minimum during the monthly management meeting—we reviewed completed jobs and sorted them by profitability. The least profitable got attention first. Then we asked the same set of hard questions:

- Did we quote it wrong? Was the original estimate built on bad assumptions about time, material, or process?
- Did the process break down? Did execution fail in a way that wasn't the estimator's fault?
- Can we improve the method? Is there a better fixture, program, or workflow we haven't tried?
- Should we outsource it? Is there a partner shop better equipped to make this part profitably?
- Do we need to raise the price? Has the market shifted, or were we leaving margin on the table?
- Or should we simply stop doing it? Is this a job, or a customer, that doesn't belong in our shop anymore?

Sometimes the answer was to increase pricing. Sometimes to fix execution. Sometimes to fire the job—or the customer. Without numbers, none of those decisions are possible. When numbers aren't trusted, real solutions stay hidden. Instead of data, you get opinions. That formal "kill the losers" process we religiously followed, significantly increased our company's overall profitability and enterprise value. It was one of the most impactful exercises we did that led to our 8-figure exit at a strong multiple.

These exercises are critical to maintaining profitability. To this day, I remember one egregious example of a part we needed to not make again at the quoted price. It was a titanium engine mount for a business jet application. About 8" cubed, and with features from many angles and some very long and deep corner radii, it was complicated and expensive. But it was far more expensive for our shop than it was for our customer.

I was the one who estimated the job, calculating our setup, cycle time, and cutting tool costs to the best of my knowledge. We had little experience in machining titanium, and my inexperience was shown in its full glory when time came to machine the parts. The setup probably took 4 times longer than I estimated, but the cycle time and cutting tool consumption was where I really screwed up. The cycle time was easily 5x what I thought, and the cutting tool consumption was nearly as much as what we had quoted for the entire part.

It was a very rough learning curve, which resulted in 10s of thousands of losses on that job. We did it only once, but if a process to review and adjust hadn't been in place, we could have easily accepted more orders for that part. After all, our client was probably tickled pink that they could get that part for a fraction of what it was worth on the market.

Meanwhile, specific part numbers lose money year after year. If the overall company is losing money year after year, it will eventually disappear. Even profitable shops can be far less profitable than they should be because they tolerate hidden losses inside individual jobs. Feelings replace facts, and feelings are expensive.

The Chart of Accounts That Matter

The way expenses are structured—and misunderstood—distorts how owners see their business. One of the biggest misconceptions is around "variable" costs, especially direct labor. On paper, labor looks variable. In reality, it's mostly fixed. You can't just cut a machinist's hours when work slows without risking losing them entirely. Skilled people don't stick around waiting for inconsistent paychecks.

The same is true for machines. When you buy a machine—financed, leased, or paid in cash—it carries a fixed annual burden: payments, maintenance, floor space, utilities, depreciation. A machine sitting idle isn't neutral. It's a liability. Many owners dramatically underestimate how underutilized their equipment actually is.

A simple evaluation framework becomes powerful here. Disciplined shops score their customer base against a consistent set of criteria. Over time, the patterns are hard to argue with. Some customers energize the business; others quietly drain it. A practical starting point:

Bucket	What's in it	Why it matters
Direct cost of goods sold	Direct labor, out-of-pocket costs (material, tooling, outside processing), direct overhead (machine cost per hour)	If these aren't accurate, nothing else in the system is
SG&A (indirect overhead)	Admin wages, office expenses, marketing, software, insurance, rent, utilities	The fixed cost of being open. Has to be spread accurately across billable hours
Through-put	Revenue generated per labor hour, per machine hour, per work center	Not technically an account, but the lever with the largest profit impact

Many shops fixate on cutting SG&A—saving a few thousand dollars on office expenses—while ignoring the much larger opportunity: increasing output from the same labor and equipment. A modest increase in throughput can have a far greater impact on profitability than squeezing administrative costs. Throughput is the lever almost no one pulls hard enough.

A poor chart of accounts blurs these distinctions. It mixes direct and indirect costs, hides machine burden inside general overhead, and makes it impossible to see where profit is created or destroyed. Clean categories create clean decisions. Without clean decisions, job costing becomes guesswork.

What Job Costing Needs to Be Real

If the data going in is sloppy, the output will be meaningless—no matter how sophisticated the software. Before job costing can work, a few non-negotiables have to be in place.

First, accurate labor tracking. Labor is the largest cost in most shops, the first area distortion creeps in. Time has to be tracked to jobs, and ideally to activities within jobs: setup, programming, run time, inspection, rework. If you're paying someone for forty hours, at least 95% of that time should be accounted for.

Second, capturing out-of-pocket costs. Material. Tooling. Inserts. Fixtures. Outside processing. Purchased components. If money leaves your bank account because of a job, it has to land on that job. Too many shops absorb tooling or outside processing into vague overhead categories, which inflates apparent margins.

Third, understanding machine and work center burden. Every machine has a real annual cost: payments, maintenance, utilities, depreciation, floor space. That cost has to be translated into an hourly rate based on realistic utilization. A machine that costs $20,000 a year to own but only runs 1,000 productive hours has a dramatically different effective hourly burden than one running 4,000 hours.

Keith Bernardo of M&K Engineering describes what disciplined costing looks like: "We had our accountant and our CPA calculate our burden rates and how many hours we consumed over the years. We've established different burden rates to each work center. And then, each skill set, right? So, if you need a high-end programmer overshadowing a job day in and day out, that costs more."[31]

Here's the nuance: you can't charge customers more just because your utilization is low. That's not their problem. If you only have one job on a high-end machine all year, pricing that one part to cover the entire annual burden will price you out of the market. Underutilization is a sales and capacity problem, not a pricing excuse. Most shops try to shortcut this. They allow rough time cards, rely on memory, and estimate that "it probably took about two days." They don't enforce time tracking because it feels administrative. Then they're surprised when margins don't match expectations. Subjective impressions aren't cost systems.

Accurate job costing is about discipline, not perfection. If you don't measure labor, capture direct expenses, and understand machine burden, you're not analyzing profitability—you're guessing at it.

Variance Is a Conversation

Real financial visibility means you don't wait until year-end to understand performance. You know, week by week—often day by day—where you stand. You know revenue per work center. You know how much value each hour of labor is producing. You know how much you've shipped this week, how that compares to break-even, whether you're trending above or below.

31 Machine Shop Mastery, Episode 52.

Break-even shouldn't be a mystery. It should be a number you can say out loud. If your monthly overhead requires $800,000 in annual gross margin to sustain the business, you should know what that translates to in weekly or daily shipments. When you fall short, you don't panic—you adjust.

Just as important is job-level clarity. Which jobs are profitable? Which are marginal? Which consistently underperform? Without that clarity, everything feels the same. With it, patterns emerge quickly. That's where variance review comes in. Variance isn't just accounting—it's management discipline. When a job misses its target, someone has to ask why. That was our kill-the-loser process. Your shop needs the same practice too.

John Shegda of KMM Group captures the right tone for these conversations, which matters as much as the conversation itself: "You're reviewing and you say, God, we didn't make any money on this job. How did that happen? And you go back and look at it [...] not [as] this person stinks kind of attitude, but how did we mess this up from a business standpoint? And what can we do to repair that?"[32]

The goal is clarity, not blame.

These conversations shouldn't happen in isolation. Finance needs to see the numbers, but operations and sales have to be in the room. If estimating was wrong, sales adjusts. If execution was inefficient, operations improves. If pricing is below market, that's a strategic decision.

32 Machine Shop Mastery, Episode 32.

Useful data starts with focus. You can't review fifty metrics and expect meaningful action. Start with a few that matter: gross margin by job, revenue versus break-even, backlog health, utilization. As systems become more reliable, expand what you monitor. A simple, consistently reviewed set drives more change than a complex one no one reads.

Kill Your Losers Early

Most bad jobs stay alive for one simple reason: no one knows they're bad. There's a gut feeling: "This one's always a pain," or "We never seem to make money on that part." Without hard numbers, that gut feeling remains suspicion. Suspicion rarely leads to action.

There's a second reason, more emotional: fear. Owners worry that if they raise the price, they'll lose the work. If they walk away, machines will sit idle. When the shop isn't busy enough to replace that work quickly, the fear feels justified. So they keep running low-margin or negative-margin jobs because something feels safer than nothing.

There's also a market misunderstanding. Some shops assume their current price is the ceiling. They think, "If we go any higher, we'll lose it." In reality, they may already be underbidding the market. Without job costing and win-rate analysis, they don't know whether they're winning because they're excellent or because they're cheap.

What are the signals that a job needs attention? Some show up before any data system catches them. Others only become visible once accurate costing exists. Both kinds matter:

Signal type	Pre-data warning signs	Post-data confirmation
Time and process	Setups that always blow past planned hours; constant troubleshooting	Labor overruns on the same part number, run after run
Quality	Excessive rework or unusual scrap on certain parts	Actual margin consistently below target on those parts
Customer behavior	Aggressive negotiation, no collaboration on improvements	High win rate with that customer combined with thin margins
Equipment fit	A job that always seems to tie up the wrong machine	Expensive machine running it for mediocre contribution per hour
Pattern recognition	Frustration that surfaces in the same conversation repeatedly	The same job appearing at the bottom of the profitability sort, month after month

At Pro CNC, this became a discipline. We looked at every job as it moved through the floor, watching how planned and actual were shaping up. That's when you can do something about it, before a bad job gets worse. At ProShop, that turned into our Job Progress and Period Progress reports, which gave proactive alerts when a setup exceeded 120% of the target time. We also did a quick review as jobs shipped each day to spot anything that jumped out. Each month, jobs were formally sorted by profitability and the worst ones got attention first.

Sometimes the answer was to raise the price. If the customer accepted it, great. If not, that told its own story. When killing losers becomes normalized, something shifts culturally. The bar rises. The company stops settling. It stops hiding behind busyness. Conversations move from blame to improvement.

Bill Berrien of Pindel Global Precision frames the underlying principle: "If I had to give another piece of advice, it would be let go of parts that aren't a good fit. Just be honest with yourself, be honest with the customer, and do that, because it's not a good fit for a reason, and you'd be better off not having it."[33] That's the discipline at the end of all the data: knowing what to walk away from, and being willing to do it.

33 Machine Shop Mastery, Episode 25.

PART IV

People, Culture, and Standards

CHAPTER 10

The Shop Is the People

Why Culture Beats Talent Every Time

A machine shop is a team sport. No part moves from quote to cash without passing through multiple hands—estimating, programming, setup, run, inspection, shipping, invoicing—and when those hands work together well, the business compounds. When they don't, even the best machines, contracts, and intentions slowly unravel.

You can have great machines. Great customers. Strong systems. None of it holds without the right people, and the right people only stay right inside the right culture. That's what this chapter is about: not talent management as an HR function, but culture as the operating system every other system runs on top of.

A single highly skilled but misaligned employee can quietly erode morale, undermine systems, and reduce everyone around them. A team of solid, aligned people—who collaborate, follow process, and want each other to win—will out-deliver a constellation of stars every time.

This chapter looks at why raw talent fails without culture, why hiring for attitude is often smarter than hiring for experience, how apprenticeships build durable pipelines, and why replaceability is the operational design choice that protects the people you care about most.

What this chapter covers:

- Why culture beats talent every time, and what tolerating misalignment actually costs.
- Hiring for attitude, training for skill—how the strongest shops choose people.
- Apprenticeships and the pipeline you build instead of waiting for the market to hand you one.
- Onboarding that actually works in the first ninety days.
- Why people stay when they do, beyond the paycheck.
- When it falls apart anyway: how strong teams still get taken down by structural fragility.

Culture Beats Talent

Raw talent is attractive. A machinist who can program complex parts in half the time. A setup expert who rarely scraps anything. An operator who runs at 130% of everyone else's output. Owners often default to tolerating attitude problems from people like this, because the output feels too valuable to lose.

Tolerating behavior that undermines teamwork sends a message to everyone watching, and the message isn't subtle: performance excuses behavior. Over time, that dismantles trust, accountability, and the willingness to call problems out.

The math here is something most owners never run. Picture a shop with ten machinists, one of whom produces 130% of normal output. Impressive in isolation. If that person creates tension that quietly drags everyone else's output down 10–15%, the net effect on the shop is negative. One star producing 50% above average, nine others producing 10–15% below it. The numbers rarely flatter the brilliant jerk once you pencil them out.

The shift from net positive to net negative usually doesn't show up in a spreadsheet. It shows up in the way people quietly avoid working with someone, in the way communication breaks down around them, in the way good employees start polishing their resumes. By the time the cost is visible in the numbers, the best people are already gone.

Owners who have lived through this stop tolerating it. Jason Davis of D&D Enterprises is direct about the calculus: "If you want to come to work and you bring just a crappy attitude and just sour about it."[34] The pattern repeats across shops with very different cultures. Ashley Hunsaker of

34 Machine Shop Mastery, Episode 63.

HTS Coatings is dedicated to her four core values, putting it plainly: "we do tell them that we hire and fire through them."[35] Heidi and Bob Devroy of ProsperTech, whose values are Professionals, Trust, Motivated, and Teamwork, said much the same: "we hire, evaluate and fire on those."[36]

Nubia Perez of Gretna Machine Shop also treats her core values as the ultimate filter for personnel decisions, noting, "our values, we hire, we fire, we promote when we have to make a decision as to a certain employee."[37] And Justin Quinn, at Focused on Machining, describes how a defined culture shifts how he handles the toxic-but-talented case—instead of looking the other way, he now tells them, "you're a cancer to our culture. You either need to change... or you got to go."[38] The willingness to act is what separates shops with a stated culture from shops with an actual one.

The behaviors that matter long-term aren't flashy. They're easy to list and harder to enforce consistently:

- **Teamwork**: the willingness to work alongside others rather than around them.
- **Collaboration**: sharing information, surfacing problems, and supporting handoffs across functions.
- **Humility**: recognizing that no one role carries the whole business.

35 Machine Shop Mastery, Episode 67.

36 Machine Shop Mastery, Episode 30.

37 Machine Shop Mastery, Episode 103.

38 Machine Shop Mastery, Episode 04.

- **Kindness**: treating colleagues, especially newer ones, with patience and respect.
- **Discipline with systems**: following documented processes instead of improvising constantly.

Even in highly technical environments, the shops that endure are the ones where people operate within structure and respect the team around them. Technical skill is necessary. It isn't sufficient. Culture, by contrast, is both necessary and load-bearing.

Hire for Attitude, Train for Skill

If culture is the foundation, hiring is the gate.

Most owners say they want both skill and attitude, and of course they do. When the labor market tightens—and it almost always does—the temptation is to prioritize experience and hope the rest sorts itself out. That bet rarely pays.

The hardest traits to teach are not technical—they're character-based: work ethic, humility, kindness, honesty, the instinct to do the right thing when no one is watching. You can teach someone to run a five-axis. You cannot easily teach someone to care. That doesn't mean skill is irrelevant. Mechanical aptitude matters. Curiosity matters. A willingness to learn matters more than either. Between raw experience and the right mindset, the right mindset wins—experience without attitude usually produces a senior employee who turns into a problem; attitude without experience usually produces a junior employee who turns into a star.

Alan Hartmann of Hartmann's Inc. uses a two-stage filter, screening first for fit before anything else: "Number one, we want to make sure they're a culture fit. Do they work hard? Are they critical thinkers? Are they thinking outside the box a little bit?"[39] Strong shops screen for this early and intentionally. They don't just evaluate resumes. They introduce candidates to their mission, vision, and core values, and they make cultural expectations explicit before any technical conversation. The interview is a calibration exercise on both sides, not a sales pitch from the employer.

The skills safest to train internally are the technical ones tied to your specific processes—programming standards, inspection routines, documentation discipline, machine-specific workflows. Those are teachable. What isn't teachable is the willingness to follow them.

Over time, shops that hire for attitude and train for skill build something more durable than a collection of experienced individuals. They build a team that thinks the same way about quality, accountability, and ownership.

Apprenticeships and Your Pipeline

One of the most persistent complaints in machining is that the talent pool is empty. In most regions, that complaint is largely accurate. Few experienced machinists are walking around ready to contribute on day one, and the ones who are usually already have jobs they like.

---

39 Machine Shop Mastery, Episode 07.

Well-run apprenticeship programs solve this by building capability from the ground up. Done right, an apprenticeship gives young or simply inexperienced people a structured pathway into the trade. It also builds loyalty—employees who came up through your system are more likely to stay than those you pulled off the street with the highest offer.

Two common models dominate the industry. Where they break down is usually less about structure than about the discipline behind them.

Model	How It Works	Where It Tends to Fail
Internal Program	Structured training plans, in-house mentors, and skill milestones owned by the shop	Lack of focus: leadership attention drifts, mentorship becomes inconsistent, plans gather dust
School Partnership	Classroom instruction at a technical school or community college paired with on-the-job experience	Weak collaboration: educators don't know what shops need, and shops don't shape the curriculum

The shops that succeed treat workforce development as a core business function rather than a side project, and they take ownership of the outcome rather than expecting the system to deliver it. Long-term thinking is essential here. Matt Wardle of JD Machine describes how seriously his company takes this: "It's a long-term investment and really pays off when you're basically marketing to your community that you are an employer of choice and you are on the minds of people as they graduate from high school or looking for a potential place to work. They think very highly of JD Machines."[40]

Unless a shop is extremely automated, people are still the primary constraint, and a shop without a talent pipeline accumulates risk in ways that don't appear on financial statements until they're already expensive. Almost every shop feels this pressure. The question isn't whether you need a pipeline—it's whether you're building one intentionally or hoping the market solves it for you. The market won't.

Onboarding That Works

Hiring the right person is only the beginning. What happens in the first thirty to ninety days often determines whether that hire becomes a long-term asset or a short-term mistake. Onboarding should account for as much hand-holding and time investment as if the person were a paying customer.

Strong onboarding accomplishes four things at once, and weakness in any one of them undermines the others:

- **A genuine welcome.** The new employee should feel they matter from the first hour of the first day. Not tolerated. Not processed. Welcomed.
- **Clear organization.** The new employee knows who they report to, what they're supposed to be doing, and how success is measured. Chaos in week one signals a place not worth committing to.

40 Machine Shop Mastery, Episode 40.

- **Explicit values.** Core values are communicated as operating expectations, not as posters on the wall. The behaviors that get rewarded and the ones that are unacceptable are made obvious early.
- **Defined responsibilities and metrics.** The new employee knows what outcomes they own, what success looks like at 30, 60, and 90 days, and how their performance will be evaluated.

Keith Bernardo of M&K Engineering describes the spirit of the first bullet as something close to family work: "What I learned was the first three months, it's like joining a new family."[41] That framing matters. The new employee's sense of belonging is established in the first weeks; what isn't built then is much harder to add later.

Done properly, onboarding sets tone, expectations, and standards simultaneously. That work leads to a concept many owners misunderstand: replaceability. Replaceability isn't disposability. It's operational resilience.

When knowledge lives only in someone's head, the company is fragile in ways that are easy to ignore until they aren't. If that person takes vacation, things stall. If they leave, operations grind down for months. If they retire, the institutional knowledge walks out with them.

Anne Duyck of Duyck Machine describes the fix in concrete operational terms: "One of our next projects that our production manager and QA are teaming up on is

41 Machine Shop Mastery, Episode 52.

documenting that tribal knowledge."[42] That's the work. Not glamorous, not fast, but it's the difference between a shop that survives a departure and one that staggers from it.

Shops that document processes and institutionalize knowledge grow faster over time because learning compounds. Each improvement builds on the last because it has been captured and shared, not lost the moment the person who made it moves on.

Caring about people and building resilient systems aren't opposing ideas. They're complementary responsibilities. The shops that grasp the distinction are the ones that hold together when something unexpected hits.

Why People Stay

What actually keeps good people long term?

For younger generations especially, it isn't just a paycheck. It's alignment. They want to believe in the company's mission, to feel that the work matters, and to see that the company will invest in them as much as they're investing in it.

Retention, in shops that hold onto their people, rests on four pillars rather than one:

- **Mission alignment.** Employees can see how their daily work connects to something larger, and leadership reinforces that connection consistently.

42 Machine Shop Mastery, Episode 21.

- **Growth opportunity.** Mentorship, continuing education, skill progression, lateral movement, and upward pathways are real, not theoretical.
- **Thoughtful transparency.** Teams understand the economics of the business at the operational level, and have enough financial context to feel ownership without being overwhelmed by detail they can't act on.
- **Real operational trust.** People are given ownership of outcomes, not just tasks, and mistakes are met with coaching rather than blame.

Michael Tamasi of AccuRounds frames the underlying logic at the level of organizational design: "Everything we do in the organization revolves at some level around developing people, doing things better in order to grow, so our team can grow."[43] Jason Davis, on his end, points out the simple economics underneath all of this: "Retention is a huge part of our business because while workforce development is important, we also don't want our workforce to be departing. We want to make sure that we're retaining our workforce because it's so much easier to retain someone than it is to train somebody new."[44]

Transparency plays an important role in retention, though it has to be handled carefully. Operational transparency is essential—teams should know, job by job, whether they made money or lost money, and what needs to improve. Numbers grounded in the work create accountability.

43 Machine Shop Mastery, Episode 42.

44 Machine Shop Mastery, Episode 63.

At the company level, broad financial transparency can be healthy. Sharing monthly revenue, breakeven targets, and profit outcomes helps employees understand the economics of the business they're part of. Shipping $100,000 against a $97,000 target and generating $16,000 in profit is meaningful context; it lets people see the connection between execution and results. At Pro CNC, we ran this approach for years. Every month, we shared how much money we'd made or lost, jobs that had gone well, jobs that hadn't.[45] That kind of regular, structured visibility turns the business into something employees understand rather than something that happens to them.

Transparency has limits. Handing out full profit-and-loss statements or balance sheets is rarely prudent. Too much detail creates confusion or anxiety about variables employees don't control. Operational transparency about jobs and throughput is almost always healthy; raw financial transparency about executive comp, owner draws, or debt structure rarely is.

Trust shows up operationally through delegation. Real trust means giving someone ownership of an outcome, not just a task. It usually starts small—you assign responsibility, monitor results, coach through mistakes—and over time the scope expands. The owner has to be willing to let the person succeed and to let them fail without rescuing them.

Retention, ultimately, is not an accident. It's the byproduct of mission alignment, growth opportunity, thoughtful transparency, and real operational trust. Each of those elements has to be built deliberately rather than assumed.

---

45 Machine Shop Mastery, Episode 38.

When It Falls Apart

Culture and trust matter. So do systems. Even strong teams can be taken down by structural fragility, though, and a healthy backlog and good people aren't enough if the business itself is sitting too close to the edge financially or operationally.

Jereme Rogers' story is a hard example of how those conditions converge. His shop didn't go out of business because of toxic culture or lazy employees. It went out of business because of concentration risk, missing systems, and a financial structure that couldn't absorb a sudden downturn. Rogers describes the underlying weakness candidly: "Before I bought the place, we were not using ProShop. There was a lot of tribal knowledge and not a lot of organization."[46] At the same time, the company was carrying significant debt from its early days, and there wasn't enough buffer to absorb disruption. When performance dipped from two of his best setup guys getting hired away, financial pressure intensified quickly. Even with good people working hard, structural fragility caught up.

Mark Heston's story is different in shape but similar in pattern. His company had a strong backlog and plenty of work on the books. On paper, things looked solid. However, through customer concentration, internal financial pressure, and what he describes as "a hundred small problems compounding,"[47] cashflow became acute and the shop didn't make it.

---

46 Machine Shop Mastery, Episode 64.

47 Machine Shop Mastery, Episode 89

A common theme emerges across both cases. Backlog is not protection. Talent is not protection. Even a strong culture is not protection. What protects a business is margin and buffer at every layer: customer diversification, cost discipline, cash reserves, accurate cost data, and the systems that make it possible to see problems early enough to respond.

These stories aren't shared to create fear. They're shared to show reality. Machine shops don't usually fail because of a single catastrophic event. They fail because a series of manageable risks compound until one bad month tips the balance. Designing for resilience—at the cultural, operational, and financial level—is how shops survive long enough to enjoy the upside their people earned.

CHAPTER 11

Growing Pains

What Breaks at $2M, $10M, and Beyond

Most machine shops don't fail because they lack demand. They fail—or stall—because the business they built to reach one level of revenue is not the business required to reach the next, and the gap between those two businesses is rarely closed by working harder.

In the early days, growth feels straightforward. More work comes in, more hours get put in, a few more machines get added, revenue climbs. The same core group of people carries the load. Problems get solved quickly because everyone is close to the work. The owner sees everything.

Until it doesn't.

As the shop grows, complexity doesn't increase linearly—it compounds. More jobs mean more variability. More people mean more coordination. More machines mean more scheduling pressure, more maintenance, more capital at risk. What used to be manageable through effort and proximity starts to break down.

At that point, growth stops being a question of effort and becomes a question of design.

This is where leadership and organizational structure enter the picture as practical necessities. The shop can no longer rely on one person to hold everything together. It needs defined roles, clear ownership, and layers of responsibility that let decisions be made where the work actually happens.

What follows is the natural evolution every growing shop goes through, whether intentionally or by force. The question isn't whether structure will emerge but whether it will be designed or imposed by chaos. We begin with the first step most shops take as they grow: the introduction of functional leads.

The biggest challenge in scaling a manufacturing company isn't technical or financial; it's the owner's psychological transformation. A business will never grow larger than the capacity of the owner. Whether you started the shop, bought it, or inherited it, the mindset that made you successful at the beginning—often a necessary, fierce self-confidence—can eventually become your greatest bottleneck. To navigate the growth stages outlined in this chapter, an owner must shift from that initial posture to one defined by self-analysis, humility, and the ability to work collaboratively with people who are more expert in their specific domains than the owner is. The wise owner welcomes people smarter or more expert than they are.

As discussed in Chapter 2, many shop owners struggle because they continue to operate as "the best machinist" rather than the leader of a system. These growth stages can only be successfully implemented if the owner has the humility to build and trust a team of experts, transforming from a reactive firefighter into the analytical architect of the business.

What this chapter covers:

- The first real layer of structure most shops add—and why it changes everything.
- Breaking $2M and breaking $10M: two distinct structural moments most owners walk into blind.
- The stages of the owner, from Operator to Architect, and the letting-go each one demands.
- Designing what comes next, before the current way of operating becomes the constraint.

The First Real Layer

The first visible sign that a shop is outgrowing itself isn't chaos—it's friction. Work still gets done, but it takes more effort than it should. Decisions slow down. The same issues resurface in slightly different forms. What once felt smooth begins to feel heavy, and no one can quite point to a cause.

It's simple math. As volume increases, work moves through more hands, more machines, more decisions. Jobs overlap. Priorities compete. What used to be obvious becomes unclear. Who owns this job? Who is responsible for that delay? Why did this issue happen again? Without defined roles, these questions default to the owner.

The first real structural shift most shops make is the introduction of functional leads. A functional lead isn't a manager in the corporate sense. It's the first layer of ownership inside a specific domain:

- **Shop lead.** Owns throughput, setup times, troubleshooting and keeping spindles turning.
- **Scheduling lead.** Owns flow, priorities, and the alignment of the schedule with real capacity.
- **Quality lead.** Owns standards, repeatability, and the inspection systems that protect them.

These roles often emerge naturally, usually filled by the most capable or reliable people in each area. What matters isn't the title—it's the clarity. When a functional lead exists, decisions stop defaulting to the owner. Problems have somewhere to go. Responsibility settles into the system.

This shift alone can stabilize a growing shop. It reduces noise. It shortens decision cycles. It creates consistency where there was variation. For the first time, the owner isn't required to intervene in every issue, and the business starts to carry some of its own weight.

Yet this stage introduces a new constraint. Most functional leads come from the floor. They're strong technically. They understand the work. What they often haven't developed yet is the ability to lead people, manage tradeoffs, or think across the system. Shops frequently make the mistake of assuming the promotion automatically produces the skills.

Dave Kapkowicz of CK Tool names the trap from experience: "I took the best guys, and I made a managers that did not serve me well. [I] promoted [them] to their level of incompetency."[48] Technical skill doesn't automatically translate into leadership skill. Without coaching, the best operator becomes a frustrated manager—and a worse operator.

Without support, functional leads can become bottlenecks instead of multipliers. They hold onto decisions. They solve problems themselves instead of building processes. They stay reactive, pulled into the urgency of the day, without creating stability for the team. The role exists, but the function it's supposed to play doesn't.

Management doesn't mean adding hierarchy for appearance. It's about coordination. The distinction between functional leads and managers is one of the most important transitions a growing shop makes, and it deserves to be drawn clearly.

---

48 Machine Shop Mastery, Episode 35.

Role	Scope	Primary Job	What Breaks Without Them
Functional Lead	A single domain (quoting, scheduling, quality)	Owns the function; anchors responsibility and standards within it	Decisions default to the owner; problems have nowhere to go
Manager	Multiple functions and the handoffs between them	Integrates across functions; resolves tradeoffs; aligns priorities	Local optimization shifts pressure elsewhere; the owner becomes the integration layer

In smaller shops, this coordination still sits with the owner. As complexity increases, that model breaks down. Too many decisions require cross-functional alignment. Too many issues compete for attention. The owner becomes the bottleneck—not because of lack of effort, but because of structural design.

Justin Quinn of Focused on Machining, for instance, recalls, "we graduated, if you will, from that manager who wasn't really a manager, but just was great at putting out fires. I hired two great shop foremen who are process oriented. They came from very large manufacturing companies—Lockheed Martin to be specific. It's all about process and it's all about people."[49]

49 Machine Shop Mastery, Episode 04.

Introducing management layers carefully solves this. A production manager aligns scheduling with real capacity. A quality manager ensures standards are maintained and improved. And a sales leader connects demand with operational reality instead of creating constant firefights. Jim Carr of CARR Machine and Tool puts the obligation in realistic terms: "When you're an owner and a leader, you can't do everything. You have to start really thinking like an owner and you have to delegate responsibilities."[50] Easier said than done, but it's the only path forward.

The risk is overcorrection. Add too much structure too early and the shop slows down. Decisions get pushed upward unnecessarily. Communication becomes indirect. The business starts to resemble a bureaucracy instead of a production system. The goal isn't to copy large organizations.

The best shops do this deliberately. They add layers when the business demands it. They define roles clearly but keep communication tight. They build structure to enable flow, not to control it.

At its core, this stage marks a shift in how the business operates. Work no longer depends on proximity or heroics—it depends on design. Responsibility becomes explicit. Leadership begins to distribute. The owner, for the first time, can step out of the center of execution and begin acting as the architect of the business.

50 Machine Shop Mastery, Episode 03.

Breaking $2M, Breaking $10M

Growth in a machine shop rarely feels like progress while it's happening. It feels like pressure. Orders increase, machines stay busy, people work harder, and yet the business doesn't become easier to run. It often becomes more difficult, because the structure that supported the previous stage is no longer enough.

Two specific revenue thresholds expose distinct structural failures, each requiring a different kind of redesign:

Threshold	Primary Constraint	Required Shift	Failure Mode
~$2M	Coordination through conversation rather than structure	Defined roles and clear ownership at the functional level	Roles exist on paper but authority remains centralized
~$10M	Cross-functional friction; local optimization degrading system performance	Coordination as a formal responsibility; outcome-based roles	Partial structure; ambiguous authority; systems introduced but not adopted

This is where defined roles begin to matter, not as a formality but as a stabilizing mechanism. When quoting, scheduling, and quality each have clear ownership, decisions stop drifting across the organization. The quoting function becomes responsible not just for getting work in but for getting the right work in. Scheduling owns flow against real capacity. Quality protects standards.

This stage exposes a tension many owners struggle to resolve. The business requires delegation, while the instinct is to stay involved, especially when problems arise. The contradiction: roles exist, but authority remains centralized. People hesitate, not because they lack competence, but because they sense the owner still wants to weigh in.

Some shops remain in this state for years. They grow, but unevenly. Revenue increases, yet operational clarity doesn't keep pace. Over time, the gap between what the business demands and how it's run becomes visible through missed deliveries, margin compression, or constant firefighting.

Shops that move past this stage commit fully to ownership at the functional level. Decisions happen where the work is understood, not where authority happens to sit. The owner's role shifts—sometimes gradually, sometimes abruptly—from solving problems to shaping how problems get solved.

By the time a shop approaches $10M, a different limitation emerges. The issue is no longer whether roles are defined but whether the business can coordinate across those roles without friction. Each function—sales, operations, quality—can perform well in isolation, yet the interactions between them produce drag.

Susan Palma of Precision Shapes recognizes this transition as both structural and cultural: "Part of the culture that I see from being with small companies and watching companies grow, some of that culture does require a little bit of changing. You start building a little bit more structure, a little bit more process."[51]

Eric Hagopian of Pilot Precision Products describes the curve from the other side, having pushed a business through several thresholds: "The customers kind of change. Once you get over, say, 10 million, things got a lot easier between, say, 10 and 15 million. Because what happens, all of a sudden, the people you're dealing with are far more sophisticated."[52]

A second structural shift becomes necessary, one that introduces coordination as a formal responsibility. Functional ownership remains important but is no longer sufficient. The business requires a layer that aligns priorities, resolves tradeoffs, and ensures decisions in one function don't create problems in another.

As this layer takes shape, roles become more outcome-oriented:

- **Sales.** No longer measured solely by bookings, but by the quality and fit of the work entering the system.
- **Operations.** Evaluated not just on utilization, but on throughput and on-time delivery performance.

51 Machine Shop Mastery, Episode 02.

52 Machine Shop Mastery, Episode 41.

- **Quality.** Extends beyond inspection to include system integrity and prevention.

These shifts may seem incremental, but they reflect a deeper change: the business organizes around results that span functions rather than activities contained within them. This transition also forces a reconsideration of how decisions are made. Earlier stages rely on proximity and experience; scale introduces distance, physically and informationally. The owner can no longer "see" the business simply by walking the floor. Decisions require visibility through data rather than observation.

Technology, in this context, becomes less about efficiency and more about coherence. An ERP system connects information that would otherwise remain fragmented, letting different parts of the business operate from a shared understanding of reality. Formal quality systems introduce consistency that makes delegation possible.

Dave Hannah of G-Zero built this thinking into his shop from the start: "I wanted to, when I started my shop, I wanted to have an ERP system. So right away, I picked up an ERP system when it was just two of us. I knew from the beginning I wanted to have a really nice system in place."[53]

Even with these changes, many shops struggle to move beyond this stage. The structure evolves partially, not completely. Leadership roles exist, yet authority remains ambiguous. Systems are introduced but not fully adopted. The result is a business that appears more sophisticated but still behaves like a smaller one when pressure hits.

---

53 Machine Shop Mastery, Episode 28.

Breaking through these thresholds requires more than incremental improvement. It requires redesigning the business in response to its own growth. At $2M, that redesign centers on ownership and clarity. At $10M, it centers on coordination and integration.

Stages of the Owner

Structure alone doesn't carry a business through growth. It creates the conditions for scale; it doesn't guarantee it. What ultimately determines whether a shop breaks through or stalls is the maturity of its leadership, especially the owner's. As the business evolves, the role of the leader must evolve too.

Stage	Name	Primary Focus	What the Owner Lets Go Of
1	Operator	Direct execution: programming, setup, troubleshooting	Nothing yet — the dependency is the constraint
2	Supervisor	Coordinating people and work; assigning jobs	Direct execution, but escalation runs through them
3	Manager	Planning, resource allocation, consistency across the operation	Routine decisions within defined functional areas

Stage	Name	Primary Focus	What the Owner Lets Go Of
4	System Builder	Identifying patterns; eliminating root causes; defining processes	Solving the same problem twice
5	Leader of Leaders	Developing functional heads; aligning the organization	Directing the work; controlling decisions made well by others
6	Architect	Long-term design: strategy, capital, market positioning	Day-to-day execution and routine coordination entirely

The first stage is the Operator. The owner is deeply embedded in the work—programming, setting up, troubleshooting, solving problems in real time. The business grows on the strength of execution, and that execution is personal. This creates speed and quality early on, but it also creates a ceiling. Everything moves only as fast as the owner can move.

As the shop grows, the limitations surface, leading into the Supervisor. Here, the owner starts stepping back from direct execution and spends more time coordinating people and work. Jobs are assigned, priorities set, problems escalated rather than solved individually. Throughput improves because the owner is no longer in every step—but the owner still carries decisions personally.

The transition to Manager requires a more deliberate shift. Functional ownership begins to take hold, and the owner starts relying on others to make decisions within defined areas. Focus moves toward planning, resource allocation, and consistency across the operation. The shop becomes less reactive.

This is also the stage at which most owners encounter, for the first time, the psychological difficulty of letting go. Mitch Free of ZYCI describes the shift with unusual candor: "When I did everything myself, day one of the business, I didn't have to have any meetings because I knew everything. I knew what needed to be done."[54] The pull back into execution is real, even after you know better.

There's a practical standard for the same transition—one that lets owners hand off work without requiring perfection at the handoff. The pitfall a lot of shop owners find themselves in is the realization that they are the experts. They know how to do programming, set up, make fixtures, or sell better than anyone they can hire. But even if someone does something at 80% of what you can do, if they can do it instead of you, that's a win. Eighty percent and done with you not doing it is better than a hundred percent and you being in the weeds every day.[55] The math is unsentimental but accurate, and it's the math that lets an owner move from Supervisor to Manager without strangling the team in the process.

54 Machine Shop Mastery, Episode 16.

55 Machine Shop Mastery, Episode 38.

Beyond this lies the System Builder. The owner begins to see the business as an interconnected system rather than a series of tasks or departments. Attention shifts from solving individual problems to identifying patterns and eliminating root causes. Processes are defined, metrics are introduced, feedback loops are formalized.

As the organization matures further, the owner steps into the role of Leader of Leaders. Functional heads operate with clear accountability, and the owner's focus shifts toward developing those leaders rather than directing their work. Alignment becomes the priority: ensuring that different parts of the business move in the same direction without being controlled centrally.

Jason Davis of D&D Enterprises summarizes the destination in a single sentence: "I feel like one of the great things you can do is work yourself out of a job. You can find an area that needs to be improved, spend the time to work and improve it, and then find somebody who could do that."[56]

The final stage is the Architect. The owner is no longer involved in day-to-day execution or even routine coordination. The focus is on long-term design: strategy, capital allocation, market positioning, leadership development. The business operates with enough internal capability that the owner becomes optional for daily operations.

Barry Russell of Low Country Aerospace described his epiphany: "I'm never going to be able to steer the company

---

56 Machine Shop Mastery, Episode 63.

in the direction I wanted to go unless I let go of everything I'm doing because there's not enough time in the day for you to do it all. And you've got to realize you've got a really good team of people that are more than capable of doing it. And you just have to let them do it...within three to four months, there was a burden off my shoulders."[57]

Not every shop moves cleanly through these stages. Owners often operate across multiple stages at once, depending on the situation. A decision in one area may reflect the Operator mindset, while another reflects the Architect. This overlap is normal—it becomes a constraint when the owner can't recognize which mode is appropriate when.

Understanding the stages doesn't remove the difficulty of transition, but it clarifies what's required. Each stage demands the owner let go of something that once made them effective—direct control, technical involvement, immediate problem-solving.

Designing What Comes Next

Every machine shop eventually reaches a point where effort stops being the limiting factor. The owner is working hard, the team is capable, demand exists—yet the business resists further growth. At that point, the issue is no longer execution. It's design.

What this chapter has shown—from functional leads to management layers to leadership maturity—is that growth forces structure whether the owner intends it or not. The

57 Machine Shop Mastery, Episode 117

only question is whether that structure is designed or imposed by chaos.

Each stage introduces new tools, but the underlying shift is the same. The business moves from being driven by people to being supported by structure—not to remove people, but to let them operate effectively without constant intervention from the top.

There's a more personal dimension. Each stage requires the owner to give up something that once made them successful:

- Control gives way to delegation.
- Visibility gives way to systems.
- Direct problem-solving gives way to designing how problems are solved.
- Personal capability gives way to organizational capability.

This often feels like a loss in the moment, but it's what creates the capacity for the business to keep evolving. Leaning into issues around trust, ownership and letting go is essential for this transition to work well. For many, it requires some challenging internal work to make the change. But that work is worth doing.

The shops that break through aren't the most skilled or best equipped. They're the ones that recognize when the current way of operating has reached its limit and are willing to redesign before that limit becomes a constraint.

From here, the conversation moves deeper into systems. Once leadership and structure reach a certain level of maturity, the next question is unavoidable: how does work actually flow through the business, and how do you design that flow to be consistent, visible, and profitable?

CHAPTER 12

Certifications and Compliance

Certifications, Compliance, and Playing in Better Markets

Every growing shop eventually reaches a point where capability isn't the limiting factor. The machines are in place, the team knows the work, the business can deliver quality parts. Yet certain opportunities remain inaccessible, certain customers won't engage, and certain markets stay out of reach.

The issue is no longer execution. It is credibility.

This is where certifications and compliance enter the picture, though not always in a way that's immediately welcomed. Most shops encounter standards as requirements imposed from the outside: a customer requests ISO 9001, an aerospace contract demands AS9100 (soon to be called IA9100 in late 2026), a defense opportunity surfaces CMMC. The first instinct is to view them as overhead.

What standards actually do is force a level of clarity most businesses postpone. They require processes to be defined, decisions to be traceable, and outcomes to be repeatable. In doing so, they expose how the business truly operates—not on its best day, but on its average one.

That gap becomes more important as the business grows. Informal coordination, personal oversight, and tribal knowledge can carry a shop through its early stages, but they break down under increasing complexity. Standards don't eliminate that complexity; they impose a structure that makes it manageable.

What this chapter covers:

- The truth behind standards—what certifications actually do inside a business.
- ISO, AS9100, CMMC, and what each one opens and requires.
- Why compliance has to have a single owner, not be everyone's responsibility.
- Whether compliance shows up as a burden or as structure—and what determines which.
- The always-audit-ready shop, and what zero-prep audits actually mean.
- Turning the compliance burden into commercial leverage.

The Truth Behind Standards

The most common reason shops pursue certifications is external pressure, but that explanation captures only the surface. The more interesting question is why some of the best shops pursue standards even when they aren't strictly required.

Inside the business, the effect is more structural than symbolic. Standards force systems into place by requiring processes to be defined, documented, and followed. What might otherwise remain informal—how work is quoted, how inspections are performed, how corrections are handled—becomes explicit.

Tom Nathan of Total Precision has watched standards make a positive impact even before formal certification arrived: "An excellent thing that's happened to the business without even being certified yet is that it has just driven discipline through the organization. Like really, really getting to where we can be detailed and provide repeatable results, regardless of who's doing the job."[58]

As these systems take hold, the way the business thinks changes. Decisions once based on experience alone incorporate data. Teams look for patterns, measure performance, refine processes based on evidence rather than intuition.

Another shift occurs in how work is approached daily. Ad hoc solutions, still necessary at times, become less

58 Machine Shop Mastery, Episode 40.

dominant; standard work begins to define how tasks are performed, reducing variability across people and shifts. Although that initially feels rigid to some, it stabilizes the business in ways that are hard to achieve through effort alone.

Over time, these changes compound. Problems become easier to diagnose because processes are visible. Improvements become easier to sustain because they're built into the system rather than dependent on individuals. The business becomes more predictable.

Standards aren't simply a requirement to meet. They're a mechanism that pushes the business toward a more disciplined, more analytical, and ultimately more scalable way of operating.

ISO, AS9100, CMMC, and What They Open

Not all certifications carry the same weight. Each standard signals something specific to the market, and that signal determines how the business is perceived before a single part is produced.

Certification	Primary Industry	Focus	Role in the Market
ISO 9001	General manufacturing	Structured quality management system; basic process consistency	Qualifies a shop to be considered; rarely differentiates

Certification	Primary Industry	Focus	Role in the Market
AS9100	Aerospace	Risk, traceability, configuration control, plus all of ISO 9001	Required for participation in higher tiers of aerospace
ISO 13485	Medical devices	Process control and documentation tied to patient safety	Required to bid on some types of medical device components
CMMC / NIST 800-171	Defense	Protection of sensitive information rather than product quality	Required to handle controlled unclassified information (CUI) in defense work

At the most basic level, ISO 9001 establishes a foundation. It communicates that the business has a structured quality management system and can operate with a degree of consistency. For many shops, it doesn't differentiate so much as qualify them. Without it, certain conversations don't happen at all.

Other certifications operate with a different level of expectation.

AS9100, for example, is effectively a requirement for participating in higher tiers of the aerospace industry. It extends beyond general quality management into risk, traceability, and configuration control, reflecting the complexity and consequences of aerospace work. Shops considering this path have to weigh not just the cost of certification but the operational maturity required to maintain it.

There's also a strategic angle to choosing the right certification, particularly when one standard can do the work of two. Tom Nathan describes how a defense-oriented pivot reshaped his approach: "We actually started doing work with a large trucking company around the corner and they immediately said, do you have your ISO certification? We said, no, we don't really have any certification, but we do work with company XYZ ABC. The conversation started rolling on and then we started talking to people in defense and then AS9100D came up. And then in conversation with a couple of implementation people, they said, look, if you're really going to target defense, go for AS9100D."[59]

Dave Hannah of G-Zero describes the marketing payoff once certification is in hand: "We got AS9100 certified and then add that to our brochures and stuff and re-sent to people that I'd been talking to before, saying, hey, we just got our certification. Now we're a real, certified aerospace shop. Boom, we're open for business."[60]

Similar dynamics exist in other regulated sectors. ISO 13485 serves a comparable role in medical device manufacturing, where process control and documentation are directly tied to patient safety. Christian Schutte of Rise Industries

59 Machine Shop Mastery, Episode 40.

60 Machine Shop Mastery, Episode 28.

recounted, "We had been working on a major ~ implant project that needed 13485 to ~ get the order. And it was the next day after that, we received the order for this medical implant assembly that is going to really propel us to the next level... But ~ it was definitely a big ~ sigh of relief and pushed us to like, we made the right decision in doing this."[61]

In defense, certifications such as CMMC shift the focus from product quality to data security, emphasizing protection of sensitive information rather than the physical part itself. These standards do more than signal capability. They define access. In other words, a shop can't simply decide to enter aerospace, medical, or defense markets based on technical skill alone. Each industry sets its own baseline, and certifications are part of that baseline. They function as gatekeepers—not arbitrary ones, but reflections of the level of process maturity each industry demands.

The answer depends on alignment. A shop must evaluate the cost of compliance—upfront and ongoing—against the opportunities it enables. If a certification opens access to markets with higher margins, more stable demand, or better strategic positioning, the investment makes sense. If not, it may add overhead without real return.

Someone Has to Own It

Compliance touches every part of the business, which is why it's often described as "everyone's responsibility." On the surface, that idea makes sense: operators follow

61 Manufacturing Transformed, Episode 55.

processes, inspectors verify results, managers enforce standards.

The problem is that contribution and ownership aren't the same thing, and confusing the two creates subtle but persistent gaps. When compliance belongs equally to everyone, it often ends up enforced by no one in particular.

- A record is missed here because someone assumed someone else would catch it.
- A step gets skipped there because the workaround feels faster.
- A requirement is presumed to be handled in another department, and isn't.
- Small inconsistencies accumulate, surfacing later as audit findings or operational failures that could have been prevented.

What stabilizes the system is not broader participation, but clear ownership.

Someone in the organization must be responsible for the integrity of the compliance system as a whole, not just for individual tasks within it. In a smaller shop, that responsibility usually sits with the owner, whether formally defined or not. The owner is closest to customer requirements, has the most context across functions, and ultimately bears the consequences of failure. As the business grows, that ownership has to transition.

That handoff—from owner doing it themselves to a dedicated person owning it formally—is the same evolution most shops eventually live through.

As the business grows, the role becomes more structured: a QMS coordinator or quality manager, eventually a more senior leadership position as complexity increases. The point isn't to add layers for structure's sake; it's to ensure accountability has a clear endpoint. When there's a single point where the buck stops, issues are more likely to be identified, addressed, and prevented systematically.

Dave Capkovitz adds an unexpected payoff of letting someone else own the standard: "My quality guy was fantastic about holding me accountable to make sure we follow the process. And I got so close to that. I wound up trusting the process more because of him."[62]

The distinction becomes even more important when different types of compliance are involved:

- **Quality compliance.** Focuses on whether products and processes meet customer requirements: dimensional accuracy, specifications, repeatability.
- **Security compliance.** Particularly in defense, focuses on protecting information, ensuring data is handled and stored in a way that prevents unauthorized access.

62 Machine Shop Mastery, Episode 35.

Although these areas intersect at times, they operate under different constraints and require different controls, which means they can't be managed effectively without clear ownership in each domain. As the organization grows, the structure around compliance has to grow with it—one person, two, eventually a small function. The discipline scales when the ownership scales.

Burden or Structure

Two shops can face the same certification requirements and arrive at entirely different outcomes, even with similar systems on paper. The difference rarely comes from the standard itself—it comes from how the business interprets what compliance is for.

The contrast between the two postures shows up across every dimension of how the system actually operates.

Dimension	Compliance as Burden	Compliance as Structure
Processes	Documented because they have to exist; rarely followed	Documented, followed, and refined over time
Audits	Events to prepare for; cycles of last-minute fixes	Reflections of how the business already operates
Records	Assembled retroactively under deadline pressure	Generated continuously as part of normal work
Relationship to the business	Parallel to operations; layered on top	Part of operations; inseparable from execution

When compliance is viewed as a burden, the approach becomes reactive. Processes are documented because they need to exist, not because they're meant to be used. Audits are treated as events to prepare for, creating cycles of scramble followed by drift. Inside this posture, the business never quite catches up to its own standards—documentation lags reality, training is uneven, corrective actions feel like punishment rather than learning.

A different mindset produces a different result.

When shops treat compliance as a structure, it becomes part of how the business runs rather than something layered on top. Processes aren't only defined but followed and refined. Standard work begins to replace improvisation—not because it's required but because it produces better results with less stress. Documentation becomes a tool for thinking, not a chore to satisfy auditors.

This shift is often misunderstood as a loss of freedom. In practice it creates a different kind of freedom. By reducing reliance on tribal knowledge and individual memory, the business becomes less dependent on specific people being present at specific moments.

Eventually, what feels restrictive becomes stabilizing.

The impact is most visible during audits. In a reactive system, audits disrupt the business because they expose gaps. Preparation becomes a separate effort, often requiring time and attention that could be spent on production. In a designed system, audits cause minimal disruption because the evidence already exists.

This is where being "always audit-ready" starts to make sense. It doesn't mean the business is perfect or that issues never occur. It means the system is maintained continuously, so nothing needs to be reconstructed or corrected at the last minute.

Over time, the discipline reinforces itself. The habits required to maintain compliance—recording accurately, following defined processes, addressing issues systematically—carry into other areas. What begins as a response to external requirements becomes a way of operating.

The Always-Audit-Ready Shop

Being audit-ready at all times sounds unrealistic to shops used to preparing for audits as discrete events. Audits trigger a familiar pattern: documents are gathered, records are reviewed, gaps are patched. The effort is large, focused, and short-lived—and the underlying reason the gaps existed is rarely addressed.

A different approach begins with a different assumption.

If compliance is built into the way work is performed, the records required for an audit should already exist as part of normal operations. Inspection results, process documentation, corrective actions, and traceability shouldn't need to be assembled before an audit—they should be available continuously, because they exist for their own operational value.

Scott Shortess of Advanced Plastics and Machining describes what that posture looks like: "We had a customer a few years ago call us on a Friday and say, hey, we're gonna be in on Monday to do an audit. Is that okay? And I was like, sure, no problem. Because everything is in the cloud. And so we've already got everything organized."[63]

This shift depends on how systems are designed. Record-keeping can't be a task layered on top of production—anything that feels secondary is eventually neglected under pressure. The discipline has to be embedded into the workflow itself:

- Operators record what they produce as they produce it.
- Quality checks are logged in the same workflow where the check requirement was created, and where it's tied to a high-level procedure.
- Issues are captured and addressed in real time, not reconstructed later.
- Corrective actions are documented as they happen, not summarized after the fact.

When these elements are integrated properly, the need for audit preparation disappears. There's no scramble to locate missing information or recreate incomplete records, because the system reflects what's actually happening. Lori Robertson of Cutting Edge Metals describes the practical effect: "We've already had our stage one audit for as 9100

63 Machine Shop Mastery, Episode 01.

passed it with flying colors. As a matter of fact, they typically don't schedule the second stage to audit for several months after stage one, because typically companies have to go in and do things and fix things. We scheduled mine for like seven, eight weeks later."[64]

This level of readiness reveals something about the health of the business itself. A shop that can withstand an audit at any moment is a shop where risks are being managed continuously rather than accumulated over time. The audit stops being a test to pass. It becomes an indicator of whether the business is operating as intended, which is ultimately what the standard is meant to measure.

Turning Burden into Leverage

When certifications are approached narrowly, they remain a cost to manage. They require time, documentation, audits, ongoing attention—all of which feel disconnected from production and revenue. When they're integrated into how the business operates, they shift from cost to leverage.

From a market perspective, certifications shift the level at which a shop can participate. They allow access to industries and customers that would otherwise remain out of reach. More importantly, they change how the shop is perceived within those markets. That distinction often supports stronger pricing, provided the business understands its own cost structure and doesn't treat compliance as an invisible expense. Many shops misstep here.

---

64 Machine Shop Mastery, Episode 33.

If shops absorb the cost of compliance but fail to translate it into pricing or positioning, margins erode rather than improve. The advantage doesn't come from having certifications. It comes from using them deliberately.

Internally, the leverage is less visible but often more significant. The systems required for compliance reduce variability, which affects everything from scrap rates to rework to delivery performance. Processes become more consistent. Risks become more identifiable. Continuous improvement becomes structural rather than aspirational. For shops who aspire to work this way, a certification can be a good way to force themselves to follow their aspirational goals (and reap the benefits of doing so).

There's also a protective dimension. A shop operating without structure may perform well under normal conditions but is more exposed when something goes wrong. A quality issue, a missed requirement, or a security incident can escalate quickly if the systems behind it can't demonstrate that the work was performed correctly.

Over time, the combination of access, pricing power, operational stability, and risk reduction produces a different type of business. More resilient because it depends less on individual effort. More scalable because its systems can absorb growth without breaking.

Certifications aren't the end goal. They're the mechanism that forces the business to operate at a level where those advantages become possible.

CHAPTER 13

Stop Winging It

How Systems Change Everything

Most shop owners don't think they're winging it. They have systems—or at least it feels that way. There's a way quotes are done, a way jobs are scheduled, a way parts are inspected. People know what to do.

The problem is not the absence of systems. It is the type of systems that exist.

In many shops, what passes for a system is a workaround that survived long enough to become standard. A spreadsheet meant to be temporary becomes permanent; a checklist created for one customer gets applied everywhere; a piece of tribal knowledge becomes "how we do it." The result is a patchwork that feels like structure but isn't.

John Preiser of Precision Shapes describes the shape this takes once a business has grown for a while: "Right now, I've tried to get a good number on how many different spreadsheets we're running the business on, and it's like

60. That's wild and that's a function of years of just adding stuff."[65]

The full extent rarely becomes visible until someone tries to describe it out loud. Over time, this creates a business that feels stable on the surface and fragile underneath. You can see it in how problems behave. They don't disappear—they mutate. Symptoms change, but underlying causes persist.

Progress starts to feel inconsistent. You can have strong people, good equipment, and steady demand, yet still experience recurring mistakes, missed expectations, constant adjustments. At some point, the question shifts. Not "How do we fix this?" but "Why does this keep happening?" That question leads to a different way of thinking about the business—not as a series of problems to solve, but as a system to design.

What this chapter covers:

- The franchise prototype revisited—what shops are still trying to learn from a thirty-year-old idea.
- Why systems beat fixes, even when the fixes feel faster.
- Why discipline beats software, no matter how good the software gets.
- Effort vs. design—the trade-off that separates the shops that scale from the shops that stall.

---

65 Machine Shop Mastery, Episode 02.

The Franchise Prototype, Again

The idea of building a "franchise prototype" often feels misplaced in a machine shop. Most owners aren't trying to open multiple locations, and the term itself can sound more like retail than manufacturing. The principle, though, is the same.

At its core, the franchise prototype forces a different question—one most owners don't naturally ask: could someone else run this shop without you, not eventually, but reliably, within a defined system? The exercise tends to surface a recognizable set of weak points—the places where the business is held together by the owner's memory and presence rather than by anything documented:

- Quoting follows a general approach, but the actual logic varies depending on who is doing it that week.
- Scheduling lives across conversations, sticky notes, and spreadsheets, none of which fully agree.
- Quality checks are performed, but the method differs from one operator to another, and the results aren't reliably recorded.
- Customer expectations and preferences sit in the owner's head, not in any documented form.
- Process knowledge for repeat parts depends on the one person who has run them before.

Framed this way, the concept becomes less abstract and more operational. The focus shifts from how work gets done today to how it would need to be structured for someone else to execute it tomorrow. Each part of the workflow functions in isolation, and while the business continues to move, the connections between those parts are often assumed rather than designed. The franchise prototype forces those connections to become explicit.

This way of thinking doesn't come naturally, especially in environments where the day-to-day demands are immediate. When there are jobs to ship and problems to solve, stepping back to design seems like a luxury. The pressure to act keeps focus on what's immediately visible. The cost of relying on effort instead of design is what changes the perspective. When processes aren't clearly defined, the business compensates through people. Decisions depend on experience. Outcomes depend on who happens to be working that day. The business functions, but its consistency is borrowed.

At Pro CNC, we tried to build the business in exactly this way: by working ourselves out of the roles we'd once occupied. Kelsey, for example, started as one of our main setup people, programmers, and fixture designers. Over time, we built systems and trained people so those tasks didn't depend on him. I was a machinist in the first few years, but moved into estimating and sales, eventually replacing myself in those roles as well. By the time we exited, the business could run without any of us being involved every day.

Designing the shop as a franchise prototype doesn't remove problems, but it changes how they behave. Instead of recurring in slightly different forms, they become easier to trace and address at their root.

Systems Beat Fixes

Most shops don't lack solutions. They have too many of them.

Every time a problem appears, something is put in place to address it. A spreadsheet to track quotes. A whiteboard to manage scheduling. A checklist to keep inspections consistent. Each one solves something specific—and over time the result is a patchwork.

The contrast between an accumulated patchwork and a designed system shows up across every dimension of how the business actually operates.

Dimension	What Most Shops Have	What Designed Systems Produce
Origin	Fixes layered on as problems appeared, one at a time	Built as a single connected system from the start
Information	Lives in multiple places, often slightly out of sync	Captured once, flows downstream cleanly, single source of truth
Problem behavior	Mutates into new symptoms; recurring causes remain	Surfaces clearly, gets traced to source, gets resolved
Effect of fixes	Local improvement, system-wide friction	Local improvement, system-wide stability

Over time, a patchwork creates a business where information exists in multiple places, often slightly out of sync. A job is updated in one system but not another. A decision is made based on data that's already outdated. Coordination becomes manual: someone has to consolidate, translate, and reconcile information that should have been consistent in the first place.

The underlying pattern is subtle but consistent. Most fixes are applied where the problem becomes visible, not at the level where it originates. If quoting is inconsistent, the instinct is to fix the quoting tool. If scheduling slips, the instinct is to update the schedule. Each fix addresses the symptom; none address the architecture.

This is where the idea of the business as a single system becomes critical.

A machine shop isn't a collection of departments operating independently. It's a value stream, where each step depends on the one before it and influences the one after it. When one part of the system changes, the others change with it, whether the change is intentional or not.

Mark Heston of Collinear Machine describes this dynamic exactly: "Once you fix in these businesses, once you fix one of these issues, the weak link pops, it's set up really fast. You fix your schedule, now you have a labor issue. You fix your labor issue, now you have a quality issue. Etc."[66]

66 Machine Shop Mastery, Episode 89.

In other words, improvements made without considering the full system tend to relocate problems rather than resolve them. Stronger shops think in terms of flow rather than function.

Approach	Question Asked	Where It Targets the Problem
Isolated Fix	"How do we solve this specific problem?"	At the point where the symptom became visible
Flow Thinking	"How does work actually move through the business, and where did this originate?"	At the source, even when it sits several stages upstream

Instead of asking how to fix a specific issue, they step back and examine how work moves through the entire business. They look at how information is created, transferred, and used across each stage of the process.

That shift in perspective isn't immediate, but it is decisive. Once the business is understood as an interconnected system, isolated fixes start to feel insufficient. The focus moves toward integration—making sure information flows from quoting to scheduling to production to inspection without translation, gaps, or duplicate entry.

Derek Kowalski of LOC Industries describes the principle from the perspective of how work moves once integration is in place: "You try to get everyone on the same page. You do the analysis and try to figure out and just make sure that the team knows the why behind the decision."[67]

---

67 Machine Shop Mastery, Episode 46.

Visibility improves, duplication decreases, and decisions are made with a clearer understanding of their impact across the operation. The business begins to behave differently. Problems become easier to address because the system makes the connections between them visible.

Discipline Beats Software

When shops begin formalizing processes, the conversation almost immediately turns to tools. Should everything be managed in spreadsheets, moved into a database, integrated into an ERP system? The tool matters less than people assume.

Inconsistency doesn't come from a lack of tools—it comes from how people behave under pressure. The pattern repeats across every busy shop:

- An operator skips a step because they have done it a hundred times and don't need the prompt.
- A quote is rushed without fully checking assumptions, because the customer is waiting.
- A quality check is performed but not recorded, because "it looked fine."
- A program adjustment is made on the floor without being captured back in the master router.

None of these decisions seem significant in isolation, yet they introduce small deviations that accumulate. The system still exists on paper, but actual execution begins to drift away from it.

A documented process only creates value when it produces the same result regardless of who performs it. That requires more than having instructions written down—it requires the discipline to use them as designed, even when shortcuts are available.

Discipline can't be sustained through enforcement alone. If people experience the process as additional work, separate from the task they're trying to complete, they'll quietly de-prioritize it. The process has to be part of the work, not a separate layer that has to be remembered.

The solution is to design processes that are inseparable from execution. If an operator is completing a job, the system they use should require the key information to be entered as part of the job, not as a separate report. If a quality check is performed, the act of performing it should also be the act of documenting it.

Kelsey of ProShop and Pro CNC describes the design principle: "It turned out that done well, you can do normal work all day where everyone's work across the entire company is adding the little piece that makes you compliant."[68]

There's a leadership component too. People are far more likely to follow a process when they understand how it affects outcomes they care about. If consistent

68 Machine Shop Mastery, Episode 23.

documentation reduces rework, customer escalations, or rebuilds, that connection has to be made explicit.

Over time, consistency produces measurable effects that compound across the business:

- Scrap rates become more predictable because processes are followed the same way every time.
- Training time decreases because new employees aren't relying on informal instruction.
- Scheduling becomes more reliable because the inputs it depends on are accurate.
- Quality outcomes stabilize across shifts and operators rather than tracking with whoever happens to be on the floor.

Effort vs. Design

Most recurring issues inside a shop aren't independent problems. They're the result of how the business is currently set up to operate. When the same types of mistakes appear in different areas, the underlying structure is producing them.

This is why the business can feel both functional and fragile at the same time. Work gets out the door, customers are served, nothing appears fundamentally broken—yet the operation depends heavily on people compensating for what the structure doesn't provide.

Changing that dynamic doesn't come from solving problems faster. It comes from reducing how often the same problems need to be solved. When processes are clearly defined and connected, the business spends less energy reacting and more energy advancing.

This shift has consequences beyond daily operations:

- **Easier to manage.** Fewer decisions depend on memory or individual judgment.
- **Easier to scale.** The same processes can support higher volume without breaking down.
- **Less dependent on individuals.** Operational risk decreases, and flexibility increases over time.
- **Compounding rather than resetting.** Improvements made today still hold tomorrow, because they are captured in the system rather than living in someone's head.

A business built on effort can perform, but it requires continuous input. A business built on design compounds—improvements stick, capability grows, the next stage becomes possible. The shift from one to the other is what the rest of this book is about.

CHAPTER 14

Quote to Cash

Designing the Operating System of a Machine Shop

Machine shops all run on the same basic sequence. A customer sends a request, the shop reviews it, plans the work, schedules the machines, cuts the part, inspects it, ships it, invoices for it, and collects. Quote to cash. Every business in this industry depends on that flow, and every business in this industry loses money somewhere within it.

The previous chapter made the case for systems over effort. This one moves from principle to mechanism—looking at how the operating system of a shop is built, stage by stage, and where the design choices matter.

Most shops don't lack the individual components. They have a way of reviewing orders, planning jobs, scheduling, and some form of quality control. The issue is that these components are loosely connected. Information has to be moved manually from one stage to the next. Decisions made in one stage don't automatically inform the next. The handoffs are where the cost lives.

What follows walks through each stage of the quote-to-cash flow, from the moment an order arrives through the visibility required to manage the whole system in real time.

Stage	What It Decides	What Breaks if Neglected
Contract Review	Whether to accept the work, on what terms, with what risk	Hidden clauses, undetected revisions, mismatched assumptions
Planning & Programming	How the work will be executed, on which machine, with which tooling	Rework, missed tolerances, jobs that fight the floor
Scheduling & Kitting	When the work happens and whether everything needed is there	Idle machines, hunting for tools, missed due dates
Quality Planning & Execution	How conformance is built into production and verified at each step	Scrap discovered late, liability shipped to the customer
Visibility	Whether decisions get made on current reality or yesterday's assumptions	Surprises, overpromises, expediting that eats margin

The goal isn't to prescribe a single method. It's to make the design choices visible—what each stage must accomplish, who must be involved, and what breaks when it's done poorly.

What this chapter covers:

- Before you say yes: contract review as a strategic decision, not an administrative one.
- Planning before the spindle turns, and how a few hours upstream save days on the floor.
- Schedules and kits—where good operations live and bad ones quietly bleed.
- Quality built in, not bolted on, and why inspection has to be designed into the takt time.
- How visibility translates directly into profit.
- Where the money actually moves through a shop, end to end.

Before You Say Yes: Contract Review

Every job begins with a decision most shops treat as administrative but is, in fact, strategic: whether to accept the work.

Contract review is the point where the shop formally agrees to deliver a specific result under specific conditions—price, timeline, quality, capability. When it's thorough, it protects the business. When it's skipped, the consequences surface later, usually expensively.

The purpose is risk mitigation. Anything the shop agrees to that it can't deliver—or can't verify—becomes a liability the moment the order is accepted. The fine print buried in a customer's terms can include first-article inspection requirements, special packaging, traceability conditions, NDA stipulations, country-of-origin certifications. None of these are exotic. All of them affect cost and lead time, and any one of them can render a quote invalid if it was missed.

From the other side—after the damage has already surfaced—the diagnosis comes too late. Did we not do a careful enough contract review? Did we miss a clause that bit us later because it added difficulty or a requirement we didn't notice? At Pro CNC, we've asked ourselves that exact question.[69] The clause was always there. The shop simply didn't notice it in time for the noticing to matter.

What must be verified before the commitment is formalized is more specific than most shops acknowledge:

- Price, lead time, and due dates align with what was quoted.
- Drawings and models on file match the current revision level.
- Machines, tooling, and inspection equipment required for the job are actually available.

69 Machine Shop Mastery, Episode 38.

- People with the right skills are available within the committed timeframe.
- Special clauses, packaging requirements, and traceability conditions buried in the documentation have been read and understood.

The people involved matter as much as the checklist. Estimating and sales confirm commercial terms. Quality assurance verifies inspection requirements and flowdowns can be met. Production confirms capacity and capability. Purchasing confirms material and outside processing availability. The job of contract review isn't to slow the business down—it's to confirm that the conditions implied by the quote still hold when the order arrives.

Kowalski describes how his own shop hardened this stage after experiencing the alternative: "Going back down to the other system where we had to catch everything as we were going through contract review, and we were missing things all the time. So having a centralized place to access these notes makes it really easy."[70]

A formal checklist doesn't need to be elaborate—it needs to be consistent, covering every condition that could create a gap between what was promised and what can be delivered. Some ERP systems include built-in contract review workflows; some shops use standalone checklists. The tool matters less than the consistency of use.

70 Machine Shop Mastery, Episode 46.

There are situations where the right decision is to decline the work. If the customer has changed requirements between the RFQ and the PO and the shop can't accommodate those changes, the answer may be a polite refusal, or a renegotiation, not a quiet absorption of new risk. Saying yes when the conditions have shifted is one of the most expensive errors a shop can make.

There's a third scenario that's less obvious: the shop didn't fully understand the requirements when it estimated. A cursory review during quoting can miss things that contract review—if it's done properly—would catch. When that happens, contract review becomes the last chance to renegotiate or decline before the cost gets locked in.

Contract review isn't where most shops lose money in dramatic ways. It's where they let risk in quietly, one unchecked assumption at a time.

Planning Before the Spindle Turns

A job that passes contract review has earned the right to proceed, but proceeding and being ready to proceed aren't the same thing. What happens between accepting an order and cutting the first chip determines whether the job runs cleanly or fights the shop at every step.

What happens in many shops is simpler and more damaging than it sounds. The order comes in, someone glances at it, and it gets tossed to manufacturing: make this. There's no detailed plan, no upfront thinking about which machine, which tools, which fixtures, which inspection methods.

The first time those questions get answered is when the operator at the machine has to figure them out—usually under time pressure, often with incomplete information.

The better approach starts with assembling the smallest group of people who can collectively build a confident plan. That might be one person or five. What matters isn't group size—it's that the people involved understand the work end to end. Engineering reviews geometry and tolerances. Manufacturing evaluates whether existing programs and fixtures can be reused or whether new ones are needed. Quality confirms the inspection plan. Purchasing confirms material and tooling lead times.

Programming adds specificity. Assuming the shop uses 3D model-based programming, the programmer needs the customer's CAD model—or needs to create one from a 2D drawing—along with the drawing itself. From there, the programmer builds the tool paths, posts the programs, and verifies them against the model. If verification happens at the machine, the cycle takes longer and the spindle is consumed for setup rather than production.

Mark Heston describes how his shop eliminates that gap by pulling programming off the floor: "We run all DMG Mori. So we have full posts for our machines. We don't do any programming, no posting, no verification at the machine. It's all done in the office, beforehand, and ready to go."[71]

The programmer's role is more significant than many shops recognize. They shouldn't just receive instructions—they

71 Machine Shop Mastery, Episode 89.

should have input. Within the constraints of the customer's requirements, the programmer can often suggest changes that reduce setup time, simplify inspection, or improve cycle time.

Which machine the job runs on matters more than it might seem. That single decision drives tooling selection, fixture design, program structure, and scheduling. When it's answered clearly and early, everything downstream gets easier.

Heston also describes what a complete pre-floor package looks like once a shop has built the discipline to produce one consistently: "From cradle to grave, they create the inspection plan, all the gauging, the tools, the holders, the fixtures, the programs. We make all the cards. So when the machinist gets the job, they've literally got everything they need."[72]

The point isn't the level of detail—it's that the operator at the machine inherits certainty, not ambiguity. Every question that could have stopped the job has been answered upstream.

When planning is rushed, the failure modes are predictable rather than mysterious:

- Tolerances aren't held—not because the machines aren't capable, but because the process wasn't designed to achieve them reliably.

72 Machine Shop Mastery, Episode 89.

- Surface finish requirements get missed because no one flagged them in the routing.
- Parts get made from the wrong material because purchasing worked from incomplete specs.
- Jobs take far longer than budgeted because setups weren't thought through and the tools or gauges weren't on hand.
- Steps get forgotten entirely, and the shop ships an incomplete part.

None of these failures are mysterious. They're the natural consequence of sending work to the floor without a plan that accounts for reality.

The line between a job that runs cleanly and one that fights the shop at every turn is almost always drawn here. No chips are flying, no parts are shipping—but this is the stage where the shop decides whether the next dozen hours are going to be efficient or expensive.

Schedules and Kits

Planning defines what needs to happen. Scheduling defines when it happens, in what order, and on which resources. These are different problems, and shops that blur them tend to experience a stretched, anxious version of both.

Building a schedule starts with understanding what the shop actually has—not in theory, in practice. The work that has to be resourced sorts into three categories:

- **Setup.** The people, machines, and tooling required to get a job ready to run.
- **Execution.** The machines, secondary work centers, and operators required to actually produce the part.
- **Verification.** The inspection equipment, quality labs, and personnel required to confirm conformance.

Until the shop has a clear and current picture of those resources across all three categories, scheduling is wishful thinking with dates attached.

Once the resources are mapped, jobs can be applied against them. Each job moves through multiple stages, each requiring time on a specific resource. Laying those stages across available capacity—not just machine capacity but inspection and verification capacity—is what produces a real schedule.

Tools vary. Whiteboards. Spreadsheets. Scheduling software. ERP modules. The tool matters less than the discipline behind it. A whiteboard that gets updated honestly outperforms an ERP system that nobody trusts.

Scheduling determines when work is supposed to happen. Kitting determines whether it actually can.

A job scheduled to start on Monday but without its material, tooling, or inspection equipment ready isn't really scheduled—it's parked in a queue with a date on it. When that job hits the floor, the operator spends time chasing what should already be there. Spindles sit idle. Setups stretch. The schedule starts drifting from reality, and the drift accumulates fast.

What needs to be on the cart or ready to converge at the machine before the job reaches the floor is more comprehensive than most shops treat it:

- Material on hand—correct alloy, correct size, verified against the order.
- Cutting tools and holders assembled and touched off.
- Fixturing and workholding confirmed as functional.
- Inspection equipment available and calibrated.
- Programs posted and verified.
- Work instructions complete and accessible at the machine.
- Packaging materials staged for the end of the run.
- Quality plan finalized and digitally ready, not something figured out after the first part.

Jerry Mullins of Western Precision Products describes what a functioning kitting system looks like: "In ProShop, when we cue the tools, it goes to her dashboard and she can get the tools to the job and put them on a cart. So when the setup person goes to set the job up, they're all neat and tidy on the cart with the number, and they know what to get. They can take their old cart and just leave it for the tool crib person to disassemble and clean."[73]

When kitting is done properly, the list of problems that disappear justifies the effort. Machine downtime drops. Scrap rates decline. Setup times shrink. Spindle utilization improves. The operator can focus on running parts instead of hunting for what they need. When this practice is followed, we often see setup times get slashed in half.

There's a broader effect easy to overlook. When kitting is consistent, the shop stops needing to expedite its own jobs nearly as often. Due dates get met not through heroic compression but because the work was ready when it was scheduled to be.

Scheduling sets the sequence. Kitting makes the sequence real.

Quality, Built In

Quality in a machine shop isn't a department. It's a condition: either the process is producing conforming parts reliably, or it isn't. Shops that treat quality as a function separated from production tend to discover problems only at final inspection—when the cost of correcting them is highest.

Before production starts, the shop needs a complete inspection and verification plan for every step of the

73 Machine Shop Mastery, Episode 20.

process. Not just the final dimensions the customer will see, but the intermediate conditions that have to be true for the final dimensions to be achievable. A datum surface that drifts at operation three becomes a tolerance violation at operation seven. A bore that's slightly off at intermediate stage becomes uncorrectable at final. If the shop doesn't verify intermediate conditions when they're produced, it won't know to correct them until the final dimension fails—at which point the part is already scrap, or close to it.

Understanding the requirements well enough to build that plan is harder than it sounds. The shop has to confirm its machines and processes can produce the required accuracy repeatably, not just on a good day. It has to identify which features carry risk and design verification points that catch problems before they propagate. How the plan is communicated to the people doing the work also determines whether it functions as a system or sits as a document. Operators need to know which aspects of the part they're responsible for verifying, what measurements they need to take, what tolerances apply, and what to do when something drifts.

The comparison between results and requirements needs to be automatic. When an operator records a measurement, the system should immediately flag whether that value falls within tolerance. Manual comparison invites errors, especially under time pressure. What happens when a quality issue is discovered mid-run, in fact, reveals how well the system actually works. Mid-run is better than post-run—that much is obvious. What the shop is really trying to achieve is catching the issue early enough that the rest of the lot doesn't become scrap or rework.

Ultimately, the closed loop matters more than the catch itself. Identifying a deviation is only useful if the shop can adjust the process, produce a new part, re-verify, and confirm the correction holds. Quality planning and execution aren't bolted onto production. They're the mechanism that makes production trustworthy.

Visibility Is Profit

Everything covered in this chapter—contract review, planning, scheduling, kitting, quality—shares a common dependency. Each stage produces information that the next stage needs, and each stage generates information about how it's performing. If that information doesn't flow, the system doesn't function.

To run a shop well on any given day, the people responsible for production need answers to a handful of specific questions on a continuous basis:

- How is each job tracking against its time budget and its calendar?
- Is quality stable across active runs, or are processes drifting?
- Have any customer changes landed—pulled-in due dates, revised quantities, modified specs?
- Has anything in the resource picture changed since the schedule was built—a machine down, a person out, a critical tool tied up elsewhere?

The first of those questions deserves a moment on its own, because the two measurements behind it are different and both matter.

Measurement	What It Tracks	What Happens When It Slips
Time Budget	Hours allocated to produce the job profitably	Margin erodes silently even when the job ships on time
Calendar	Dates that determine whether the part ships on time	Customer trust erodes even when the job hit its hour target

A job can hit its ten-hour target and still deliver late if those hours happened a week behind schedule. A job can stay on the calendar and still lose money if it consumed fifteen hours instead of ten. Cost tracking and schedule tracking are different signals.

Beyond time and schedule, the shop needs to know that quality is stable. A process running on time but producing nonconforming parts isn't under control—it's generating cost that hasn't been recognized yet.

Customer-driven changes add another layer. Due dates shift. Quantities change. Requirements get revised. These aren't exceptions—they're normal in a job shop. The question isn't whether changes will come; it's whether the shop can absorb them without losing visibility.

Resource availability rounds out the picture. A machine down. Someone out. A critical tool tied up. A schedule built on Monday's assumptions is only useful if it's updated against Tuesday's reality.

Where this information lives changes everything about how the shop responds to it. Nathan Byman of Wolfram Manufacturing describes how visibility extends to scheduling itself, so the operator can see what's coming rather than waiting to be told: "If somebody needs to see the next job coming, they can just check their dashboard. There's no walking around asking what's next."[74]

Byman emphasizes the importance of continuous, real-time visibility into machine performance rather than waiting to review data after the fact. Instead of looking at reports the next day, a week later, or even updating a chart at the end of each hour, their custom monitoring software tracks uptime and part progress at a very granular level as it happens. Because this performance data is constantly visible to everyone on the team, they know immediately if a process is falling behind schedule and can take action to make up for the lost time right away.[75]

Who reviews this information depends on the size of the operation. In a small shop, it may still be the owner. As the business grows, it should shift to a production manager or shift lead—someone whose entire job is to keep work moving.

---

74 Machine Shop Mastery, Episode 55.

75 Machine Shop Mastery, Episode 55.

When visibility exists, every decision in the shop improves—not because the people making them suddenly become more capable, but because they're working from a complete picture. A quality problem gets addressed at the source. A schedule slip gets caught before it cascades.

The connection between visibility and profit is direct. A shop that can see its operation clearly doesn't overpromise capacity. It doesn't lose margin to expediting. It doesn't burn trust with customers.

Where the Money Moves

The quote-to-cash flow is the operating system of the business—the sequence through which every dollar of revenue is earned, every hour of capacity is consumed, and every customer relationship is either reinforced or eroded.

The shop that examines this flow as a whole starts to see its problems differently. Recurring issues stop looking like bad luck and start looking like what they are: predictable outputs of a system that wasn't designed to produce different outputs. Mike Payne once commented "I have shifted our thinking that we don't deliver parts. We deliver a collectible invoice. [Those are] steps that convert parts into money in the bank.

Closing that gap doesn't require a massive overhaul. It requires looking at how work actually moves through the business—from the moment a PO arrives to the moment payment is collected—and designing each stage so the next one inherits clarity, not ambiguity.

When this flow is designed well, the business holds together on its own—not perfectly, not without effort, but without the constant intervention that makes growth feel like a burden instead of progress.

CHAPTER 15

Where Precision Lives

What the Shop Floor Reveals About the Business

The previous chapter was about architecture: how the stages connect, how information moves between them, where the gaps live. This chapter moves to the floor itself. No matter how well the upstream system is designed, the floor is where parts get made—and where the design is either honored or quietly undone.

Most shops don't think of the floor as a design problem. They think of it as an execution problem—get the parts out, hit the dates, keep the machines running. Execution matters. But how the floor is designed to execute, what disciplines hold it together, what gets ignored or skipped when pressure rises—those choices are what separate shops that ship reliably from shops that ship anxiously.

Scott Shortess of Advanced Plastics and Machining frames the inversion that produces this result: "What are we doing on the front end? The old way was, well, we need more people out on the shop floor. The new way is, well, what can we do upstream so that the people on the shop floor aren't fighting the work?"[76]

This chapter is about the practices, disciplines, and habits between the moment a job reaches the floor and the moment the part leaves it. The argument runs through five interlocked ideas:

- Kitting as a philosophy that governs how work is released to the floor, not just a step in the workflow.
- Inspection discipline that puts verification as close to the machining process as possible, and as early as possible in the run.
- Time tracking that turns hours into the operational truth the shop can act on, not a retrospective record nobody trusts.
- Inventory and WIP management that treats unfinished work as the liability it actually is.
- What the floor looks like when all of this comes together, and what separates a culture of compliance from a culture of improvement.

Some of this will feel familiar. Some of it will feel like a mirror held up to problems you've been living with long enough to stop seeing. Either way, the floor is where the business's design is tested—and where most of the failure modes show up.

76 Machine Shop Mastery, Episode 01.

Kitting as Philosophy

Chapter 14 covered kitting as a step in the quote-to-cash sequence. Here, it deserves a deeper look—not as a task but as a philosophy that shapes how the floor operates. The distinction isn't small. As a task, kitting is something you check off. As a philosophy, it governs what the shop accepts onto the floor in the first place.

What must be prepared before a job reaches a machine is extensive, and every item exists for the same reason: to ensure the machinist can walk up to the workstation and produce the first good part without ever leaving it. That's the test. If the machinist has to walk somewhere else—to find a tool, track down a gauge, locate a fixture, pull up a drawing—the kitting wasn't complete. Every trip away from the machine is time the spindle isn't turning, and time the spindle isn't turning is time the shop is consuming cost without producing revenue.

The standard is uncompromising. The fixture should be identified in advance and on the cart or pallet. The inspection equipment needed for the first part should be at the machine, assuming the work can be done there and not on a CMM. The wrenches you need. All these simple things. The machinist should show up at the machine with a pre-kitted job and a clean machine that's been torn down from the last job, and they should never have to leave that machine before they get a first good part off in their hands. Anything short of that is a hidden cost the schedule will eventually expose.

What needs to be ready before the job starts splits cleanly into two categories, and both have to be complete:

- **Digital deliverables.** Setup notes, tool lists, work instructions, drawings, programs posted and verified, the inspection plan finalized and accessible at the machine.
- **Physical deliverables.** Material pre-cut and staged, cutting tools assembled in their holders and touched off, workholding and fixturing ready, any special measuring instruments or gauges kitted on the cart, custom fixtures complete and at the workstation.

Nothing about this list is surprising. What's surprising is how rarely all of it is in place when the job actually starts.

Matt Boucher of Machinosaurus describes what a functioning kit looks like once a shop has standardized on the cart as the physical unit of readiness: "Every job gets a cart. The cart has the material, the tools, the gauges, the fixtures, the inspection equipment. When the job is ready, the cart rolls to the machine."[77]

Ownership of kitting is collaborative but has to land somewhere specific. Programmers and planners set the stage—their deliverables have to be complete before physical kitting can begin. On the floor, a designated kitter or tool crib lead assembles the physical components when those roles exist. In the early days of my shop, the machinists would often do their own kitting of the next jobs while

77 Machine Shop Mastery, Episode 37.

their current jobs were running. A final check confirms readiness. Without a single point of accountability, kitting becomes everyone's responsibility and no one's job.

When this discipline isn't in place, the cost is measurable. Matt Fortner of Progress Machining describes what poor kitting actually looked like when his shop quantified it: "you could see through the analysis of that setup that we were walking, the percentage was wandering around 15%. We were basically spending two hours of this setup walking back and forth to the tool room because we didn't have the right tool."[78]

Readiness is a checklist, not a glance at the cart. The same one, every time. When that discipline is in place, the recurring problems that plague most shop floors begin to disappear—not because the people improved but because the inputs they're working with finally make their improvement possible.

Kitting done right doesn't just prevent waste. It changes the rhythm of the floor. Work flows instead of lurching. Machinists focus on machining instead of hunting. The schedule holds because the inputs to it are reliable.

Inspection That Catches Things

First article inspection and first part inspection aren't always the same thing. The first part off the machine is often the first article part, but the inspection requirements may be different. The first article is what gets formally

78 Machine Shop Mastery, Episode 93.

documented and submitted to the customer. The first part is the operator's internal verification that the setup is correct.

The part should first be checked by the machinist who made it, ideally before it leaves the machine. While the part is still in the workholding, certain features can be measured directly—a quick check with calipers or a micrometer can catch a major issue before it's removed from the fixture and can be adjusted. This isn't a substitute for formal inspection; it's a safety net that catches the problems formal inspection would discover hours later.

Jereme Rogers of TK Machine describes the layered version of this discipline: "The way we would run is you'd set up your machine, get a good part, somebody else would have to verify that. And then the operator is responsible for verifying those parts as they're running. And then everything would go for a final inspection before it goes out the door."[79]

Checkpoint	Who Performs It	When It Happens	Purpose
Setup Verification	Machinist + second qualified person	Before production starts, on the first good part	Confirm the setup produces a conforming part before committing to the run
In-Process Checks	The operator running the job or QC depending on requirements	At defined intervals during the run	Catch drift, tool wear, and process shifts before they propagate

79 Machine Shop Mastery, Episode 64.

Checkpoint	Who Performs It	When It Happens	Purpose
Final Inspection	QA/QC or another qualified machinist	Before the part leaves the floor	Confirm what every prior step has already established

Setup is verified before production starts, the operator owns running checks, and final inspection confirms what every prior step established. None of the three is optional. Removing any one introduces risk the others can't fully cover.

From there, the second check—whichever form it takes—adds the necessary layer of assurance. In larger shops, this typically means submitting the part to the QA or QC department for formal inspection. In smaller shops, it may mean another machinist trained on inspection signing off. What matters is that the verification is independent: not the same person who made the part.

Ken Frankel of Three Sigma Mfg describes the cultural counterpart—pushing ownership of quality out to the people running the work: "We don't have set inspectors. We don't have people who only inspect parts and improve them. We have everybody out in our shop who's running a job responsible for that. And we get a signed off double check. Depending on the expense of the part, we might go for a triple or quadruple check."[80]

80 Machine Shop Mastery, Episode 11.

Before full production begins, two things must be confirmed: the quality is verified and the process is stable. These aren't the same conditions. A single good part proves the quality is achievable. Process stability requires running enough parts to confirm the result is repeatable.

The inspection plan has to be defined before production, not figured out on the fly. How frequently will parts be checked? Which dimensions? Using what equipment? The answers depend on the tolerances, the geometry, the customer's requirements—and they have to be established up front.

The most common way inspection breaks down isn't deliberate skipping—it's that the process wasn't designed to include it. When a takt time is calculated based only on machining, inspection becomes the thing that gets squeezed when the schedule tightens. The fix is to design inspection into the takt time from the start, not bolt it on after the schedule is already too tight to absorb it. At Pro CNC, that meant breaking the in-process checks across multiple parts as needed to fit into the takt time. If we had 50 in-process dimensions for a complex part, we would check dims 1-5 on one part, 6-10 on the next, and so forth until we checked all 50 dims every 10 parts. So, essentially, we did 10% IPC, but we actually put eyes and gauges on every single piece which was a benefit itself, and those checks fit into the takt time rather than being much longer every tenth part.

Where the Hours Go

A shop that doesn't know how long its jobs actually take can't price accurately, can't schedule reliably, and can't identify where it's losing money. Time tracking on the floor is the foundation of every operational improvement that follows.

Ideally, labor is tracked in software, as close to real time as possible. Some shops still record time on paper—job cards, job tickets, handwritten logs. That can be accurate in theory, but it's not actionable. Pages get lost. Entries get reconstructed from memory at the end of shift. The data exists, but nobody trusts it enough to act on. Real-time software, by contrast, makes the data visible while the work is still happening, which means a problem can be addressed before it propagates across the rest of the run. An even more ideal situation is to also directly track machine hours in addition to labor hours, which provides an objective source of rich data which time tracking alone can't entirely provide.

A shift lead or production manager should be able to see, at any point in the day, how every person and every machine is performing against the targets set. The categories matter, because they tell different stories: setup time, run time, inspection time, indirect time.

Category	Examples	What It Reveals
Direct Labor	Setup, running, inspection, programming, troubleshooting	Where time is going on revenue-producing work, and where the process is consistently overrunning the quote
Indirect Labor	Estimating, purchasing, cleaning, training, continuous improvement	How much overhead the shop is absorbing into the cost of doing business

If setup consistently runs over target, that's a different problem than if run time is the issue. If inspection is taking longer than estimated, the tolerances may be tighter than the estimate assumed. If indirect time is high, the shop is losing capacity to non-value-added activity it hasn't identified.

The real value emerges when actual time is compared to planned time. This is the foundation of job costing—and it only works if two conditions are met. First, the planned time has to be realistic. An estimate built on hope rather than data produces a comparison that punishes the floor for the estimator's mistakes. Second, the actual time has to be captured honestly. If operators feel that tracking time accurately will be used against them, they'll game the numbers.

Lori Robertson of Cutting Edge Metals describes what changes culturally when shops actually share the comparison: "I'll show them the quoted versus actual report. We made $1,500 on this job, or whatever the case may be. And it's interesting to watch them get excited. We really did it. We really nailed it."[81]

When gaps between planned and actual time surface—and they will—the shop has a limited set of options:

- **Invest in the process.** Better tooling, better fixturing, better programming, better methods—anything that brings the actual time down toward the plan.
- **Outsource the work.** If another shop can do it more efficiently, let them, and redeploy the freed capacity to work the shop is better positioned to win.
- **Raise the price.** If the work is genuinely harder than the original estimate captured, the customer needs to be paying for that difficulty.
- **Fire the customer.** If a trend exists where a customer's work is overwhelmingly unprofitable, firing the customer may be the right choice.

Each is a legitimate response, and the right one depends on specifics. But none of them are available if the shop doesn't have accurate data on what's actually happening versus what was estimated.

This is what we at Pro CNC called our "kill the losers" process—a systematic review of jobs where actual costs exceeded estimates, followed by a decision about what to change. The name is blunt, but the discipline is honest: surface the losers, decide what to do, and don't leave the same jobs to keep losing the same money next quarter.

81 Machine Shop Mastery, Episode 33.

The Weight of Unfinished Work

Inventory in a machine shop isn't inherently bad, but it's never free. Every piece of raw material on a shelf, every partially machined part waiting between operations, every finished good in the cabinet represents cash the shop has spent and not yet recovered.

Finished goods inventory exists when the customer requires it. A blanket order, a long-term agreement, a customer who needs parts shipped faster than they can be made—these are legitimate reasons. The shop knows it's carrying inventory, prices the cost into the work, and the customer is paying for the convenience. Many shops also carry finished goods inventory because of repeated overruns, or at-risk decisions to build in larger lots without a written client commitment to buy those parts. Both are risky and ideally mitigated with better systems to limit their occurrence.

Work in progress is where the real risk accumulates.

WIP looks like activity. It's actually liability, and the costs are easier to itemize than most shops realize:

- It ties up cash in parts that can't be sold yet.
- It takes up physical space the shop could be using for value added activities.
- It has to be moved around, which introduces handling risk every time a part changes location.

- It can become obsolete if customer requirements change, or orders are canceled.
- It can get damaged (the longer it sits, the more likely it is to happen; that's just what happens in shops).
- It hides problems—a hundred parts scattered across five operations make it very hard to see where things actually stand.

The work feels busy, but the output isn't flowing.

The antidote is shorter lead times and one-piece flow. Instead of batching—machining all hundred parts through the first operation, then moving the batch to the second—the shop processes parts through every operation in sequence, one at a time or in small groups, ideally without setting them down between stages.

At Pro CNC, we had a phrase for the cleanest version of this principle: "bar to box." The idea was to move the part from raw material to finished, packaged product in one continuous flow, with as little queuing as possible between operations. In its ideal state, we would cut a piece of material on a small, right-sized bandsaw next to the machine, machine multiple operations across one or more machines, inspect parts, install hardware, deburr, wash, dry and package finished parts within the takt time. We didn't always achieve it—sometimes the geometry or the outside processing prevented it—but the principle drove every design decision we made.

The benefits compound. Lead times shorten because parts aren't waiting in queues. Scrap exposure drops because problems are caught immediately. Cash flow improves because parts are converted to revenue faster. We could often ship partials of hot jobs the same day we started a setup.

Not every job lends itself to one-piece flow. Complex parts with long cycle times, multiple outside processes, or specialized heat treatments may require batching at certain stages. But the principle should be the default and the deviation should require justification.

This principle is why 5-axis machines are such a game changer. Even when a part doesn't require simultaneous multi-axis cutting, a 5-axis machine allows parts to be machined complete or nearly complete in one workholding, removing countless wastes from a batch and queue process. The key is to then try and flow the remaining steps to finished parts in a box as soon as possible.

What "Good" Looks Like

Most of this book has focused on what goes wrong and why. That's intentional—shops learn faster from diagnosing real problems than from admiring abstractions. But at some point, the picture of what right looks like has to be drawn.

A shop operating at "good enough" is profitable on paper. The owner takes home a reasonable income. The bills get paid. The doors stay open. But on the floor, the texture of how work actually moves tells a different story. Setups stretch. Operators wait. Quality drifts. Schedules get rebuilt midweek.

Dimension	"Good Enough" Floor	Excellent Floor
Operating Mode	Reactive; problems are solved as they appear	Schedule-driven; people execute against a plan
Knowledge	Tribal; lives in people's heads	Documented; lives in the system
Machine Uptime	Inconsistent; inputs aren't reliably staged	High; inputs are kitted and ready before the job starts
Cash Flow	Tight; work moves slowly through the shop	Steady; work converts to revenue without lingering
Culture	Survive the day	Improve the system while running it

"Good enough" is survivable. But it is fragile.

The floor looks different in a shop that has moved past survival into discipline. Work is schedule-driven. People know when things need to happen and they're executing against a plan rather than improvising. Kits are ready. Inspection is integrated. Time tracking is real. WIP is contained. The floor is calm—not because nothing is happening, but because the things that are happening were designed to happen.

What separates the best shops from the rest isn't a single practice. It's a culture, and that culture shows up in specific observable behaviors:

- People are invested—they care about the work, not just the paycheck.
- They're not only executing the process—they're improving it.
- There's a feedback mechanism where machinists can flag waste, suggest improvements, and contribute ideas that get acted on.
- Feedback is specific—tied to a part number, a process step, a recurring issue—not vague complaints that disappear into the air.
- The bar for trying a small improvement is low—the cost of trying is generally lower than the cost of debating.

Angie Holt of Rathburn Tool & Manufacturing describes what an active feedback loop looks like in practice: "We have an idea board that the operators suggest, and we give rewards for those that submit."[82] Matt Wardle of JD Machine also explains how to keep that mechanism alive over time, drawing on advice he received early in his career: "I came up with it and it's a quarter size sheet of paper and says, 'What's the problem? What's the solution and who's going to do it?' I was mentored by a good, a good friend who says, if you respond to those ideas, they will keep coming."[83]

These shops are actively working on lean improvements: not as a corporate initiative or a poster on the wall, but as a daily practice of identifying and removing waste. The

82 Machine Shop Mastery, Episode 31.

83 Machine Shop Mastery, Episode 49.

feedback loop closes: someone spots a problem, suggests a fix, the fix gets tested, the fix gets adopted or revised.

Kelsey highlights how they formalized improvement by building it directly into every employee's daily responsibilities, rather than making it someone else's job: "We did something very smart, which is that part of your job is 3% improvement. But I expect that. I expect that all the time. I expect you to time track system improvements at a rate of 3%."[84]

Discipline, in this context, doesn't slow people down. It speeds them up. When the process is designed to support value-added work rather than compete with it, the team can focus on the work that actually produces value.

Built to Excellence

The shop floor is where the business's design meets reality. Every decision made upstream—in contract review, planning, scheduling, systems—either supports the floor or burdens it. But the floor isn't a passive recipient of upstream design. It's where excellence is built moment by moment.

Kitting treated as philosophy rather than procedure means jobs arrive ready to run. Inspection designed into the takt time rather than squeezed around it means quality is built into the work. Time tracked honestly means the shop knows where it's winning and losing. When WIP is managed, deliberately, cash isn't locked up in unfinished work.

84 Machine Shop Mastery, Episode 23.

None of this is theoretical. Every practice described in this chapter is something real shops do, every day, to produce real results. The difference between the shops that do it and the shops that don't isn't talent—it's the willingness to design the floor as carefully as the parts that get made on it.

That's shop floor excellence. It's not perfection, it's control.

CHAPTER 16

Never Finished

Why the Best Shops Are Always Fixing Something

Systems create stability. That's the core argument this book has been building—through structure, through leadership, through the design of the quote-to-cash flow and the disciplines that protect the shop floor. None of that is enough by itself. Stability without improvement becomes stagnation, and shops that stagnate eventually slip behind the ones still moving forward. The work of running a great shop never finishes.

Continuous improvement is one of the most talked-about concepts in manufacturing and one of the most poorly executed. The language is everywhere—lean, kaizen, waste elimination, value stream mapping. The practices are well documented. The frameworks are mature. What separates the shops that actually produce gains from the ones that produce binders is discipline—not new tools, not new training, but the willingness to do the unglamorous work week after week.

This chapter covers what continuous improvement actually looks like inside a machine shop, across five threads:

- Lean thinking translated to the daily reality of the floor rather than the language of the textbook.
- Kaizen events as the mechanism for resolving problems too large for daily improvement to reach.
- Employee-driven improvement, and what separates a system that compounds from one that quietly dies.
- Automation as an amplifier of whatever the process already is—good or bad.
- How to keep improvement going when the pressure to ship parts threatens to push everything else aside.

The theory is not the issue. The daily practice is.

Lean, Without the Lecture

Lean is simple at its core: everyone in the shop understands the difference between waste and value-added work, and the business has formal processes to identify, document, and eliminate waste. Sustaining that distinction at the daily, weekly, and monthly level is what separates a lean shop from one that has merely read the book.

Day to day, lean means the people doing the work are trained to recognize when they're adding value and when they're not. A machinist running a part is adding value. That same machinist walking across the shop to find a missing gauge isn't. Waiting on the right material is waste. Rework is waste. Producing parts that aren't needed yet is waste. Recognizing these patterns by name—and acting on them—is the foundation.

Awareness alone doesn't produce results. There has to be structure: a way to capture what people see, prioritize it, act on it, and verify the action worked. Document, prioritize, eliminate—and then check.

The toolkit available to a shop trying to put this into practice spans a wide range of cadences and scopes:

Tool	Cadence	Best Used For
Daily Habits (e.g., 2-Second Lean)	Every day	Building improvement into the rhythm of the shift so it never disappears entirely
Kaizen Newspapers	Weekly review	Capturing the steady stream of small wastes that nobody would ever schedule a meeting for
Value Stream Mapping	Periodic, project-based	Examining how work flows through the entire process and identifying where value is leaking
Full Kaizen Events	Several days, targeted	Tackling bottlenecks and cross-functional problems that newspapers can't solve one ticket at a time

Each of these tools has a place. Daily habits keep the rhythm alive when nothing dramatic is happening. Kaizen newspapers create a steady drumbeat of incremental improvement. Value stream mapping identifies the bigger problems that small fixes won't reach. Kaizen events resolve those bigger problems when they rise to the top of the priority list. Strategic A3s align the team on the few changes that have to happen this year and the metrics that will tell whether they worked.

Kaizen newspapers, in practice, are large notepads posted in each area where anyone can write down a waste they've identified and, ideally, a proposed solution. Each week the kaizen team for that area reviews entries, decides what to act on, and tracks results. The mechanism is simple. The hard part is responding to entries consistently enough that people keep contributing.

At Pro CNC, we had a very active kaizen newspaper process. There were several of them in different areas of the company: the front office, planning, production, prototyping, engineering, assembly, etc. Everyone was trained on the 8 wastes to the point where they would recognize when they were performing one of them, and record it on the newspaper.

To make this work, we held regular weekly meetings with a rotating crew of employees in each area to work through and solve those wastes. How did we maintain this over time? We required 5% kaizen time tracking of every employee, right inside of ProShop. We set it as a requirement for each person and tracked against that target in their reviews.

Were we perfect at it? Certainly not. But we were good enough that we completed thousands of kaizen newspaper tickets over the years. Some significant individual improvements were born out of that system, but the real magic was from the thousands of little ones, completed week after week, year after year. It had a dramatic effect on the overall efficiency of the company.

Target - Against WOs %:	90%
Target - Kaizen %:	5%
Target - Training %:	3%

Time tracking targets set on the user page of each employee in ProShop. The kaizen target of 5% sits alongside work order and training targets—a small configuration choice that turns improvement from an aspiration into a number a person is measured against.

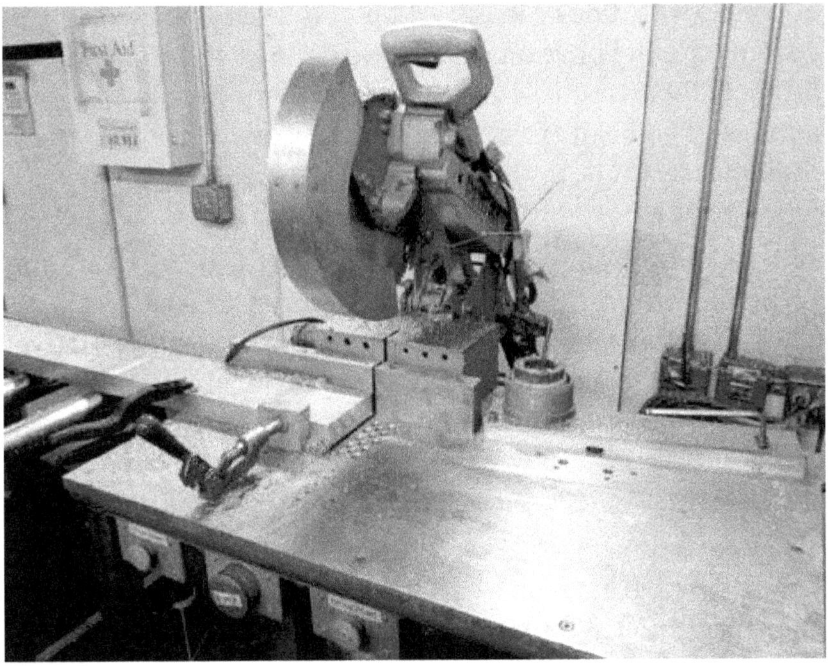

A one-piece-flow chop saw and dovetail router station, built in response to a single kaizen newspaper ticket. It let an operator cut one piece of stock and dovetail it in place—no WIP, no waiting, no transportation to a saw department, no motion to a CNC machine for dovetail prep. Four of the eight wastes eliminated by one bench.

Which lean principles deliver the fastest payoff depends on the shop, but a few consistently rise to the top. 5S—sort, set in order, shine, standardize, sustain—addresses what is probably the single largest source of waste in most shops: time spent looking for things. Tools, gauges, fixtures, drawings, programs. A 5S program done well removes that waste entirely, and the time recovered shows up in spindle utilization, first-part success, and operator focus. For us, 5S and our Pre-Processing Checklist dramatically shifted the time we wasted looking for things.

Michael Tamasi describes the same principle applied beyond the floor itself: "We look at not just the manufacturing portion of what we do, our office closet, our finance department, our HR. Everywhere people work, 5S applies. If you can't find what you need in your office in less than five seconds, your office isn't organized."[85]

Where shops go wrong with lean isn't usually in the principles—it's in the discipline required to sustain them. The most common failure is treating lean as an initiative, something the shop is doing this quarter, instead of as a permanent operating philosophy. The initiative produces a burst of activity, a few wins, and then quiet decay back to the baseline.

Leaders who treat lean as a shop-floor exercise—something the machinists need to do—while leaving the office untouched are sending a clear signal: lean doesn't actually apply to leadership. Lean applies to the entire business or to none of it.

---

85 Machine Shop Mastery, Episode 42.

Kaizen That Sticks

The daily drumbeat of small improvements creates a baseline of continuous progress. Some problems, though, are too large, too embedded, or too cross-functional to be solved through incremental fixes. Those require a different mechanism: a focused, time-bounded event involving the people closest to the problem, working together for several days to redesign how that part of the operation runs.

Deciding when a kaizen event is needed comes back to the theory of constraints. There's always a bottleneck somewhere in the operation, and a well-targeted kaizen event opens it up. The bottleneck might be a specific machine that produces parts too slowly. It might be an inspection process that consistently delays shipping. It might be a setup procedure that eats most of the available capacity on a high-demand work center.

The impact matters because the bottleneck sets the pace for the entire system. Even a small improvement in throughput at the constraint produces an outsized effect on the shop's overall capacity. A five-percent improvement at a non-bottleneck does almost nothing. A five-percent improvement at the bottleneck reshapes the whole operation.

Nate Bourgeois of Ouroboros Space and Defense describes the diagnostic moment that triggered a major kaizen-style overhaul in his own shop: "I read that book, *The Gold Mine*, and realized we're having bottlenecks somewhere. We're running into a pile up of components and WIP and we're stagnating at QC. We thought, 'let's take one of the people who's tacking stuff up or running the line and move them over to QC, and our throughput went from 276 parts a week to over 1500 parts a week. And we were able to drop the total staff requirement of the department to three people."[86]

Machines are a natural focal point for kaizen events because they're where parts are made. If jobs consistently take longer than estimated on a particular work center, that's a signal. It might indicate a slow setup, suboptimal tool paths, an inefficient layout, or a workholding system that creates more variation than necessary.

Setup reduction is one of the highest-leverage kaizen targets in any shop, often yielding dramatic results simply by stopping the process to ask what is actually necessary and what is being done just out of habit. However, uncovering that wasted time requires more than just a mandate from management. Who participates in a kaizen event, for instance, matters as much as the methodology itself.

A few principles separate events that produce lasting change from events that just apply a fresh coat of paint:

- Include the people who actually work in the area being improved—all of them if the team is small, the key representatives if it is large.
- Pick participants respected by their peers, who can carry the change back into the daily rhythm of the work.

86 Machine Shop Mastery, Episode 48.

- Choose people who understand how their area connects to the rest of the operation, so the changes don't just relocate the problem.
- Make sure the people affected by the new process had a hand in designing it, so the buy-in is genuine rather than coerced.

A kaizen event designed without the input of the people who do the work will produce solutions that look good on paper and fail on the floor.

The harder question is what happens after the event ends. Improvements that aren't sustained aren't improvements—they're experiments that were abandoned. The most important factor in making changes stick is incorporating them into the standard work, the formal processes that govern how the operation runs day to day.

Auditing reinforces the change. Someone—a lead, a supervisor, the continuous improvement owner—needs to check frequently in the weeks after an event to confirm that the new process is being followed. Without that follow-through, the team drifts back to the old way within a month, and the kaizen event becomes another exercise people went through that didn't actually change anything.

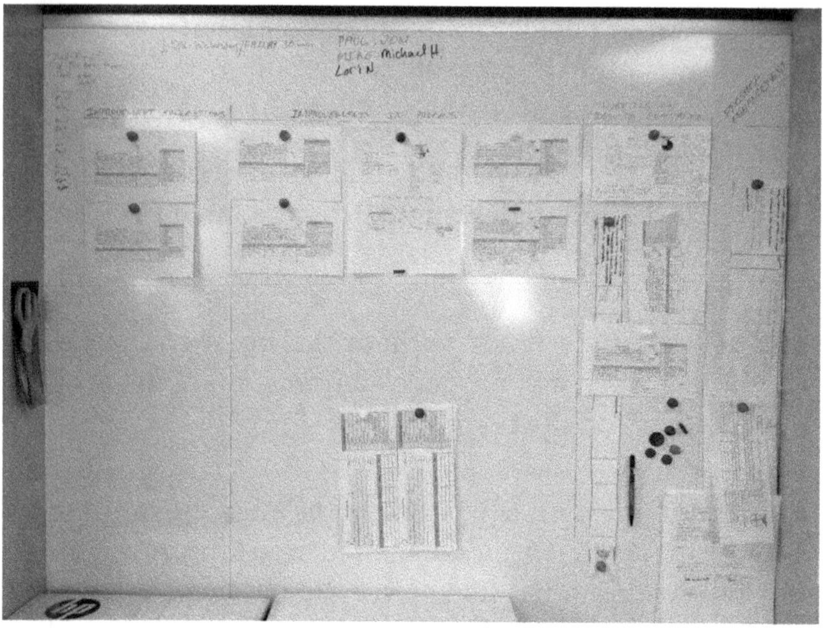

The office kaizen board at Hill Manufacturing. The leadership team was as active in the kaizen newspaper system as anyone on the floor—a signal that improvement wasn't something the office asked for and the shop delivered. Two details are worth noticing. The long, narrow tickets came from other departments, but the source of the waste traced back to the office, so that's where the ticket lived and where it got solved. The far-right column is reserved for ProShop enhancements: problems best answered by a new software feature rather than a small physical fix. Hundreds of features were initiated this way over the years.

When the Floor Brings the Ideas

The people closest to the work see the most waste. They know which setups take too long, which tools are always missing, which steps in the process feel redundant, and which workarounds have quietly become standard. A shop that doesn't have a structured way to capture that knowledge is leaving its best improvement opportunities on the table every day.

Nate Ankrom of Genuine Machine Products describes how he digitized the process right at the point of work. Because his shop places a computer at every work center, they use custom software to manage multiple, highly specific feedback loops. "One's called the voice of the floor," where operators can submit general improvements, alongside dedicated digital loops for updating fixturing and managing new product integrations.[87]

The specific tool matters less than whether the system behind it is credible. Whether ideas keep flowing or quietly stop comes down to a small set of factors that distinguish a living improvement culture from a dying one:

Dimension	What Kills the Culture	What Sustains It
Response to ideas	Suggestions collected but rarely acknowledged or implemented	Visible action on submitted ideas, even when the answer is no
Speed of action	Slow enough that the link to the suggestion disappears	Fast enough that the contributor sees the outcome
Leadership posture	Lean pushed onto the floor while the office stays untouched	Leadership uses the same channels and applies the same discipline to itself
Connection to mission	Improvement framed as busywork or compliance	Improvement tied directly to a stronger, more secure business

87 Machine Shop Mastery, Episode 43.

Employees will contribute ideas exactly as long as they believe leadership is taking those ideas seriously, acting on them, and making visible changes based on the feedback. The moment that belief breaks, participation collapses—and rebuilding it is much harder than building it the first time.

This is the single most common way shops kill their own improvement culture. Leadership asks for ideas, collects them, and then does nothing—or does something so slowly that the connection between the idea and the action is lost. The signal employees take from that is unambiguous: my contributions don't matter. A key to solving this is to let the team solve it themselves, empowered by leadership, but not requiring leadership to accomplish it. That dovetail station seen above was executed by the team in our horizontal pallet pool department.

Evaluating and prioritizing ideas requires a simple framework. A two-box or four-box matrix—effort versus impact—works for most shops. High-impact, low-effort items go first. How the idea affects throughput, scrap, cost, quality, or safety becomes the screen for what gets attention.

What encourages participation is the inverse of what kills it: people see their ideas implemented. They see the result. They see leadership engaged in the same process—not pushing improvement onto the floor while doing nothing about their own areas. They see public recognition for contributions. They feel ownership over the changes their work produces. That's the culture worth building.

What Automation Reveals

Automation is appealing for obvious reasons. Machines don't call in sick, they don't lose focus, and they can run lights-out. Automation doesn't solve problems, though—it amplifies whatever is already happening in the process underneath.

Scott Harms of MetalQuest Unlimited frames the rule in terms a shop owner can apply directly: "This is common sense. It's all about process control. If you don't have process control, don't put a robot on something because it's going to make it more out of control."[88]

The principle is straightforward: if you automate a process that produces scrap, you'll produce more scrap, more quickly. Scrap is one of the eight wastes, and automating it doesn't eliminate it—it accelerates it. The same logic applies to every other category of waste embedded in the process.

Before automating anything, a few prerequisites have to be in place—or the automation will lock in problems instead of removing them:

- **Full understanding of the process.** Not just the step being automated, but what feeds it and what receives it downstream.
- **Stable process behavior.** If the process produces variable results depending on who's running it or what shift it is on, automation will preserve that variability rather than eliminate it.

---

88 Machine Shop Mastery, Episode 62.

- **Resolved upstream waste.** Scrap, rework, and motion waste have to be addressed at the source before the machine speeds them up.
- **Downstream capacity to absorb the change.** A faster machining cycle that overwhelms the inspection step downstream hasn't improved throughput—it has moved the bottleneck.

The exception is when the automation itself improves stability—a robotic arm that loads parts with more consistent positioning than a human operator, for instance, or a probe that verifies dimensions the operator might miss. In those cases, automation reduces variability rather than amplifying it.

Shops that automate too early tend to make the same mistake: they don't understand the full value stream they're affecting. They see a bottleneck, apply technology, and create a new bottleneck somewhere downstream. The right sequence is process before automation—fix the system, then accelerate it.

When Things Get Busy

The word "continuous" in continuous improvement isn't aspirational—it's structural. Improvement has to be built into how the business operates, reviewed, measured, owned, and protected, or it will be displaced by the daily pressure of producing parts.

How often improvements are reviewed and measured depends on their scope. A simple process change with an obvious impact can be checked within a day or two of implementation, then again a week or two later to confirm the change has held. Larger improvements—a new layout, a new system, a new procedure—need review on a longer arc: a month after implementation, a quarter after, a year after. The discipline is to actually do the review, not just plan it.

Every improvement, regardless of size, should ultimately be measurable in dollars. Whether the gain comes from increased throughput, reduced scrap, shorter setup times, or lower material waste, it should translate into a financial result the shop can point to.

Ownership of continuous improvement evolves as the shop grows. In the earliest stages, it's the owner—there's no one else. As the business scales, it makes sense to assign a continuous improvement lead, and eventually a full continuous improvement function with dedicated staff. The role isn't separate from operations—it's embedded inside them.

The real threat to continuous improvement isn't a lack of tools or frameworks. It's pressure. When the shop is busy—when due dates are tight, when machines are running at capacity, when every hour feels spoken for—the first thing to get sacrificed is the time set aside for improvement work.

Shops that sustain improvement under pressure share a recognizable set of disciplines:

- **Keep it visible.** Improvement metrics, kaizen boards, and project status are part of the daily or weekly rhythm, not something reviewed quarterly.
- **Bring the floor into the room.** Improvement meetings include the people doing the work being improved—either as standing members or on rotation.
- **Track recurring offenders.** A rolling top-N list of the parts driving the cost of quality builds a pipeline rather than waiting for problems to be brought to it.
- **Celebrate wins.** Recognition reinforces behavior. Improvements that get noticed get repeated.
- **Protect the time.** Not unlimited time, not at the expense of customer commitments, but enough that the work doesn't disappear when the floor gets busy.

Mitch Olson of Olson Custom Designs describes how his shop institutionalized that rhythm: "In the last year or so, we've started a meeting on Friday afternoons. Literally, it's called a continuous improvement meeting." During these meetings, they talk about what didn't work that week, what they want to try next, and exactly who is responsible for moving each solution forward.[89]

---

89 Machine Shop Mastery, Episode 66.

Angie Holt describes the complementary discipline of measurement—keeping a running view of where cost of quality is actually concentrating: "We do a top five every month. What are the top five parts that are driving the cost of quality?" Once they identify those most expensive errors, they attack them by assigning an engineer and running a Kaizen event to ensure the problem is solved.[90]

Continuous improvement doesn't require perfection. It requires consistency. A shop that makes one small improvement every week—fifty-two per year, compounding—will look dramatically different in two years than a shop that runs the same operation every day.

Stability and Momentum

Systems create stability. Improvement creates momentum. Neither is sufficient without the other. A shop with strong systems but no improvement culture will perform consistently at whatever level it has reached and slowly drift downward as conditions change. A shop with an improvement culture but no systems will produce sporadic gains that don't hold.

The shops that win are the ones that do both. They build systems that create predictability, and they improve those systems in ways that create compounding gains. They treat waste not as inevitability but as opportunity. They treat employee ideas as fuel for the operation, not noise to be managed.

90 Machine Shop Mastery, Episode 31.

This isn't the dramatic part of running a machine shop. It isn't a new machine on the floor or a marquee customer won. It's the quiet, steady work of getting a little better every day—one kaizen ticket, one closed loop, one improvement at a time. That work, done consistently, is what separates the shops that last from the shops that don't.

PART V

The Call

CHAPTER 17

Myths and Realities of a Top Shop

What Top Shops Actually Look Like

Every industry has its top performers, and every industry has stories owners tell themselves about what makes those performers different. Machining is no exception. Walk into ten shops and ask what separates the best from the rest, and you'll get ten different answers. Better machines. Better customers. Better people. Better luck. Better timing.

The data tells a different story. When you look at the shops consistently performing in the top quintile of the industry—the ones that show up year after year in benchmarking surveys, that produce two to three times the industry-average revenue per employee, that maintain net margins double the industry norm—the differences cluster in a small number of areas. And those areas have very little to do with luck.

This chapter is about that gap. Not to flatter the top performers, but to make explicit what they're actually doing differently, and to give shops below that line a clearer view of what "getting better" would actually mean. Four threads run through it:

- What "top shop" actually means once the surface myths are stripped away.
- How benchmarking data should be used—and the ways it's most often misused.
- Where shops can identify their own weak spots without waiting for a crisis.
- Which key performance indicators actually drive improvement rather than simply describing what already happened.

The thread through all of it is the same one this book has been pulling on since the beginning. Performance isn't about heroics. It's about architecture.

What "Top Shop" Really Means

The most widely referenced benchmark in the industry is the Top Shops survey published annually by Modern Machine Shop. The survey assesses shops across four pillars and honors the top twenty percent in each as well as the composite top performers. The pillars themselves are a useful diagnostic for any shop wanting to understand where it sits.[91]

---

91 Modern Machine Shop, Top Shops survey. https://www.mmsonline.com/zc/top-shops

Pillar	What It Measures	Common Signals of Strength
Machining Technology	The equipment, automation, and digital infrastructure on the floor	Modern multi-axis machines, in-process probing, automation, real-time data capture
Shop Floor Practices	How work moves through the floor and how variability is controlled	Documented setups, kitting discipline, low scrap, high spindle utilization
Business Strategy	How the business decides which work to take and where to grow	Clear specialization, deliberate margin management, structural investment
Human Resources	How the shop attracts, develops, and retains its people	Apprenticeship programs, core values, low turnover, retention of senior talent

Underneath that structure, the patterns that separate top shops from the rest reduce to three: people, process, and performance. Those words are easy to nod at and surprisingly difficult to operationalize.

Most of the myths owners hold about what makes a shop great fail when held up against these three dimensions:

- **Good machines make a good shop.** They don't. A shop can have the most capable equipment on the market and still underperform badly if the process surrounding those machines is weak or the people operating them are misaligned. Machines amplify whatever business they sit inside of.

- **Growth means top-line revenue.** Top shops are not indifferent to revenue, but they are far more disciplined about the bottom line. They concentrate on the categories of work that produce the strongest profit, not the categories that produce the most volume, and they accept that those two things are rarely the same.
- **Scale equals excellence.** Top shops are denser, not larger. A thirty-person shop with strong systems will consistently produce more revenue per head, and more profit per head, than a hundred-person shop running on heroics.

The expensive spindles in a poorly run shop will sit idle, run inefficiently, or produce work the system around them can't price, ship, or invoice correctly. The hundred-person shop without systems will spend an outsized share of its capacity on coordination overhead that the thirty-person shop with systems doesn't need.

When the myths fall away, what remains is something less glamorous than the language of "world-class" suggests. Top shops are businesses that have done the unglamorous work of building people, refining process, and measuring performance long enough that the work compounds.

Reading the Benchmark

Benchmarking is most useful when it's treated as a mirror rather than a map. The data describes what top shops are doing—it doesn't prescribe what every shop should do. A small shop serving high-mix, low-volume customers shouldn't try to match the spindle utilization of a production shop. A new shop shouldn't expect the revenue per employee of a thirty-year-old operation. Comparisons matter, but context matters more.

A handful of metrics deserve the most attention. Revenue per employee is probably the single most diagnostic number in the industry, with one caveat: it can be misleading when material cost per job varies dramatically between shops. Industry average sits around $150,000–$180,000 per employee. Top shops typically land between $300,000–$400,000. Specialized shops in extremely specialized markets can exceed $500,000, with the rarest (as discussed in Chapter 6) exceeding $1,000,000 per employee.

Profit margin is the second metric worth tracking carefully, and the tiers are well established across the industry.

Net Margin	Performance Tier	What It Typically Reflects
6–9%	Industry average	A functional business operating without significant pricing power or cost discipline
10–15%	Strong performance	A shop with disciplined costing, market-aware pricing, and reasonable specialization
20–25%	Top quartile	A highly specialized shop serving a high-value niche with limited competition

Most shops underestimate how far their margin is from the top quartile, partly because the comparison is uncomfortable and partly because they don't have the cost accuracy required to know exactly where they sit. The 6–9 percent industry average gets reported as "fine," but it's actually a structural warning sign: a shop operating in that range has very little buffer for the next downturn.

Spindle utilization rounds out the short list of high-leverage metrics. A machine that runs four hours out of every eight is half the asset a machine that runs seven out of eight is, regardless of how new it is. Top shops consistently track this number per work center, and they treat sustained low utilization as a signal that something upstream is broken—not as a complaint about the operators.

Many other metrics get tracked across the industry, but most of them are either downstream consequences of the three above or vanity numbers that describe activity rather than outcome. A shop that improves revenue per employee, margin, and spindle utilization will improve almost every other metric automatically.

How shops should use benchmarks once they have access to them depends on where the business currently sits. The first step, often skipped, is to participate in the survey itself. If a shop can't produce its own numbers cleanly enough to fill out the questionnaire, that's the diagnosis. The data isn't the problem—the lack of measurement is. In MakingChips episode 456 Brent Donaldson, editor-in-chief of Modern Machine Shop, drives that point home: "It is sometimes the case that shops taking the survey for the first time realize they don't have the tools to track some of these metrics to begin with... back to the point — if you're not benchmarking, you're guessing. A lot of shops are still at that level. Taking the survey itself could be a valuable lesson in learning that you need the capability to measure yourself."

No shop would run production without measuring the dimensions that determine whether a part conforms to print. Yet many owners run the business itself without measuring the metrics that determine whether it succeeds. That's the same discipline this book keeps returning to: build the business with the same precision you build the part.

Once a shop has its own numbers, the temptation is to attack every gap at once. That impulse usually produces no meaningful improvement anywhere. Top shops focus on two or three metrics at a time and drive sustained gains on those before moving to the next set.

The deeper shift these benchmarks reveal isn't in any single number but in how the owner thinks about the business. A typical shop owner thinks about the machining process—how to make this part faster, more cheaply, with fewer setups. A top shop owner thinks about the business that surrounds the machining: the systems, the people, the financial structure, the customer mix. The machining is downstream of those choices.

Looking across multiple years of survey data, the pattern is remarkably stable. The shops in the top quintile consistently invest at higher rates in apprenticeship programs, defined core values, team-based decision-making, and capital equipment. None of that is glamorous. All of it compounds.

Finding the Soft Spots Before They Crack

One of the most damaging beliefs in the industry is that high performance is supposed to feel like heroics. Owners normalize the effort it takes to hit ninety-five percent on-time delivery, a ten percent margin, or twenty-five-percent annual growth—as though those numbers should require a sprint.

Top shops achieve those same numbers with dramatically less effort, because well-engineered systems do most of the work that heroics would otherwise have to do. One shop, before adopting a proper ERP system, hit ninety-eight percent on-time delivery by walking the floor every morning, chasing every open job for many hours per day. After adopting the ERP, the same number was produced automatically, with a fraction of the time investment.

The diagnostic question for any shop is whether high performance, when it occurs, feels like a sustainable rhythm or a sprint that can't be repeated next week. If a delivery rate is being hit only because someone is heroically expediting jobs every day, the system isn't producing the result—the person is, at unsustainable cost.

Top shops identify constraints before those constraints become crises. They pay structural attention to where the business is weakest, even when nothing is currently on fire. They review where work is queuing, which machines are sitting idle, which customers are silently drifting, which procedures are being shortcut. The review is regular, scheduled, not triggered by a problem.

The signals that a system is underperforming are consistent across shops, even when the underlying causes differ:

- Recurring firefighting that everyone has come to treat as the normal texture of the day.
- Sustained overtime that the team came to expect rather than fought against.
- A steady undercurrent of stress and burnout in the people closest to the work, particularly the experienced operators and leads.
- The pattern of having to throw money at problems—expediting fees, overnight shipping, rework, customer credits—to keep commitments from breaking.

Each is a symptom of a system that wasn't designed to absorb the conditions it's now operating under. Individually they look like operational facts of life. Cumulatively they're the unmistakable signature of a business in need of structural improvement.

The most useful exercise an owner can do, periodically, is to list the things the business consistently has to compensate for—and ask which of those would disappear under a stronger system. Most of the answers fall into the categories this book has already named: estimating, scheduling, kitting, inspection, communication, training. The fix is usually upstream of the symptom.

The Four Numbers That Matter

Most shops measure too much. They produce reports nobody reads, track numbers nobody acts on, and confuse the act of measuring with the act of improving. Top shops measure less but with greater discipline. The KPIs they track are chosen for impact—each one tied directly to a decision someone will make based on the number.

Four indicators consistently rise to the top across high-performing shops, each with a clear owner and a different lens on the operation.

KPI	What It Measures	Who Owns It
Overall Equipment Effectiveness	Machine availability, performance, and quality combined	Production manager
First Pass Yield	Whether the first part off a setup is conforming rather than scrap	Cross-functional: programming, floor leads, QA
Quote Turnaround Time	How quickly the front end can respond to RFQs	Sales manager, GM, or owner
Win Rate	Whether quoted pricing matches the market the shop actually serves	Sales manager, GM, or owner

Overall equipment effectiveness, or OEE, captures whether a shop has a "green light culture"—whether machines are running when they're supposed to be, at the rate they're supposed to run, producing good parts. The number combines availability, performance, and quality. Top shops track it per work center, with daily reviews.

First pass yield is a cleaner indicator than total scrap rate because it isolates the moment where most preventable failures happen—the transition from setup to first part. A shop with strong first pass yield has its kitting, programming, and verification disciplines in place. A shop with weak first pass yield is paying for those gaps every time it starts a new job.

Quote turnaround time and win rate sit on the commercial side of the business. Both belong to whoever owns the sales function—a dedicated sales manager in larger shops, the owner or a generalist in smaller ones. A quote that arrives three days after the customer expected it tells the customer something about the shop's discipline before any work is done.

Achieving strong numbers on quote turnaround and win rate depends on a system underneath them that few shops have fully built: accurate costing, fast estimating, market-aware pricing, and a feedback loop that translates lost quotes into better quotes next time.

Cadence matters as much as the metrics themselves. KPIs should be reported daily where the data supports it, summarized weekly for review, and discussed in a defined forum by the people who actually own them. Daily review without action is a calendar entry. Weekly action without daily visibility is improvisation.

From Data to Action

Knowing where the gaps are isn't the same as closing them. Most shops can identify, within an hour of honest conversation, the three or four things most holding their business back. The harder question is which of those to attack first, and the answer is usually different from what owner instinct suggests.

Top shops decide what to fix first by combining two filters:

- **The lowest hanging fruit.** Changes that require modest effort to implement but produce visible improvement quickly. Early wins matter, not because they're the most important improvements, but because they build the credibility and momentum that harder changes require.
- **The biggest opportunity.** The change that, if successful, would produce the largest sustained improvement in the business.

Sometimes those two filters point to the same project. More often they point to different ones, and the right answer is to run both in parallel: a quick win to demonstrate that change is possible, alongside a structural improvement that addresses the deeper constraint.

Top shops can be great in one category and merely adequate in another. The composite excellence the benchmarking surveys describe is unusual; the more common pattern, even among high performers, is strength concentrated in a few dimensions with deliberate investment in the others over time.

Cadence for closing performance gaps depends on the metric. Some can be reviewed daily with very little overhead—spindle utilization, on-time delivery, scrap counts. Others require weekly or monthly attention. The discipline isn't in the frequency. It's in the consistency: the same metrics, in the same forum, every week, until the gap is closed.

The most common failure in turning benchmarks into action is metric overload. A shop that tries to improve fifteen things at once will improve none of them, because attention is the binding constraint. The discipline is to pick three, work on three, finish three—then pick the next three.

What separates the top quintile from everyone else, in the end, isn't access to better information. The benchmarking data is public. The metrics are well understood. The practices that produce strong performance are documented everywhere. What separates the top shops is the willingness to do the unglamorous work, every day, until the numbers reflect it.

CHAPTER 18

Something Someone Would Buy

Designing a Valuable Company Through Systems

Most shop owners don't think about selling their business until they have to. The reasons are obvious: selling is far away, the business is functional, and the day-to-day demands consume whatever attention isn't taken by family and life. The work of building a valuable business and the work of running a business feel like two different things—until they intersect, usually at exactly the worst time.

This chapter is about that intersection. Not selling specifically, but the more useful frame: building a business someone, eventually, would actually want to buy. Whether that someone is a strategic acquirer, a private equity firm, a competitor, an employee, or family, the criteria are roughly the same:

- Strong fundamentals—clean books, predictable margins, accurate cost data.

- Low dependence on any single person, especially the owner.
- A diversified customer base, with no single account that would threaten the business if lost.
- Real systems—documented, repeatable, used.
- A team that can run the operation without constant intervention from the top.

Those criteria don't apply only to companies on the market. They apply to every company that wants to compound value over time, whether the value ever gets realized through a sale or not.

What follows is a tour through what makes a company valuable, why the owner's relationship to the business is the single largest determinant of that value, and how the choices made in daily operations either build optionality or quietly destroy it.

What Buyers Pay For

Buyers, regardless of category, are looking for one thing first: an absence of risk. Everything else flows from there. They want a company with strong fundamentals—clean books, predictable margins, accurate cost data. They want low dependence on any single person, especially the owner. They want a diversified customer base. They want real systems—documented, repeatable, actually used. They want a team that can run the operation without constant intervention from the top.

Buyers walk away when they perceive too much risk in any one of these categories. Transparency is the price of entry for a serious conversation. They need to fully understand the business—warts and all—before they'll commit. A shop that resists transparency, or presents a too-clean version of itself, raises the only red flag that matters: what are they hiding?

In practice, the diligence conversation tends to circle the same short list. If you want to know how a buyer sees your shop, look at what they ask for:

- Clean financials
- Customer concentration understood
- Owner role documented
- Equipment list current
- Maintenance and calibration records organized
- Quality system functioning
- Key employees retained
- Quoting and job costing visible

Nothing on that list is exotic, and that's the point. The work of becoming sellable is mostly the work of being able to answer ordinary questions without hesitation.

Value, in this context, isn't the same as size or reputation. A larger shop isn't automatically a more valuable shop. A well-known shop isn't automatically a more sellable shop.

Value is calculated from a specific formula, and the formula rewards profitability, predictability, and independence from the owner.

Mike Payne of Hill Manufacturing explains what SDE actually captures, and why it's the more relevant figure for owner-operated machine shops. "In this industry," he says, "people are buying what you call seller's discretionary earnings. Seller's discretionary earnings is basically EBITDA, but it's also the money that flows through that will not continue to flow through. So, if you pay for a personal car and your family cell phones and all those types of things... I'm going to pull those back out of the expenses and I'm going to get to a number of SDE, which is basically EBITDA plus discretionary expenses."[92]

Either way, the formula is the same: a base number representing profitability, multiplied by some factor that reflects how risky, scalable, and attractive the business is. The base number is finite. The multiple is where the work pays off.

The spread across profiles, in practice, looks something like this:

Shop Profile	Typical Multiple	Why
Owner-dependent, undifferentiated, concentrated customers	1.5–3x	Buyer sees a job, not an asset; the business may not survive the owner's exit

92 Machine Shop Mastery, Episode 24.

Shop Profile	Typical Multiple	Why
Some decoupling, modest systems, mixed customer base	3–5x	Functional, but the buyer is still pricing in transition risk
Professionally run, mature systems, leadership team in place	6–10x	Buyer is acquiring a sustainable operation that runs without the seller
Specialized, defensible niche with strong margins	10x+	Buyer pays a premium for pricing power and limited competition

It's tempting to say that organized equipment records, inventory, calibration records, and maintenance records add to the multiple. But that's too literal. They may not create a separate valuation line item at all. However, they do affect buyer confidence. They help the buyer believe the business has been professionally managed—and belief can move the multiple.

Mike Payne has been on both sides of these transactions and notes how management needs dictate value: "If this company cannot survive—without the intervention of a management team, in particular, my management team—that's a much lower multiple: three, then another acquisition we've done that I literally can buy it and it's going to keep on going. Maybe now you start looking at six, seven, eight, nine, ten."[93]

93 Machine Shop Mastery, Episode 24.

Mike Fritz of American Precision Partners describes the baseline most owner-operator acquisitions actually fall into: "When I look at a business, it's usually one and a half to three times multiple." While that multiple can slide based on the strength of the shop's management, customer concentration, and equipment, Fritz notes that scale itself eventually shifts the math entirely. He explains that for shops below $1.5 million in EBITDA, the 1.5 to 3 range is standard across the board. However, the moment a shop jumps above that $1.5 million EBITDA threshold, the valuation multiple jumps to a six, simply because a business of that size attracts a significantly larger pool of interested buyers[94]

A shop without strong technology, without growth, with concentrated customers, and with deep owner dependence can expect a two-to-three-times multiple in most markets. A top shop—professionally run, well-systemized, with a real management team and diversified customer base—can earn five to ten times or more. The work of moving from one end of that range to the other is what this chapter is about.

Working Yourself Out of a Job

If owner dependence is the largest single drag on valuation, then decoupling the owner is the largest single lever for increasing it. The work isn't glamorous. It's mostly a long, patient sequence of handing off responsibilities the owner has historically held.

94 Machine Shop Mastery, Episode 57.

Where the owner remains essential, even at the end of this process, is at the top: setting the vision, providing resources, allocating capital, and removing obstacles. Everything else can—and should—be handed off.

- They should not be working on the shop floor.
- The office should function without them.
- Key customer relationships should be carried by other people.
- Quoting should not be reliant on them.

Each handoff, in isolation, looks small. Taken together, they describe the transition from owner-operator to owner.

The standard for whether a function has been successfully handed off is roughly eighty percent. The new owner of that function doesn't need to perform it as well as the original owner did. They need to perform it well enough that the business doesn't miss the owner doing it. If the result is consistently in the right range, the handoff is complete.

Standard operating procedures in every position make this possible. The premise of the E-Myth is that every function should be designed so that a competent person could step into it without inheriting a decade of tribal knowledge.

This is how it played out in my own exit from Pro CNC. None of it would have been possible without having already kind of worked ourselves out of a job. If you intend to one day exit your business, that's something worth understanding now—and worth building strategic plans around, over many years. The phrase "over many years" is the part most owners want to skip and can't. Working yourself out of a job isn't a project. It's a posture maintained across the entire arc of running the business.

The first role an owner should remove themselves from depends on what they're specialized in. An owner who is an expert machinist should remove themselves from the bench first, because that's where their presence creates the most distortion. An owner who is the primary salesperson should remove themselves from customer-facing work first. The right first move is the one that frees the most owner time and exposes the most hidden risk.

Buying back time, at scale, often starts with an executive assistant. The work an owner does in a typical week isn't all owner-level work. Much of it is calendar management, inbox triage, scheduling, follow-ups—work that an EA can absorb for a fraction of the cost the owner's time actually represents. Most owners resist this hire because it feels indulgent. The math, when they finally look at it, says the opposite.

Mike Fritz uses a single diagnostic question to surface owner dependence faster than any financial analysis. "The number one question I ask when I come to buy a company is how dependent is the business on you?" he explains. "Because owners often struggle to grapple with that concept, he follows up with a more practical test: "The one question I ask is how much vacation did you take last year?"[95]

95 Machine Shop Mastery, Episode 57.

The answer tells him exactly how well the shop functions without the owner present. An owner who can spend all summer out fishing in Florida, or who takes a full month off to go hunting every year, is running a business where the success is decoupled from the owner's time. Buyers like Fritz know which businesses can truly run themselves long before due diligence begins.

EBITDA, Not Revenue

Most shop owners track revenue more closely than profitability, because revenue is the number that feels like progress. It's also the number that most reliably misleads them. A shop can grow revenue and destroy value at the same time, taking on work that adds cost faster than it adds margin.

Revenue growth doesn't say anything about profitability on its own. Profitability is EBITDA, and EBITDA is what gets multiplied to produce value. A shop with rapidly growing revenue and stagnant or deteriorating profit is moving sideways, or backward, at higher cost. Mike Payne has watched this pattern play out repeatedly: "What a lot of people in all industries make the mistake of, when they start to prepare to sell, is they start to grow what they think looks good, right? Maybe that's top line revenue... The reality is I'm buying EBITDA." He advises sellers, "Let's not grow the company, let's grow the value of the company."[96]

The work, when an owner gets serious about EBITDA, begins with the P&L and ends with a deep understanding of every

96 Machine Shop Mastery, Episode 24.

line on it. Cost structure. Gross margin by category. Where overhead is actually going. Which jobs and customers produce the most profit per hour of capacity. Where waste exists that nobody's named.

The operational decisions that improve EBITDA fastest cluster in four areas:

- **Gross margins.** Where the largest dollars live. Understanding gross margins and optimizing them across product families is the single highest-leverage analytical exercise most shop owners can do.
- **Scrap rate.** Every scrapped part is a unit of cost without a unit of revenue attached. Scrap directly compresses gross margin.
- **Labor efficiency.** Labor is typically the largest line item in any shop's overhead. Its productivity has an outsized effect on throughput, spindle utilization, and the absorption of fixed overhead.
- **Overhead structure.** Some shops normalize the amount of effort it takes to run them rather than recognizing effort as a symptom of a broken system.

A shop that hires an expediter to improve on-time delivery is treating a symptom rather than fixing the process that produces missed deadlines. The expediter is a real expense. The broken process is the underlying liability. Fixing the process eliminates the need for the role.

Mike Payne breaks down the financial leverage of operational improvement in the simplest math: "You can have a company with a half million dollar EBITDA and you want to grow it to $700k times 3." At a standard 3x multiple, that $200,000 operational improvement translates directly to an extra $600,000 in your pocket. But if fixing those operational issues also allows the business to run without you, it increases the multiple itself. Taking that new $700,000 EBITDA and applying a 4x multiple grows the value of your business by over a million dollars.[97]

Scenario	EBITDA	Multiple	Value	Gain
Starting point	$500K	3x	$1.5M	—
Grow EBITDA only	$700K	3x	$2.1M	+$600K
Grow EBITDA + lift multiple	$700K	4x	$2.8M	+$1.3M

The multiplier effect on the multiplier is the entire game, and most owners don't see it until they're standing on the other side of a transaction. The work that lifts the multiple—decoupling, systems, diversification—pays back on both axis at once: more EBITDA, applied to a higher multiple, produces a compounded gain that no amount of revenue growth alone can match.

The decisions that hurt EBITDA, on the other side, are largely the absence of the disciplines this book has been building toward. No systems. No KPIs. Owner involvement that creates distortion. Customer concentration. Pricing built on hope. Each of these doesn't just drag EBITDA—it drags the multiple applied to that EBITDA.

97 Machine Shop Mastery, Episode 24.

Mike Fritz speaks bluntly to owners who resist hiring management because the numbers "don't work": "A lot of owners may look at their numbers and go, Mike, the numbers just don't work... It doesn't work to hire another person". He agrees that the math might be tight, which is why he tells them their first mission must be to drive up their revenue. By generating enough new income first, an owner can afford to hire a replacement to run the daily operations without having to sacrifice their own salary.[98]

Systems Are the Multiplier

Buyers care about systems during due diligence because systems are the mechanism through which the business will continue to function after the transaction. A buyer purchasing a shop is purchasing the ability of that shop to keep producing without the previous owner. Systems are what make that continuity possible.

The systems that carry the most weight during diligence are the ones that reduce operational risk and ensure performance through transitions:

- **Sales and marketing systems.** A repeatable process that delivers revenue and profit without the owner's personal involvement at the front of every deal.
- **Documented procedures.** Institutional knowledge that lives in the company rather than in any one head.

98 Machine Shop Mastery, Episode 57.

- **ERP or equivalent.** An accurate, real-time view of operations that makes the business legible to someone who hasn't been running it for years.
- **Scheduling and execution.** Disciplined enough that the owner doesn't need to personally know the status of every job to keep the floor moving.
- **Quality systems.** Repeatable processes that produce conforming work without heroic intervention.

Each is something a buyer will examine. Each one either lifts the multiple or pulls it down.

How processes are documented matters as much as whether they exist. Documentation that lives in binders no one consults isn't real documentation. The standard the strongest shops apply is whether the documentation actively shapes behavior—whether following it is the path of least resistance for the people doing the work.

Matt Boucher of Machinosaurus describes what this looks like from the buyer's side, reflecting on a recent acquisition. Instead of paying a massive premium, he paid a 2x multiple—or $200 for $100 in earnings. However, he explains that "if, you know, the earnings had been a hundred dollars, but the business had had more process, more definition... then maybe I would have had to pay $400 for it, um, or $300 for it". The systems are what gives the buyer confidence that the business will keep running, and a highly systemized business can easily command double the valuation multiple.[99]

99 Machine Shop Mastery, Episode 37.

Mike Fritz puts the same point in sharper terms regarding the need for standard operating procedures: "I know it's crazy to everybody to think about that, but you have one document that says day one, day two, day three, day four, day five. Here's the first five days of every time we train a lathe operator". Documenting those baseline processes allows a buyer to come in and keep the shop operating seamlessly.[100]

Mike Payne adds a practical clarification that often catches owners by surprise: "I'm not taking any of your cash and I'm not taking any of your debt. So there's no reason to build up millions of dollars of cash in the bank, right? Cause I'm not buying that. You're taking it with you". Buyers are purchasing the business, the systems, the equipment, and the team; the cash on hand stays with the seller.[101]

Concentrated But Stable

Customer concentration is one of the most carefully scrutinized factors in any acquisition, and the conventional wisdom—that diversification is always safer than concentration—is more nuanced than it looks.

What often isn't obvious to shop owners is that deep concentration can also be safe under specific conditions. The shape of the relationship matters as much as the percentage.

---

100 Machine Shop Mastery, Episode 57.

101 Machine Shop Mastery, Episode 24.

There's a barbell logic at work: extreme concentration can be either the most dangerous or the most stable configuration, depending on what holds the relationship in place.

Consider the difference between two shops, each with a single customer accounting for ninety percent of revenue.

Scenario	What the Customer Buys	Replacement Time	Buyer's View
Single customer, commodity parts	Standard parts any shop could produce	≈30 days	Extreme risk; deal-killer
Single customer, engineered assemblies	Custom assemblies, IP-protected fixturing, design participation	≈18 months	Defensible concentration; manageable

The first concentration is genuinely dangerous, and a buyer will price the risk accordingly. The second looks similar on paper but is structurally different, and a sophisticated buyer will see it that way.

Eric Hagopian of Pilot Precision Products describes the strategic shift his shop made to become harder to replace: "In order to become more, you know, as we say now, sticky, you know, we needed to go and move up the food chain". The philosophy, he explains, was to pursue business tied to an assembly number rather than a part number, ensuring customers needed them for more than just individual components.[102]

The general principle great shops apply is to specialize by product type while diversifying by customer and industry. A shop that's the best in its region at a specific class of work—titanium aerospace brackets, tight-tolerance medical components, production Swiss—can have many customers across many industries, all of whom value the same capability.

The trap most shops fall into is the opposite: generalist on capability, concentrated on customer. They'll take any work they can win, and they wind up over-reliant on whatever single customer happens to be sending the most volume.

Building for Options

This is why owners should design their business as if they intend to sell it, even if they never plan to. The E-Myth makes this argument explicitly, and it applies as forcefully to a shop owner planning to hand the business to a family member or run it for thirty more years as it does to one preparing for an exit. Optionality compounds. Constraints compound.

The design choices that keep future options open are essentially the ones discussed throughout this chapter:

102 Machine Shop Mastery, Episode 41.

- Designing for scale, even at small size.
- Eliminating tribal knowledge by documenting processes as they're developed, not retroactively.
- Building redundancy into key roles so that no single departure cripples a function.
- Investing in systems early enough that they grow with the business rather than being retrofitted under pressure.
- Maintaining customer diversification even when one large account would be easier to serve.

Each of these decisions sacrifices short-term convenience for long-term optionality, and the cumulative effect is a business with substantially more degrees of freedom in every direction.

John Shegda of KMM Group describes the time horizon required: "Even though it's way down the road, a lot of these things you have to start planning long in advance and start navigating your company towards an end goal that might take a decade to get to."[103]

What's hardest to retrofit later is culture. Systems can be built in a year if the will is there. Documentation can be produced in months. Customer diversification, in directional terms, can be improved over a couple of years. Culture takes much longer.

103 Machine Shop Mastery, Episode 22.

The shop that has spent ten years operating with owner dependence as the central organizing principle can't shift to a culture of distributed ownership in a single year.

The systems described throughout this book support that cultural shift, because they create the structure within which autonomy can actually function. A team can't take ownership of an area that isn't defined. A leader can't make decisions about information they don't have access to.

Designing for optionality isn't a technique. It's a posture. It's the willingness to build the kind of business that doesn't require the owner to be sitting at its center, and to do that work long before any specific exit is on the table.

CHAPTER 19

Leaving Well

On Selling, Succession, and Stewardship

The previous chapter argued that the discipline required to build a sellable business is the same discipline required to make one worth owning. This chapter is where that argument meets the actual mechanics of exit. The transition itself—who buys, on what terms, what happens to the people and customers and culture—is shaped almost entirely by decisions made long before any deal is on the table.

What gets resolved in advance—who can buy the business, what they'll pay, how smoothly the handoff goes, what happens to the people who stayed loyal for decades—is mostly set years before the documents get signed. The owners who exit cleanly are usually the ones who started preparing five to ten years out.

This chapter covers the full arc, from the foundational documents that should be in place at the very beginning of a partnership through the deal killers that surface at the very end:

- The buy-sell agreement most owners skip, and what its absence costs.
- Family transitions, and why "fair" and "equal" are not the same thing.
- The four buyer types, what each one actually wants, and how to match a shop to the right one.
- What real preparation looks like across a three-to-ten-year horizon.
- The deal killers that surface late in the process, often after months of work.
- Stewardship: what the owner owes the buyer, the employees, and the legacy of what was built.

The Document Most Owners Skip

The single most overlooked piece of preparation work isn't a system or a process—it's a document. Every business with more than one owner should have a buy-sell agreement in place from the very beginning of the partnership. Most don't. The cost of that omission is invisible until the moment something happens that triggers the need for one, at which point the cost is enormous.

A buy-sell agreement is, in effect, a business prenuptial. It's a binding contract that dictates what happens to a partner's shares if they leave, die, or are otherwise forced out. If a partner dies, does their spouse become a co-owner of the company? If a partner gets divorced, does their ex receive part of the business? If a partner decides to leave, what is the company obligated to pay them, and on what schedule? None of these questions have automatic answers. They have to be negotiated.

The agreement has three core components:

- **Trigger.** What specific events allow for a buyout. Death, disability, voluntary departure, termination, divorce, bankruptcy—each possibility should be addressed in advance, before any of them are happening.
- **Price formula.** How the business will be valued at the moment a triggering event occurs.
- **Funding.** Where the money actually comes from. Life insurance policies on each partner are a common mechanism for the death scenario. For other scenarios, the agreement may rely on a structured payout from the company's cash flow over time. The point is that the funding mechanism is identified before it's needed.

Heidi Devroy of ProsperTech describes how this scenario planning unfolds in practice: "We were able to button some things up with the lawyer and have another consultant that would sit with the four of us and ask some questions about how it would affect us personally. And then we ran through some scenarios because you have to think of what if you die mid succession. Are all the ducks in a row with the other kids?"[104]

Solo owners don't need a buy-sell in the same way—there's no partner to buy out. But the underlying logic still applies: decide the hard things while everyone is calm, healthy, and aligned, so that when the hard things happen, the structure is already in place.

When Family Inherits

Family successions are some of the most emotionally complex transitions in any industry, and machining is no exception. Many family transitions are far more difficult than they need to be, and the difficulty compounds in predictable patterns.

The complexity intensifies when multiple family members are involved at different levels. Consider a shop owner with three children, one of whom works in the business and wants to take it over while the other two have no operational involvement. If the parents pass and the estate is divided equally among the three, the operating child now has to either run a business they only one-third own or buy out their siblings under emotional pressure that nobody designed for.

The mistake underneath that pattern is confusing fair with equal. Treating heirs fairly doesn't always mean giving them

104 Machine Shop Mastery, Episode 30.

identical shares of the operating business. It can mean balancing the business against other assets—real estate, life insurance, retirement accounts—so the operating heir ends up with the business and the others end up with equivalent value in different forms.

Matt Wardle of JD Machine describes the arrangement his family worked out when he took over the shop: "The deal was, I would take over the business and own the business and I bought out my four older sisters. We worked out an arrangement there such that I could continue to reinvest in the business but still take care of my sisters."[105]

Buying out non-operating heirs is technically possible but requires care. A note from the operating heir to their siblings can't be structured in a way that financially burdens the company to the point of destabilizing it. Better to use non-operating assets as the balancing mechanism if they exist.

There's also a variable families often skip past too quickly: whether the heir who works in the business actually wants to own it. Working in a shop and being responsible for it are very different roles. An heir who has been operating happily as a senior employee may find ownership terrifying. Better to discover that before the documents are signed.

Universal advice is hard to give—families differ enormously in how they communicate and handle conflict. One approach that has worked well for shop-owning families involves:

---

105 Machine Shop Mastery, Episode 49.

- A structured meeting cadence, typically twice a year.
- A strict agenda set in advance, so the conversation stays focused.
- A neutral location, away from the shop and the family home.
- Outside advisors present—a lawyer, an accountant, or a family business consultant who can keep the discussion grounded in facts rather than emotion.

Anne Duyck of Duyck Machine describes the succession planning board her father-in-law, Andy, built to separate family ties from business operations. To ensure the business remains in the family while keeping operations in the hands of capable leaders, Andy expanded the board—originally just himself and his wife—to include their children. However, Anne notes that working in the business itself is based strictly on merit: "I do quality coordinating because I'm good at it, not because I'm Andy's daughter-in-law." She adds, "It's a family business, but you gotta be good at what you do. You don't get to stay cause you're related."[106]

The cadence matters as much as the content. Issues addressed twice a year for five years are issues that get resolved long before they become urgent. Issues addressed for the first time when an urgent event forces them to surface are issues that often blow up the family along with the deal.

106 Machine Shop Mastery, Episode 21.

The Four Buyers (and What Each Wants)

Outside of family successions, four buyer categories account for almost every transaction. Each looks for different things, pays different multiples, and fits different kinds of shops.

Buyer Type	What They're Buying	Typical Multiple	Best Fit
Owner-Operator	A business with strong fundamentals and room to grow under fresh attention	2–4x	Owners who want to leave after a transition; smaller deals
Strategic Buyer	Synergies, capabilities, certifications, or market access (1+1=3)	4x+	Shops with niche capabilities a larger buyer wants to absorb
Private Equity	A platform for roll-up, growth, and resale at a higher multiple	Variable; rises with scale	Larger, higher-performing shops above PE's size threshold
Family Office	Stable cash flow, permanent hold, medium growth, generational wealth	Lower than strategic; flexible structure	Owners who want to stay involved through a longer transition

Owner-operators are looking for a business with strong fundamentals and real opportunity to keep growing—often a shop that's a little tired, where fresh attention to sales and marketing, business processes, and capital investment can unlock growth. They tend to pay lower multiples than other buyer categories because they're bringing operating skill to the table along with capital.

Strategic buyers are running 1+1=3 math. The acquisition has to provide synergistic value beyond the target's standalone financials—expansion of customer base, entry into a new industry, access to capability, geographic coverage. They tend to pay higher multiples because they can extract value from the combination that a financial buyer can't.

Private equity has become a far more visible category in machining over the past decade. PE firms typically bring business savvy rather than technical expertise, and they tend to deploy a roll-up strategy—acquiring a platform company, then bolting on additional acquisitions over time. They have specific financial criteria, usually requiring a minimum EBITDA threshold below which the deal isn't worth their time.

Family offices behave similarly to PE firms but on a different temporal logic. They're typically wealthy families or high-net-worth individuals deploying capital they don't need to recycle on a fund timeline. Family offices can hold acquisitions indefinitely. That patience often translates into different negotiating dynamics—and sometimes different cultural fit with sellers who want their business to continue operating the way it always has.

Which buyer category is right depends primarily on scale. Small businesses don't register on the radar of most PE firms or family offices—writing a two-million-dollar check is too small to justify the diligence work. Mid-sized businesses ($1M-$5M EBITDA) sit in the most contested zone, with multiple buyer types competing. Larger businesses tend to attract PE and strategic interest almost exclusively.

What can surprise sellers is how directly some buyers want to insert their own leadership immediately after closing. Here's how this played out at Pro CNC. When we signed our deal—I think it was January 30th, 2014—the very next Monday morning, my two partners, Kelsey and Darcy, didn't come back to work. The new owners wanted them out the door. The detail is worth attending to because it cuts against most sellers' assumption that the transition will unfold gradually. In some deals it does. In others, the new ownership has its own thesis, its own team, and no interest in retaining the old leadership beyond what the contract requires.

The Years Before the Deal

Across every buyer category, the patterns of what gets examined during diligence are remarkably consistent. Owners often get surprised by how deep buyers want to go. PE firms and family offices typically run the most exhaustive diligence; strategic buyers run nearly as much; even owner-operators examine the business carefully when they're putting their own money on the line. There's no shortcut around it.

Mike Brown of Computer Integrated Machining describes the framing he's working under now: "I find myself in a fairly fortunate position with... having those conversations, if you will, right now. He isn't waiting until he is forced to make a decision; instead, he is starting these conversations early because he knows it takes about three to five years to get a business fully prepared for a sale."[107]

The arc of preparation, condensed, looks like this:

Time Before Sale	Primary Work
5–10 years out	Begin candid family or partnership conversations; build the leadership bench; design for decoupling
3–5 years out	Realistic valuation; gap analysis; ERP and systems; customer diversification; engage an advisor
1–2 years out	Clean financials; polish SOPs; catalog assets; accelerate loan payoffs; pass the three-week vacation test
Final months	Broker, tax attorney, CPA engaged; teaser and full book prepared; run a competitive process

Most preparation work consists of disciplines this book has been arguing for from the start. Better systems. A more capable ERP. A balanced management team with real bench depth. Building redundancy. Customer diversification. None of it specific to selling; all of it producing a business that's worth more whether you sell or not.

Something important to note is that owners should avoid buying significant new equipment on loans in the final years before a sale. Most acquisitions transfer the business

107 Machine Shop Mastery, Episode 45.

free and clear of prior liabilities. If the owner just took on $800,000 of equipment debt, the buyer essentially has to pay for that equipment again on top of the purchase price.

When the time comes to actually run a process, the team assembles: a broker, a tax attorney, a CPA who can prepare the financials in the form buyers expect, and often a transaction advisor. Each plays a specific role; trying to skip any of them tends to cost the seller substantially more than the fees would have.

Owners often arrive at this stage with one persistent misconception: that their business is worth more than it actually is.

Jereme Rogers of TK Machine describes the trap from the perspective of someone who later bought a shop priced this way: "I think what the previous owners valued it at, there's a lot of sentimental value there that doesn't equate into profits." While the founders built it, ran it, and put their lives into it, buyers inevitably learn that the market doesn't pay for sentimental value—it pays for cash flow.[108]

Deal Killers

When deals collapse late in the process, the cause is almost always due diligence and legal review. A handful of patterns surface repeatedly:

- **Stale inventory.** A business claims significant

108 Machine Shop Mastery, Episode 64.

inventory value, and diligence reveals that most of it is unsellable.

- **Customer concentration.** When a single customer accounts for too much of the revenue, the deal becomes a referendum on that single relationship.
- **Funding gaps.** The buyer's math doesn't add up to the purchase price, and what looked like a financed deal turns out to be something else.
- **Deal fatigue.** The owner gets pulled out of the business to prepare for the sale, the numbers slip, and the buyer revises the offer downward in response.
- **Quality-of-earnings issues.** Buyers determine that reported revenue or profitability isn't sustainable—that it was distorted by one-time events that won't recur.

Mike Fritz describes the stale-inventory trap from the buyer's side: "You go into finished, you say, we made a thousand of these. Great. But you sold six in the last eight years". Because he refuses to buy parts that will sit on a shelf forever, he audits the last 12 months of part numbers and simply tells the seller they can keep the inactive stock.

Customer concentration is another major red flag. "Number one is extreme customer concentration is when you are, you know, 75 plus percent, you're tied into one customer," Fritz explains. While a buyer will see that as extremely risky, it isn't always an absolute deal killer—Fritz actually bought his first shop knowing a single customer made up

75% of their business, but made it his immediate goal to drive up new revenue to lower that concentration.[109]

Funding gaps can be more subtle. Eric Hagopian describes the moment he caught one during his own attempted exit. He learned from his own banker that the buyer's planned lender couldn't actually fund the transaction because the purchase price exceeded their "house limit." Hagopian was shocked: "How do you come to the deal table without the money?" While he temporarily salvaged the deal by setting the buyers up with his own bank, he ultimately killed the transaction when he caught them fabricating a strategic connection at Boeing, realizing that if they lied about their money and connections, he couldn't trust them."[110]

Deal fatigue is a phenomenon every owner going through a sale eventually encounters, and most don't see coming. The owner is trying to keep running the business while simultaneously responding to a flood of diligence requests. Performance slips. The numbers the buyer is examining start to look worse than the numbers that triggered the offer.

Eric Hagopian describes the toll plainly: "I spent basically a year working on putting a deal together, which meant that other people in the business—my brother and our other teammates—had to shoulder the burden of my not being around because I was working pretty much full time on the exit."[111]

---

109 Machine Shop Mastery, Episode 57.

110 Machine Shop Mastery, Episode 41.

111 Machine Shop Mastery, Episode 41.

Key person risk is another deal killer that surfaces late. Buyers often interview the top two or three customers as part of diligence. If those customers say they work with the shop because of the owner specifically, the deal is suddenly contingent on that owner staying involved—usually beyond what the seller had planned.

And then there are wild cards entirely outside the business itself. Economic headwinds can shift mid-deal. Global uncertainty can spook buyers. A buyer's financing source can dry up unexpectedly. None of these are predictable. All of them have killed deals that were otherwise heading to close.

Stewardship After You're Out

What a good exit looks like, in hindsight, is one in which both buyer and seller end up satisfied. Communication was clear throughout. Expectations were set early and held. Things didn't change at the last minute. The price was fair. The transition was clean.

The seller's responsibility to the buyer, beyond the contractual terms, is to be ethical and play fairly. That means disclosing the skeletons in the closet, or better, getting rid of them before the process starts. A buyer who discovers a problem in diligence loses confidence in everything else the seller has represented.

The transition usually involves the seller staying with the business for some period after closing. When Pro CNC sold, the new owners asked for two years; we agreed on one. The owner's job during that period is to be useful but not to interfere with the new ownership's direction.

Keith Bernardo of M&K Engineering describes how he approached the post-sale transition with strict transparency for his buyers: "I did have to stay for a period of time." However, he was very clear with them upfront that while he would help out in some capacity for as long as it made sense for both parties, he was ultimately selling the business because he had other aspirations to pursue.[112]

Responsibility to employees, during and after the sale, deserves explicit attention. The seller can't guarantee employment for every person indefinitely, but the deal can be structured to make sure the new ownership has aligned incentives to take care of the team. Anti-displacement clauses, retention bonuses for key personnel, and clear cultural commitments are all available. "If I sell," Mike Brown says, for instance, "I'm going to sell to a company that can take care of my people and also give them an opportunity to grow."[113]

Mike Payne, who bought Hill Manufacturing from Cheryl Hill, describes the same principle from the buyer's side: "She wanted to be proud of Hill Manufacturing for the rest of her life. So the way she structured the deal, she didn't sell to the highest bidder. She sold the company to the people who would carry on what she had built."[114]

---

112 Machine Shop Mastery, Episode 52.

113 Machine Shop Mastery, Episode 45.

114 Machine Shop Mastery, Episode 24.

When Pro CNC ran its sale process, the highest offer wasn't the offer that was accepted. The company offering the most money was planning to close the Bellingham location, move the machines to Romania, and lay off the team. We took less money to sell to a buyer who would keep the shop running, keep the people employed, and continue building on what we'd started. None of us regret it.

A good exit, in the end, isn't primarily about price. It's about leaving behind a business that survives the transition—one whose employees are taken care of, whose customers continue to be served, and whose culture continues to hold.

Every owner eventually leaves. The work of this chapter, more than anything else, is to make sure that the leaving happens in a way the owner would actually choose if they could see it from the outside.

CHAPTER 20

Something Worth Keeping

Why Excellence Is the Only Option

This book has spent nineteen chapters on the work of building a profitable, durable machine shop. Quoting and pricing. People and culture. Leadership and structure. Quality and compliance. Systems, KPIs, transitions, exits, and so on. The argument throughout has been that machining isn't just a business that happens to make parts; it's a foundational activity that anchors families, communities, supply chains, and the broader industrial base.

The case is structural, not romantic. The activity inside a machine shop—taking elemental material and converting it into something of substantially higher value—has economic and social effects that compound outward through every relationship the shop touches. The job is hard. The work matters. And the standard the industry has to hold itself to is higher than ever.

This chapter closes the book with four threads:

- Why shop decisions ripple through families and communities, and the responsibility that follows.
- What a meaningful legacy actually consists of—beyond equipment, buildings, and a sale price.
- How great shops build a culture of pride and pass that pride to the next generation.
- Why "good enough" is no longer good enough, and what excellence demands now.

The thread underneath all four is gratitude. For the work, for the people who do it, and for the readers who have stayed with this argument long enough to consider what it asks of them.

What You Owe the People

Shops and the communities around them are completely interwoven. The most direct connection is the obvious one: shops employ local people in solid jobs. The less obvious connection—and the one that matters more for the long-term health of both—is that those jobs create value that doesn't exist before the parts are made.

When a shop starts with a chunk of raw material and ends with a part worth many times more, that added value distributes outward. It goes to the material supplier, the cutting tool maker, the machine builder, the truck driver, the inspector, the local accountant, the kid whose tuition gets paid by a machinist's wages. Each part shipped is an injection of value into the surrounding economy.

We're at an inflection point in the history of this country. For decades, manufacturing jobs left North America. Factories shuttered. Local economies hollowed out. The country has finally started to understand that decoupling from production decoupled us from the resilience that production provides. Reshoring is real. The shops in business now are positioned to participate in that reversal—if they're ready.

The decisions that matter at this scale are the decisions this book has been arguing for. A sales- and marketing-driven organization that creates positive sales pressure. Documented systems that let the business absorb growth. Accurate cost data that makes pricing decisions defensible. A team that can run the operation without constant intervention. The discipline that produces a sellable business is the same discipline that produces a community-strengthening one.

Courtney and Andy Silver run Ketchie, Inc., a precision manufacturing shop in North Carolina, and they run a program called Opportunity Knocks that brings high school seniors into the shop for a few hours a week over a semester. The students get exposure to skilled manufacturing as a real career path, not the fallback option many of them have been told it is. The shop gets visibility into the next generation of potential employees—and a chance to demonstrate, in person, what modern manufacturing actually looks like.

Opportunity Knocks is itself based on a program called Craftsman with Character, started by Dave Hataj of Edgerton Gear in Wisconsin. Dave has written extensively about what it looks like to treat shop ownership as community stewardship rather than purely as a business venture, and the model has spread to shops across the country who recognized the same need in their own regions.[115]

Profitability, in this context, isn't the goal. Profitability is the fuel that lets the company serve its mission. Without margin, none of the rest is possible. The shop can't pay better wages, can't invest in apprenticeships, can't fund the school programs, can't survive the next downturn.

Beyond profitability, the right word for what an owner owes their team and their community is stewardship. The shop owner is in a position of real power—employing people directly, providing for their families, shaping the daily experience of the work. That power carries obligations. To treat people with dignity. To pay fairly. To create the conditions for them to do good work. To recognize that the business exists not just for the owner but for everyone whose life it touches.

The flip side defines itself. A shop owner who runs the business without kindness, without empathy, without integrity creates a particular kind of vacuum. High turnover. Disengagement. People who only show up for the

115 Machine Shop Mastery, Episode 106.

paycheck. The shop produces parts, but it doesn't produce anything beyond that.

The dignity dimension is worth naming explicitly. There's a long tradition of political thought—cutting across left and right—that argues people fundamentally seek dignity, and that meaningful work is one of the central sources of it. A machine shop that gives its people work they can take pride in, in a physical environment that treats them as adults, is participating in something larger than a transaction.

There's an old comparison that captures the deeper version of this. In medieval Europe, the cathedrals took generations to build. The bricklayers and stonemasons who worked on them often never saw the finished structure. When asked what they were doing, the apocryphal answer separates the laborer from the craftsman: one says "I'm laying bricks," the other says "I'm building a cathedral." The work is the same. The meaning is entirely different.

What Actually Lasts

A meaningful legacy in this industry isn't measured by the sale price at the end. It's measured by what continues to exist, and to do good, after the original founder is no longer present. The frame is different from the one most business books offer, and it's the one that matches what shop owners actually build.

What that produces, concretely, is more varied than most owners realize when they're inside the daily work:

Category	What It Looks Like
Durable goods	Parts in service across machines, vehicles, aircraft, and infrastructure that continue to add value years after they were made
Homes and families	Houses bought on shop wages; college educations funded by shop wages; family stability built on the back of a stable job
New businesses	Former employees who went on to start their own shops, suppliers, or service companies in the same community
Skilled people	Machinists, programmers, supervisors, and leaders trained at the shop who carry that capability forward wherever they go next
Philanthropy	Schools, nonprofits, Boys & Girls Clubs, churches, and community organizations supported with time, money, and attention
Community memory	The collective recollection of a business that was a pillar of the place—that did right by its people and meant something to those around it

The list isn't exhaustive. It's suggestive of how distributed the actual legacy of a great shop becomes once it has been running long enough. The parts continue to circulate. The employees keep families going. The next generation of operators learns from the people the founder trained. The community is stronger because the shop was there.

There are manufacturing businesses in the United States that are five and six generations old, more than 150 years in continuous operation. What the original founders built was an enduring presence that continues to add value across decades. That kind of compounding is available to almost any owner who treats the business as something worth building for the long term.

The investments that produce this kind of compounding are the ones this book has described throughout. Building systems before they're strictly necessary. Documenting processes as they're developed. Investing in apprentices before the labor shortage becomes desperate. Diversifying customers before concentration risk becomes existential.

Pride and Mastery

Pride in the work is one of the quieter signatures of a shop that has been built well. It can't be manufactured by slogans, mission statements posted in the break room, or recognition programs. It comes from how the daily work is actually treated by the people running it.

The foundation is simple, and surprisingly few shops actually build it. The team has to know that leadership cares about them. Not in the abstract, and not in the language of corporate communication, but in concrete ways. Pay that reflects the value of their work. Equipment that works. A clean facility. Safety taken seriously. Real attention to who they are as people.

Gratitude is the second pillar, and it's one of the most underused tools in any owner's leadership repertoire. Owners are in a position of structural power relative to their employees. The power differential is real, and the relationship works only if the owner uses that power well. Saying thank you. Recognizing good work directly. Treating mistakes as learning rather than punishment. None of it expensive. All of it cumulative.

The architecture supporting pride is the same architecture this book has been describing. A mission that's clear enough that everyone can articulate what the business is for. Core values that govern decisions, not posters. Defined roles that let people own their work. Real feedback loops that turn individual effort into team-level improvement. Growth opportunities that let employees see a future inside the company.

Passing pride to the next generation is the work that turns a single great shop into a sustained tradition. It happens through a small number of consistent practices:

- Mentoring younger employees deliberately, not as an additional duty but as a central part of how the shop operates.
- Investing real time and attention in the new generation, so that their work is recognized and their growth is supported.
- Telling people, directly and often, that what they do matters—because it does, and because they may not hear it anywhere else.
- Showing up in schools and community institutions, bringing students into the shop, demonstrating that skilled manufacturing is a real career with real dignity attached to it.

The Opportunity Knocks program that Courtney and Andy Silver have built at Ketchie Inc., which was inspired by Dave Hataj's (MSM Episode 106) Craftsman with Character program at Edgerton Gear, are two examples of what this looks like at scale. Dave and Courtney also discussed this topic on episode 534 of the MakingChips podcast. They aren't the only ones. Across the country, shop owners are quietly running similar efforts—high school visits, internships, apprenticeships, in-shop training programs—because they recognize that the next generation of machinists isn't coming from anywhere else.

The students who walk through a shop on a high school visit are seeing something most of them have never been told existed: skilled work, performed at a high level, in a clean and well-run facility, by people who clearly take pride in it. That image, planted at seventeen, becomes a real career option in ways no career fair ever will.

The Final Charge

There has never been a more interesting time to be in machining. Demand is rising. Work is coming home. The defense industrial base is rebuilding. Aerospace, medical, and space are growing. The shops in business right now are positioned to participate in the most significant industrial reshoring this country has seen in two generations—if they're ready.

And the bar has never been higher. The same factors that produce the opportunity also produce the competition. Customers expect more. Better quality. Tighter delivery.

Faster quoting. Better communication. Stronger systems. The shops that thrive will be the ones that meet that bar; the ones that don't will be quietly replaced by the ones that do.

Good enough is no longer good enough. Excellence is the only survival strategy that actually works at this moment in the industry—both technically and in terms of leadership. The shops that try to coast on yesterday's standards will find that yesterday's customers have moved on.

The standard the industry should hold itself to going forward is the one set by the best shops in it. If shop owners really grounded themselves in the reality of what they're actually doing—that every part they make ripples outward into systems and communities and lives—the work would feel different. The decisions would feel different. The standard would feel different.

The case for excellence is, in the end, a case for taking the work seriously enough to do it the way it deserves to be done. It's a case for treating the daily decisions of running a shop as the meaningful work they are, not as administrative obligations that get in the way of the "real" work of making parts.

The final message of this book is gratitude. Deep, considered gratitude for what shop owners actually do. The work is hard. The hours are long. The pressures are constant. The recognition, from outside the industry, is rare. And yet shop owners keep showing up, keep making the parts, keep paying their teams, keep serving their customers, keep their communities anchored.

Machine shops are simultaneously the most essential business in modern industry and one of the most challenging to run. Everything in the physical world that matters—every aircraft that flies, every car on the road, every medical device that saves a life, every piece of energy infrastructure that powers a city—starts in a machine shop somewhere. The people who run those shops are the foundation of every other accomplishment that follows.

The owners of those shops are, in the most direct and literal sense, the superheroes of superheroes. They aren't always told this. They may not feel it on the hard days. The expectation of recognition shouldn't be the reason they do the work. But the recognition is owed.

If this book has made the case well, if it has helped fuel the passion that brought owners to this work in the first place, and if it has inspired even one shop to take a step toward the next level of excellence, then the months of writing and the hundreds of conversations that produced it will have done their job.

Go build.

INDEX

#

5S, 268
- *See also* lean manufacturing

9/11, 72, 77

A

AccuRounds, 177
- *See also* Tamasi, Michael

Advanced Plastics and Machining, 211, 245

aerospace industry, 77, 130, 203

always-audit-ready shop
- compliance embedded in daily work, 200, 210
- zero-prep audit accounts, 211

American Precision Partners, 7, 121, 302

Ankrom, Nate, 273

apprenticeships, 172, 337
- capital investment enabled by profitability, 334
- talent pipeline and retention, 168, 173
- *See also* skilled trades pipeline

AS9100, 200, 202
- aerospace focus and requirements, 203

AS9100D as market-access differentiator, 204
- externally imposed requirement reframed as structure, 199
- *See also* certifications and compliance

Athena Manufacturing, 153

automation, 264, 275–76

B

backlog, 134, 161
  leading indicator, 53, 102, 123–33, 135
bar to box, 257
benchmarking, 284–89
  See also Top Shops survey
Bergman, Jack, 39
Bernardo, Keith, 158, 175, 329
  See also M&K Engineering
Berrien, Bill, 163
billable hours, 140, 144
Boeing, 327
Boucher, Matt, 248, 309
Bourgeois, Nate, 269
  difficulty of machining business, 36
  flat shop rate corrected, 142
  specialization over generalism, 111
  See also Ouroboros Space and Defense
break-even, 159–61
brilliant jerk, 169
Brown, Mike, 323, 329
brute force and heroics
  antithesis of architecture and design, 187, 284
  experienced at Pro CNC, 76, 85
  liability in tight-tolerance work, 57, 118
  long hours, firefighting, and personal sacrifice, 26–27, 40–42
  masking systemic failures, 28, 42, 132
  system-driven shops outperforming heroics-driven, 285–86, 290
  traded for clarity and structure, 6, 22, 43, 86–87
built-in quality, 238, 261
  condition of process, not department, 238–40, 252
  See also inspection discipline
buy-sell agreement, 317
  cost of skipping, 316

solo owners, 318
See also family succession
Byman, Nathan, 242

C

capital intensity, 25, 29, 35–36, 56
Capkovitz, Dave, 40–41, 138, 185
Carlson, Kristin, 21
CARR Machine and Tool, 187
Carr, Jim, 187
Carrico, Matt, 77
cash flow, 87, 90, 99
endpoint of shop failure, 101, 179
erratic without customer fit, 118
improved by one-piece flow, 258
lag between winning work and payment, 100
sales pipeline and revenue shipped, 133–34
start-from-scratch versus acquisition, 88–89, 91, 93–98, 104, 325
structural crisis in busy shops, 34–37, 85–86, 92, 102–3
certifications
See certifications and compliance
certifications and compliance
burden versus structure posture, 209, 211
certification types and market access, 132, 199–205
ownership versus diffuse responsibility, 206–8
pricing and positioning leverage, 212–13
See also AS9100
chart of accounts, 152, 156–57
C&K Tool, 40–41, 185
CMMC, 199–205
CNC machine, 29
collaborative quoting, 125
Collinear Machine, 220

See also Heston, Mark
company culture, 103
first-order concern for owners, 103–4
hardest to retrofit in transition, 313–14
hiring for attitude and fit, 168–69, 171
improvement versus compliance, 273–74, 279
legacy in exit and succession, 315, 330–31
complexity, 99, 182
compounding nonlinearly with growth, 63–64, 119, 181, 186
compounding with capital and margins, 35–37
managed through standards and structure, 200, 204–7
stacking technical variables in machining, 32, 57
underestimated by new owners, 33–34, 88–89, 91–92, 100–104
compliance ownership
accountability gaps from diffuse responsibility, 206
organizational evolution and scaling, 207–8
Computer Integrated Machining, 323
Concise Manufacturing, 146
construction, 28–30, 37
continuous improvement, 280
employee feedback and daily responsibility, 260–61
meeting rhythms and kaizen events, 278–79
ownership and financial accountability, 277
structural design choice, not slogan, 262–64, 276
See also kaizen events; lean manufacturing
core values
hiring and firing through, 170
operating expectations, not posters, 175, 338

See also hiring for attitude
cost burden shift, 148
cost of goods sold, 140
cost of quality, 278–79
COVID, 20
Craftsman with Character, 334, 339
culture beats talent, 167–68
customer concentration risk, 179, 298
acquisition due-diligence scrutiny, 299, 308–9, 326
concentrated but stable configurations, 310–11
diversification rules and profit-percentage metric, 134–35, 300, 312
EBITDA multiples and valuation impact, 301–2, 307
proactive mitigation before existential, 337
Wardle's near-catastrophe at JD Machine, 103
warning signs and structural danger, 102
See also customer diversification
customer diversification, 180, 312–13, 337
See also customer concentration risk
customer evaluation framework, 117, 156
Cutting Edge Metals, 149, 211, 254
See also Robertson, Lori

D

D&D Enterprises, 131, 169, 195
Davis, Jason, 169
employee retention economics, 177
vendor reliability, buyer's-side definition, 131
working oneself out of a job, 195
deal fatigue, 326–27
deal killers, 316
due-diligence and legal-review patterns, 325–26
funding gaps and

fabricated buyers, 327

key-person risk, 328

See also customer concentration risk; due diligence

defense industrial base, 339

delegation

enabled by quality systems and ERP, 191

growth-stage surrender of control, 63, 197

management layers and centralized authority, 187–89

trust and outcome ownership, 178

See also owner as bottleneck

Devroy, Bob, 170, 317

Devroy, Heidi, 170, 317

dignity of work

dimension of meaningful work, 335

eroded by offshoring, 18

discipline

beating software as consistency driver, 85, 222–23, 236

building a sellable business, 23, 113, 286, 315, 333

cultural value in enduring shops, 171–73

distinguishing higher EBITDA tiers, 111–12, 287

forced into Pro CNC through hardship, 43, 79–81

imposed by certification and compliance, 132, 201, 209, 211

job costing and variance review, 140, 159–62, 255

KPI focus and consistency, 288, 292–95

mirroring machining tolerance discipline, 1, 67, 82, 262, 289, 293

non-optional in complex, thin-margin shops, 25–28, 37, 84, 180

reshoring opportunity requiring, 22, 24

sales and pricing

process, 125–28, 135, 235
shop-floor operational practices, 234, 247–50, 259–61, 291
sustaining continuous improvement and lean, 263, 268, 273, 277–79, 290
walking away from ill-fit work, 110, 163
discipline beats software, 222–23
due diligence, 308–9, 323
See also deal killers
Duyck Machine, 175, 320
Duyck, Anne, 175, 320
Dyer, Dwain, 146

E

E-Myth Revisited, The, 47, 50
applied to machining, 49, 51–57, 65–66, 75
paired with Goal, The, 48, 58–60, 67, 312
See also Gerber, Michael; technician vs. owner
EBITDA Growth Systems, 138
EBITDA margins
absolute EBITDA unlocking aggressive multiples, 113
specialization achieving 50–60% margins, 112
EBITDA vs. revenue, 305
See also valuation multiple
Edgerton Gear, 334, 339
See also Hataj, Dave
effort vs. design, 224–25
effort-impact matrix, 274
eight wastes, 266–67, 275
See also lean manufacturing
employee retention, 176–78
entity structure, 96
estimating vs. pricing, 138
accurate cost data and spindle uptime, 143–44
adjusting the two numbers, 141
four cost buckets and

overhead rate, 139–40
measuring estimating accuracy, 145–46
pricing vs. cost-plus markup, 137, 142
See also job costing; quoted versus actual

excellent floor, 261
contrasted with "good enough" floor, 258–59
designed control versus perfection, 260, 262

executive assistant, 304

expediter, 306

F

family office, 322

family succession
buying out siblings, JD Machine, 319
emotional complexity of transitions, 318

family meeting governance, 320
See also buy-sell agreement

feast-and-famine cycles, 53, 123, 126, 130

firm fixed-price, 31, 37

first pass yield, 293
See also scrap rate

first run right, 147

first-article inspection, 230, 249
See also inspection discipline

Five Whys, 41

five-axis machining, 36, 258

fixed costs, 36

flat shop rate, 142
See also machine burden rate

flow thinking, 221

Focused on Machining, 170, 186

Formula SAE, 73

Fortner, Matt, 92–93, 249

four buyer types, 316, 321–23

four cost buckets
cost-classification framework for estimating, 139
prerequisite to separating estimating and pricing, 140

See also indirect overhead

franchise prototype, 50, 216

decoupling owner from daily execution, 63

definition and E-Myth concept, 57–58, 61

designing shop as if to franchise, 60, 62

making implicit workflow connections explicit, 59, 217–18

Frankel, Ken, 251

Free, Mitch, 3, 194

See also ZYCI

Fritz, Mike, 304, 310

financing management hires and SOPs, 308

neglect of demand-building, 121

run business as if selling it, 7, 309

stale finished-goods inventory trap, 326

valuation multiples and owner dependence, 302–3, 305–7

functional leads, 182–86

G

G-Zero, 191

generalists vs. specialists

adaptability vs. compounding knowledge, and margins, 112–13

breadth as liability with growth, 109–11, 114

networks of specialists vs. price competition, 119

See also niche focus

Genuine Machine Products, 273

Gerber, Michael, 47, 56–57

See also E-Myth Revisited, The

Giddens, Allison, 31, 115

See also Win-Tech

Goal, The, 47–50, 58–60, 83

See also Goldratt, Eli; Theory of Constraints

Goellner, Nick, 2

Gold Mine, The, 269

Goldratt, Eli, 47, 58

See also Goal, The; Theory of Constraints

good enough is no longer good enough, 332, 340

gratitude, 337–40

Gretna Machine Shop, 170

gross margin, 160–61, 306

growing pains, 181–83, 191–92

H

Haas, 48, 74

Hagopian, Eric

- funding gap in attempted exit, 327
- growth thresholds and structural change, 190
- “sticky” shift reducing concentration risk, 311
- *See also* Pilot Precision Products

Hannah, Dave, 191, 204

Harms, Scott, 94, 275

- See also MetalQuest Unlimited

Hartmann, Alan, 172

Hartmann’s Inc., 172

Hataj, Dave, 334, 339

- *See also* Edgerton Gear

Heikoop, Kelsey, 73

- replaced in shop-floor roles, 218
- sales discipline, 74–75, 126
- spreadsheet tools and systems thinking, 76, 84, 223, 261
- *See also* Pro CNC

Heston, Mark

- programming pulled off floor, 233–34
- structural fragility from customer concentration, 179
- weak-link dynamic in shop systems, 220
- *See also* Collinear Machine

high-mix low-volume, 147, 287

high-volume low-mix, 147

Hill Manufacturing, 2, 272, 300, 329

Hill, Cheryl, 329

hiring for attitude, 171–72

- *See also* core values

Holt, Angie, 260, 279

HTS Coatings, 170
Hunsaker, Ashley, 169

I

in-process inspection, 252
inbound marketing
contrasted with outbound, 129
visibility and credibility mechanism, 128
weighting by growth ambition, 130
See also outbound marketing
indirect overhead, 140, 144, 148
See also four cost buckets
industrial base
national stake of shop ownership, 24, 331
reshoring window and responsibility, 22, 339
inspection discipline, 246
first article vs. first part, 249
layered checkpoint verification system, 250–51
pre-production inspection planning, 247–48, 252
See also built-in quality; first-article inspection
inventory, 94, 246, 256, 325–26
ISO 9001, 202
standards as structure, 199–201
subsumed by AS9100, 203
ISO 13485, 203–5

J

JD Machine
employer-of-choice investment in employees, 260
family succession and ownership transfer, 319
local economic and community impact, 15, 102
See also Wardle, Matt
job costing

actual-vs.-planned time comparison, 254
prerequisites for accurate data, 153, 158–59
Swiss shop case study, losses revealed, 151–52
win-rate analysis and pricing, 160–61
See also estimating vs. pricing

K

kaizen events
corrective action for quality costs, 279
triggering via theory of constraints, 264–65, 269
worker input and post-event auditing, 270–71
See also continuous improvement; setup reduction; Theory of Constraints
kaizen newspapers, 267
leadership participation at Hill Manufacturing, 272
posted notepads and area team review, 266
weekly review cadence in improvement framework, 265
Ketchie, Inc., 333, 339
See also Silver, Courtney
key person risk, 328
kill the losers, 161
cultural shift toward accountability, 163
profitability review process defined, 154, 255
variance review as management discipline, 160
warning signs and triggers, 162
kitting, 236–38, 247–49, 261, 293
See also quote to cash
KMM Group, 60, 103, 160, 313
See also Shegda, John
Kowalski, Derek, 221, 231
KPIs (key performance indicators), 284
high-impact indicators and ownership, 292–93

sale-readiness discipline alongside SOPs, 7

L

labor tracking, 246
- foundation of operational improvement, 253
- operator trust and honest capture, 254
- prerequisite for job costing, 158–59

lean manufacturing
- daily practice versus corporate initiative, 260–61, 264
- Five Whys root-cause analysis, 41
- frameworks known but poorly executed, 262–63
- tools mapped to cadences, 265–68
- *See also* 5S; continuous improvement; eight wastes

legacy, 332, 337
- community and generational impact, 336
- meaning beyond sale price, 333–35

letting-go problem
- loss of identity and self-worth, 66
- price of building durable systems, 60, 65
- *See also* technician vs. owner

LOC Industries, 221

Lockheed Martin, 186

Low Country Aerospace, 195

low-hanging fruit, 294

M

M&K Engineering, 158, 175, 329
- *See also* Bernardo, Keith

machine burden rate, 158–59
- *See also* flat shop rate

machine shop as system
- cascading delays experienced at Pro CNC, 82

embodied in ProShop ERP, 84–85
interconnected living system, defined, 3, 83, 86
patchwork fixes versus integrated design, 220
Machine Shop Mastery
origin under MakingChips brand, 2
machine-specific costing, 142–43
Machinosaurus, 248
MakingChips Podcast, 2, 339
managers vs. functional leads
functional leads as first structural shift, 184
management layers relieving owner-as-bottleneck, 187
operator to architect rungs, 192, 194
promoting technical performers, bottleneck risk, 185
scope and role compared, 186
Marzilli Machine, 5
Marzilli, Jamie, 5
mentoring, 338
MetalQuest Unlimited, 94, 275
See also Harms, Scott
metric overload, 295
model-based programming, 233
Modern Machine Shop, 284, 288
Mosey, Bob, 12
Mullins, Jerry, 237
multiplier effect, 14–15
Muthana, Aneesa, 18

N

Nathan, Tom, 201–4
national security
erosion from offshoring and foreign dependence, 17–19
strong machining base and defense readiness, 13–16
net margin, 283, 287
Newman, John, 153

niche focus, 111
- customer curation and fit, 116–18
- generalists versus specialists, 109–10, 112–13, 120
- inbound marketing to defined niche, 128
- intentional versus accidental concentration, 122
- prerequisite for scalable systems, 119, 121
- reduced job-level losses, 153
- saying no to out-of-niche work, 114–16
- *See also* generalists vs. specialists

non-recurring costs, 148–49

Northside Machine Company, 14

O

offshoring, 14, 17–19
- *See also* reshoring

Olson Custom Designs, 278

Olson, Mitch, 278

onboarding, 174–75

one-piece flow, 257–58, 267
- *See also* work in progress

operational transparency, 177–78

Operator to Architect, 183
- $10M threshold and role shift, 190–91
- personal surrender at each transition, 183
- six developmental stages defined, 192–94
- stages operating simultaneously, 196

opportunity cost, 115

Opportunity Knocks, 333–34, 339

optionality
- design choices building or destroying it, 312–13
- gained by shops through business excellence, 23, 298
- lost through offshoring, 19
- posture reducing owner dependence, 314

Ouroboros Space and Defense, 36, 111, 142, 269
See also Bourgeois, Nate
outbound marketing
aggressive growth and new markets, 130
proactive outreach tactics, 129
See also inbound marketing
overall equipment effectiveness (OEE), 292
owner as bottleneck, 124
mindset shift toward humility, 182
revenue ceiling and stalled growth, 63, 186–89
See also delegation
owner as psychological transformation
difficulty of letting go, 194
mindset as scaling constraint, 182–83, 195
surrenders at each growth stage, 196–97
owner decoupling
long-term posture, not project, 302–5
sequential handoff of responsibilities, 303, 324
See also three-week vacation test; valuation multiple
owner-operator buyer
profile and target shops, 321
typical purchase multiples, 302

P

Palma, Susan, 189
paper travelers, 84
Pareto principle, 153
paths into machining ownership, 89
misaligned expectations of machinists and outsiders, 92
three entry routes enumerated, 90–91
Payne, Mike
acquisition mechanics on cash and debt, 310

collectible invoice, parts as, 243
Hill Manufacturing acquisition, 329
MakingChips Podcast co-ownership, 2
profit over revenue growth, 305–6
SDE and management dependence, 300–301
Peerless Precision, 21
Perez, Nubia, 170
personality assessments, 55
Pilot Precision Products, 190, 311
See also Hagopian, Eric
Pindel Global Precision, 163
Pioneer Service, 18
positive sales pressure, 77, 115, 128
Precision Shapes, 189, 215
Preece Machining & Assembly, 49
Preece, Nick, 33, 49
Preiser, John, 215
pricing power, 112
pride in the work, 40, 332
emerging from organizational architecture, 336–38
eroded by chaos and poor planning, 39
machinist identity, 52, 66
passed to next generation, 335, 339
private equity
exhaustive due diligence, 323
roll-up strategy and multiples, 322
Pro CNC, 43, 79, 178
financial vulnerability and cash pressure, 98, 102
founding by inexperienced college graduates, 71–75
in-house software becoming ProShop, 2, 83–85
kill-the-losers profitability review, 154, 162, 255
operational struggles forcing systems discipline, 76–78, 80–83, 126, 230

owner exit and sale, 218, 303, 323, 328–30
See also Heikoop, Kelsey
process discipline, 132
Progress Machining, 92, 249
ProShop, 73, 179
documentation as byproduct of work, 223
enforcing discipline over flexibility, 43, 84–87
hidden cost and margin exposure, 39, 151
kaizen tracking and continuous improvement, 266–67, 272
origins at Pro CNC, 2, 71–72, 83
progress reports and proactive alerts, 162
ProsperTech, 170

Q

quality-of-earnings, 326
Quinn, Justin, 170, 186
quote to cash, 227–35, 239, 241–44, 263
contract review, 228–32
kitting, 236–38, 247, 261
pre-floor planning, 229–35
scheduling, 234–36, 240–42
shop floor, 245–46
See also kitting; visibility
quote turnaround time, 293
quoted versus actual
report shared for cultural engagement, 149, 254
target ratio of 100%, 141, 146–48
See also estimating vs. pricing

R

Rathburn Tool & Manufacturing, 260
replaceability, 62, 168, 175–76
reshoring, 14, 20–22, 333, 339
See also offshoring
revenue per employee, 113,

283, 287–88
revenue thresholds, 183, 188–89
RFQs (requests for quote)
Pipeline metrics, 123–24, 127, 133–35, 292
    Quoting process, 125–26
    See also sales funnel
Robertson, Lori, 211
    closing estimating feedback loop, 149
    sharing quoted-vs.-actual reports with operators, 254
    See also Cutting Edge Metals
Rogers, Jereme
    buyer on inflated business valuation, 325
    layered in-process quality verification, 250
    shop closure from concentration risk, 179
Russell, Barry, 195

S

sales funnel
    pipeline health and diversification, 134
stages and metrics, 127, 133
    See also RFQs (requests for quote); sales system
sales system, 124
    continuous operation and demand selectivity, 126–28
    funnel metrics and measurement, 133–35
    inbound and outbound channels, 129–30
selling trust and certainty, 131–32
structure replacing personality-dependent selling, 121–23, 125
    See also sales funnel
scalability test, 5
Schutte, Christian, 204
scrap rate, 306
    See also first pass yield
self-awareness, 55
seller's discretionary earnings (SDE), 300

selling trust
  certainty as customer purchase, 130, 132
  procurement as risk mitigation, 131
sentimental value trap, 325
setup reduction, 270
  See also kaizen events
Shegda, John, 60, 160, 313
  See also KMM Group
shipbuilding, 16
Shortess, Scott, 211, 245
Silver, Andy, 333, 339
Silver, Courtney, 333, 339
  See also Ketchie, Inc.
skilled trades pipeline
  casualty of offshoring, 16–18
  multiplier effect, 14–15
  rebuilding education pipelines, 19, 173
  See also apprenticeships
Small Business Development Center, 77
SOPs (standard operating procedures)
  role handoffs and owner independence, 303, 310
sale-readiness discipline, 7
spindle utilization, 285–88, 295
standard operating procedures
  See SOPs (standard operating procedures)
standard work
  baseline replacing improvisation and judgment, 81, 202, 209
  embedding kaizen improvements, 271
starting vs. buying a shop, 89–90
  compounding commitments, deliberate design, 104
  two paths and risk profiles, 91–96
stewardship, 315–16
  community stewardship model, 334
  post-sale transition conduct, 328–30
strategic A3s, 266
strategic buyer, 321–22

structural debt, 64
structural fragility, 168, 179–80
supply chain resilience
national-security and defense-readiness vulnerability, 16–20
systems-first principle, 63, 216
systems beat fixes, effort versus design, 217–19
systems before growth, not after, 63, 65

T

takt time, 229, 252, 261
Tamasi, Michael, 177, 268
See also AccuRounds
technician vs. owner
blind spot as structural failure, 53–54
contrasting dimensions of each role, 51–52
core distinction defined, 43, 49–50
E-Myth entrepreneurial myth, 55–56
letting-go problem and identity, 66–68
See also E-Myth Revisited, The; letting-go problem
Theory of Constraints, 58, 269
See also Goal, The; Goldratt, Eli; kaizen events
thin margins, 25, 30, 35–37, 101, 138
See also tolerance
Thomas Register, 76
Three Sigma Mfg, 251
three-to-five-year sale preparation, 324–25
three-week vacation test, 324
See also owner decoupling
throughput, 26, 67
bottleneck improvement and kaizen, 269–70
defined and framed, 27–28, 38
local efficiency trap, 59
profit lever, 157, 277
protected by standard

work, 80–81
shop lead's domain, 184
Theory of Constraints and flow, 48, 60, 82
visibility problem in busy shops, 39–40, 178
TK Machine, 250, 325
tolerance
business discipline, 1, 36
margin risk in fixed-price quoting, 35
missed, as cause of scrap, 30–31, 37
procurement and inspection controls, 131, 239
See also thin margins
Tomahawk missile, 21
Top Shops survey, 284
four pillars and honorees, 284
participation as diagnostic, 287–88
unglamorous consistency versus data access, 286
See also benchmarking
Total Precision, 201
tribal knowledge, 62, 83
documented processes, 22, 62, 83, 216–17, 223–24, 303

U

undercapitalization, 97–98

V

valuation multiple, 300, 321
operational improvement payoff, 307
ranges by shop profile, 301–2
systemization and documentation effect, 308–9
See also EBITDA vs. revenue; owner decoupling
value stream, 220, 276
See also value stream mapping
value stream mapping, 265
See also value stream

variable vs. fixed costs, 36, 156

variance review, 152, 159–60

visibility, 3, 86

- employee financial transparency, 178
- financial and job-costing transparency, 152, 159
- operator-level scheduling dashboards, 242, 293
- quoting pipeline and revenue forecasting, 127
- systems and ERP replacing owner observation, 58, 78, 191, 197
- throughput management and chaos prevention, 38–40, 228
- translation into profit, 229, 241, 243
- *See also* quote to cash

visibility is profit, 240–43

W

Wardle, Matt

- customer overconcentration risk, 102
- economic impact of family shops, 15
- employee suggestion system, 260
- family business succession, 319
- workforce development as investment, 173–74
- *See also* JD Machine

Western Precision Products, 237

what buyers pay for, 298–99

where the dollar goes, 143–44

win rate, 292

- pricing calibration and diagnostics, 125, 142, 161
- sales-funnel metric tracked systematically, 123–24, 126–27, 133–34

Win-Tech, 31, 115

- *See also* Giddens, Allison

Wolfram Manufacturing, 242

word of mouth
single-industry concentration risk, 122
starting point for new shops, 121
unrepeatable versus systematic selling, 123
work in progress, 256–61
See also one-piece flow
work on the business, not in the business, 3
World War II, 11, 16

Z

ZYCI, 3, 194
See also Free, Mitch

ACKNOWLEDGMENTS

Precision manufacturing is a team sport, and this book is no different. I've spent thirty years in this industry, and I'm mindful every day that I haven't taken a single step on this journey alone. To the hundreds—likely thousands—of people I've collaborated with, learned from, and shared a shop floor with: thank you. You are the heart of this industry, and your wisdom is woven into every page of this book. While I can't name everyone, there are several people whose support made this work possible.

To my wife, Kara: thank you for being my anchor. Your unending love, patience, and support through the early mornings, late nights, and the beautiful chaos of building businesses have meant everything to me. To my boys, Evan and Dane: I'm so proud of the men you're becoming. And to my parents, Patti, Dale, Sharon (RIP) and Bob (RIP), and my siblings: thank you for being my lifelong cheering section.

To my original partners at Pro CNC—Kelsey, Darcy, Mark, Tim, and Mason: we took a naive leap into the unknown together, and I wouldn't trade that journey for anything. Thank you for the trust and the partnership that started it all.

To my partners at ProShop—Kelsey and Matt: I'm still in awe of what our shared vision has become. Thank you for your expertise, your cool heads in the heat of growth, and your tireless dedication to helping other shops succeed.

To Nick and Mike at MakingChips: our partnership over the last few years has been a highlight of my career. Thank you for your friendship and for providing a platform to champion the #MetalWorkingNation.

To Mitch Free: thank you for your leadership, your friendship, and for setting the stage with your foreword. Your belief in this mission is a constant inspiration.

To Tom Dorr: your guidance was a lifeline when we needed it most. Pro CNC and ProShop owe much of their existence to your insight.

Finally, to the many podcast guests who have shared their stories with me: you are the co-authors of this book. Thank you for your vulnerability, your humility, and your dedication to this craft. You are the quiet heroes of our economy, and it is an honor to tell your stories. Let's keep building.

A NOTE TO READERS

If this book helped you see your business more clearly, make a better decision, or strengthen the way your shop operates, I would ask you to do two things.

First, leave an honest review wherever you purchased the book. Reviews help other machine shop owners decide whether this is worth their time. More importantly, they help the ideas in these pages reach the people who can put them to work.

Second, share the book with someone who may benefit from it: a shop owner, a successor, a production leader, a machinist preparing to take on more responsibility, or anyone committed to building a stronger manufacturing business.

This matters because the challenges facing American manufacturing will not be solved by a handful of large companies or institutions. They will be solved shop by shop, leader by leader, and decision by decision.

A stronger machine shop creates better jobs, develops more capable people, supports its community, and adds resilience to the industrial base. When one shop improves, the effect extends far beyond its walls.

That is the mission behind this book.

If these pages have helped you, your review and recommendation can help carry that mission further. They can put the book in the hands of another owner who is tired of firefighting, another leader ready to build better systems, or another manufacturer determined to create something that lasts.

The work matters. Helping others do it better matters, too.

CONTINUE BUILDING

A book can clarify what needs to change, but the work happens inside the shop.

The resources below are designed to help machine shop owners and manufacturing leaders continue applying the ideas in these pages, strengthen their systems, and build more capable businesses.

ProShop ERP

ProShop ERP is a digital manufacturing ecosystem built specifically for machine shops. It brings together shop management, quality systems, documentation, scheduling, inventory, and compliance in one platform.
Learn more at:
[www.proshoperp.com]

Machine Shop Mastery Podcast

On the *Machine Shop Mastery Podcast*, I speak with shop owners, manufacturing leaders, and industry experts about the decisions, systems, and practices behind stronger manufacturing businesses.
Listen at:
[www.machineshopmastery.com]

MakingChips Podcast

On the *Machine Shop Mastery Podcast,* I speak with shop owners, manufacturing leaders, and industry experts about the decisions, systems, and practices behind stronger manufacturing businesses.
Listen at:
[www.makingchips.com]

Manufacturing Transformed Podcast

The *Manufacturing Transformed Podcast* explores the transformational journeys of shops that are powered by ProShop.
Listen at:
[https://proshoperp.com/podcast/manufacturing-transformed-podcast/]

Additional Tools and Resources

Visit this book's website: www.disciplinetoprofit.com for additional materials.

Manufacturing excellence is never built through information alone. It is built by applying what we learn, measuring what changes, and continuing to improve.

The work does not end with the final page.
It continues in the shop.

ABOUT THE AUTHOR

Paul has spent his career around machine shops, not in a classroom talking about them. He co-founded Pro CNC, his own precision machine shop, right out of college and ran it for 17 years — including pulling it back from the edge of bankruptcy in 2002. That turnaround is where much of this book comes from.

Today he's a co-founder and Chief Industry Evangelist of ProShop ERP, built specifically for precision manufacturers in aerospace, defense, and other regulated industries. He hosts the Machine Shop Mastery podcast and Manufacturing Transformed, the ProShop podcast, and co-hosts MakingChips. Much of the book's inspiration—and its 50+ quotes—comes straight from the shop owners he's interviewed on Machine Shop Mastery. *Precision Manufacturing, Precision Business* is his first book.

Connect with Paul on LinkedIn: https://www.linkedin.com/in/paulvanmetre/

www.ingramcontent.com/pod-product-compliance
Lightning Source LLC
LaVergne TN
LVHW021741071126
851857LV00039B/576